Major League Bride

D1131891

Major League Bride

*An Inside Look
at Life Outside the Ballpark*

KATHLEEN LOCKWOOD

McFarland & Company, Inc., Publishers
Jefferson, North Carolina, and London

For my mother
Eileen Casey Murphy
whose inner strength I admire
and who taught me the power of
Faith, Hope and Love.

LIBRARY OF CONGRESS CATALOGUING-IN-PUBLICATION DATA

Lockwood, Kathleen.
  Major league bride : an inside look at life outside the ballpark /
Kathleen Lockwood.
    p.   cm.
  Includes index.

  ISBN 978-0-7864-4560-8
  softcover : 50# alkaline paper ∞

  1. Baseball—Social aspects—United States. 2. Lockwood,
Kathleen. 3. Wives—United States—Biography. 4. Lockwood,
Skip. 5. Baseball players—United States—Biography. I. Title.
GV867.64.L64 2010
796.357'640973—dc22   2009046140

British Library cataloguing data are available

Cover photographs ©2010 Shutterstock

Manufactured in the United States of America

*McFarland & Company, Inc., Publishers
  Box 611, Jefferson, North Carolina 28640
  www.mcfarlandpub.com*

Acknowledgments

I will be forever grateful to the strong, supportive women across the country who welcomed me into their caring communities.

I remember fondly the fanatically supportive fans of the Milwaukee Brewers, the California Angels, the New York Mets and the Boston Red Sox who shared with me their love of this great game and the myriad fellow baseball wives who touched my life in so many places and in so many ways, most especially Nancy Hegan, Mary Lou Lee, Rosemary Lonborg, Ruth Ryan, Maryann Sanders, Nancy Seaver, Peggy Slayton and Mary and Roxanne Valentine.

I appreciate the new owners of the Boston Red Sox who have graciously welcomed back old members of the team and I especially value the support of Lou Gorman, Pam Ganley, Rod Oreste and the Boston Red Sox Booster Club.

For preparing me for this magic carpet ride I would like to thank my college advisor, Sr. Therese Higgins of Regis College, Weston, MA, who long ago encouraged me to find my own voice in this noisy world, as well as the workshops offered by the New Hampshire Writer's Project. Thanks also goes out to the staff of the Rye Library who, over the past five years, scoured the interlibrary listing system and secured every book I requested. This library truly is the heart of the community.

I would like to thank my husband and my children, Meghan, Maura, Kara, Casey and Erin, for perpetuating my belief that life continues to be a mystifying adventure and my son-in-law, Louis, and my daughter-in-law, Ashley, whose snow-driven and rain-soaked weddings reminded me of the futility of careful planning.

Finally, I would like to acknowledge the supportive power of prayer and the soothing force of music in our lives.

Table of Contents

Introduction

Opening Day

THE GLORY OF LOVE

This is the story and the glory of my life as the wife of a professional baseball player. For over a decade, my day-to-day existence rested on the ability of my husband to successfully throw a tiny leather ball over ninety-five miles an hour past a large wooden bat. I had no control over the action on the field; still, the outcome of the pitcher vs. batter battle drastically determined the quality and tranquility of my days. I shared this gloriously nerve-racking life with a constantly changing cadre of women whose lives were also manipulated by the maneuvers of major league management, moving over 35 times in the course of my husband's association with nine different professional teams. At 22 I thought we had it all, lost that life at 26, regained that glorious gift at 27, and saw it all slowly wither away by the time I turned thirty-something. Through all the ups and downs, I definitely laughed more than I cried and belted out the National Anthem more often than I sang the blues.

My memoir chronicles my life as an impulsive ingénue bride to that of a seasoned veteran wife, fostered by the friendship of some truly special spouses. It is a diary of growth. It is a journal of struggle. It is an account of bizarrely truthful stranger-than-fiction events involving extremely eccentric teammates. It is a manual of survival. But most of all it is a story of love. From finding a little glimmer of sunlight through the clouds on that rainy morning in June 1970, when I became the wife of the young *bespeckled* Milwaukee Brewers pitcher, Skip Lockwood, until we reached the end of the rainbow in Denver, Colorado, during the summer of 1981, I was caught up in a strange and surreal existence. The people with whom I shared these incredible escapades some might consider exceptional, but the core emotional experiences themselves are universally shared with strongly committed women all across our country.

My husband and I inhabited the same statistical environment, but our remembrances are light years apart. Skip's life centered around the ballpark. He had a mission to accomplish. Constantly on stage, he played many different roles in the nightly performance between the lines. Action characters interacted with ever-changing variables—good high-inside hitters, free-swinging left-handers, batters who loved low fastballs, great bunters and fearsome long-ball belters who faced raw fire, nasty curveballs, finicky forkballs and challenging changeups. The settings added intrigue to the action—the friendly confines of Fenway Park with its scary green monster wall, Shea Stadium on Sunday afternoons when the blare of the jets from LaGuardia drowned out the chatter on the infield, early and late season wind-chill warnings in County Stadium, Santa Ana lung-searing smog at the Big A in Anaheim, along with high attitude wind tunnels in Denver's Mile High Stadium.

My life centered around my husband. I was the player's wife, the supportive spouse, nutritionist, short order cook, airport chauffeur, moving specialist, real estate agent, interior decorator to a slew of shaggy green-and-gold carpeted temporary flats, social secretary, wardrobe consultant, massage therapist, sounding board, confidante and lover. We hold disparate memories of this time period. Skip remembers who hit what pitch on what count, the childish pranks in the clubhouse, the endless hours spent icing his shoulder or groin, the anguish of giving up a bases-loaded dinger, the ecstasy of striking out the side, the catharsis of the competition. I remember the special friendships, the overwhelming camaraderie and compassion among the wives tempered by the occasional jealousy and back stabbing, the loneliness of long road trips, the anxiety that accompanied the insecurity, the constant packing and unpacking, the dismay at overhearing Milwaukee's GM blaring in the wives section how he was going to get rid of the entire inept team, the joy of joining in passionate standing ovations, the delight in purchasing a permanent home in the city in which we were playing (three times) and the anguish of learning (over the radio) that we had been traded and would have to uproot again.

Forty years ago I vowed to unconditionally love my husband for better and for worse, in good times and bad. Looking back, we have had over thirty-eight wonderful years of wedded bliss and more than our share of weeks and months of depressing dark days. How did our marriage manage to survive the turmoil, the trades and the temptations? A deep love for each other, a strong belief in a higher power, and a huge dose of humor helped us through.

Music has always been a calming presence in my life. Perhaps it's the influence of my Emerald Isle ancestry that the first words I can remember hearing are those to the Irish lullaby tune of "Too Ra Loo Ra Loo Ral" that spurned this musical connection. Whatever the origin, I often remember people and events in the light of the songs that were playing on the radio at the time. Almost everyone in my generation can remember where they were when they learned that President John F. Kennedy was shot. I was perched in the front row of my theology class trying to comprehend the unfathomable words that echoed through the intercom. An eerie chill swept into that room. The silence was deafening. Perspiration soaked my starched white blouse and bled into my green blazer. Barely breathing, with heavy hearts and tear-filled eyes, my classmates and I stared in disbelief as our innocent and invincible world shattered. My thoughts rarely go back to that claustrophobic classroom; however, the emotions of that day come to mind whenever I hear the soulful restrains of *"Hey, Jude."* Unable to bear the grief alone, I commiserated with other stunned students in my friend Mary's basement that night, replaying the first Beatles' album over and over again as we tried to make some sense of this senseless shooting. Throughout this book, I refer to songs and lyrics that reflect the mindset and mood of a particular time period in my continuing journey through the changing seasons of my life in baseball.

My introduction into the world of baseball coincided with my initiation into adulthood during the tumultuous decade of the 1970s. The country's disillusionment with the Viet Nam war was growing as protest rallies spread across the nation. Civil rights laws might have been registered in the books, but they still had a long way to go before becoming a reality. The Camelot dreams of the White House had turned into a Watergate nightmare. The women's movement had opened up new and exciting options for young women, but many soon discovered that "free love" was not totally free of deception and heartache. The high cost of personal fulfillment often came at the expense of a devoted spouse and family. Some skeptics in the media posed the question, "Is God dead?" while subversive cults preyed on lost souls who had forgotten how to pray. To deal with the daily uncertainty and turmoil in professional baseball, I found comfort in my faith, reflecting and refocusing on the true meaning of life in the company of a community of believers on Sunday mornings.

From the first freshman convocation to our final graduation ceremony, every major assembly during my four years at Regis College in Weston, Massachusetts, began with the community intoning a musical adaptation of John Donne's "Meditation 17." Donned in Fair Isle sweaters and a-line wool skirts, my classmates and I would form a circle, cross our arms, hold hands and chant:

> No man is an island, no man stands alone
> Each man's joy is joy to me, each man's grief is my own
> We need one another, and so I will defend
> Each man as my brother
> Each man as my friend.

Two weeks after singing this mantra at my college commencement, I floundered in an alien apartment in Brown Deer, Wisconsin. Alone and unglued, I sat on the floor unloading the plethora of rectangular, brown, packing boxes containing the major portion of my worldly goods, wishing I had just one friend with whom I could share the joy of my recent wedding to distract me from my present lonely state. I had just come off my all-too-short, road-trip honeymoon to Detroit and Cleveland and had arrived the previous evening in Milwaukee in a car crammed with cartons, having driven myself back to this unfamiliar, sparsely, furnished apartment. My new husband would be away for another week as he continued on that long road trip with the rest of the Milwaukee Brewers; I would have also preferred to fly on, but we had already stretched the limits of the team's tolerance as well as our limited checking account. So there I sat, sprawled out on the multi-colored shag carpet, surrounded by mounds of bubble wrap, serenaded by the Righteous Brothers' soulful strains of an "Unchained Melody" over the radio (we did not yet own a television). A short while later my doorbell rang. Nancy Hegan, the wife of one of Skip's teammates, was at the door. Her familiar Bostonian accent, along with an invitation to share dinner with her and her two-year-old son, rejuvenated my spirit. Suddenly I was no longer adrift alone on a solitary island; I was being embraced by the baseball community, by another young wife who understood my need for companionship. Though I have traveled far and wide in the ensuing years, nothing will ever erase the significance of that first dinner invitation that transformed my despondent demeanor to delight at being welcomed by a simple benevolent gesture.

Nancy and I became close friends during our time in Milwaukee and still remain connected through Christmas cards (in years that I happen to be organized and actually get them mailed). Unfortunately, the instability inherent in the world of major league baseball makes it difficult to maintain the close friendships that develop during any particular season. But just as the seasons come and go and transform our lives every year, I retain lasting memories of exceptionally giving women with whom I have had the pleasure of sharing their joy and their grief and who, throughout our years in baseball, helped to take the edge off of my personal loneliness by offering the priceless gift of friendship. A multitude of magnanimous teammates have touched my life during Skip's challenging cross-country career. While I never adequately voiced my appreciation at the time, countless acts of simple kindness extended to me by Nancy Hegan, Rosemary Lonborg, Maryann Sanders, Nancy Seaver, Ruth Ryan, and a host of other angels helped to make this dislocated spouse feel comfortable in her new home. Hopefully I have "paid this favor forward" by the way I have attempted to live my life and smoothed the base paths of other young wives as I journeyed through the baseball seasons of my life.

THE CIRCLE GAME

Baseball is a seasonal game played by young boys in dirt fields throughout America. For a special few, the baseball seasons continue to go round and round into adulthood. However, the heart of the game of baseball is rooted in childhood, and the professional athletes who are most successful continue to enjoy playing games and, like Peter Pan, refuse to grow up.

These boys marry young girls who are forced to grow up quickly and assume the role of the responsible adult. It is the baseball wife who must organize the day around her ballplayer's schedule. Preparing nutritious meals and making sure her athlete has time for an afternoon nap is a must. If there are young children in the household, they must be kept busy so as not to disturb Dad's pre-game routine. Depending on the circumstances of the previous night's game, the morning paper can either be placed quietly on the breakfast table or must be conveniently lost. There is a fine line a baseball wife must walk between chief cheerleader and personal anger management therapist.

In the inevitable event that her husband is traded, he is expected to report to the new team immediately, often on the next plane. The new ballplayer is usually excited about the opportunity to play in a different city and receives a thunderous welcome from his new fans when he arrives at the ballpark for the first time. The baseball wife is left behind to clean the apartment, pack up the car and the children, leave her friends and support system behind, and move to the next town on her own. When she eventually arrives in town, she faces the insecurity of trying to fit in with a new group of wives who might resent the fact that her husband just took over the coveted position of one of their inner circle. Next, she must secure an apartment that will rent on a short-term basis, locate the grocery store, and restock the pantry and refrigerator, all before the team returns from its road trip. No wonder Wendy-girl decided to leave Neverland!

At one time I thought that it was only the wives of professional athletes who were thrust into this protective custody role. I now recognize this same quintessential quality in strong and supportive women from all walks of life. The gift of creating an oasis of serenity has been bestowed on countless families across our country by ordinary women just "doing what needs to be done at the time." The military bride whose husband can be deployed at any time, the politician's spouse who needs to maintain a serene presence in her home state as well as entertain constituents in Washington, DC, the corporate weekday widow whose husband is constantly traveling, the family of the firefighter who can be sent to "put out the fires" anywhere at any time, and the wife of the doctor who is constantly managing life-and-death situations all recognize the need to provide a sanctuary for her hero to regroup in the comfort of home.

The seasons continue to go round and round throughout our life. We all experience the calming serenity of spectacular summer sunrises, the brisk wake-up call of the autumn winds, the caustic chill of winter squalls and the life-affirming reawakening of hope with the first buds of spring. Throughout the changing seasons of my own life, I have discovered that the secret to happiness is hanging on to your dormant dreams during the dark winter nights long enough to enjoy them in the sunshine of your life.

1

Return to Pooh Corner

QUE SERA SERA

Miracles happen every day. I consider it a miracle that I, the granddaughter of an Ellis Island immigrant who was greeted in America by signs indicating IRISH OR CATHOLIC NEED NOT APPLY, was personally welcomed to the White House by President and Mrs. Jerry Ford to the 1975 Presidential Prayer Breakfast. I find it even more miraculous that I was able to maintain my sanity during the remainder of that tumultuous season. Relieved at being traded away from Anaheim over the winter, my husband went from being elated for the opportunity to play in Shea Stadium, New York, with the Yankees to being devastated over being released in the final days of spring training in Ft. Lauderdale, the morning after he had pitched three hitless innings. A few phone calls and a few flights later, Skip could (not) be found hiding out in a Phoenix hotel under the tutelage of Charles Finley, so that Charlie himself could "stick it to the Yankees for not placing Skip on waivers." Two months later my husband emerged from the desert heat with a renewed "heater" and, through an early morning, hung-over negotiating session with the ever-opportunistic Charlie O in another Phoenix hotel room, ended the season up in Shea Stadium as the closer for the New York Mets. Welcome to the unpredictable world of major league baseball! No one could ever prepare for this true life, fairytale existence, but let me take you back to my childhood to see how I was nurtured to face the uncertainties of nature.

One of my earliest memories finds me staring into a small glass jar filled with earthy tufts of grass, covered by punctured wax paper. Inside this container lay a little green caterpillar that required a daily misting of water and a diet of freshly picked pansy stems. Day after day, my eighty-year-old grandfather Casey and I would tend to the flowers in our rock garden as we patiently waited for this homely caterpillar to transform itself into a beautiful butterfly. Softly singing Irish ditties to the plants under his care, while filling my young mind with mischievous tales of the "wee people" from the old country, this gentle man taught me to believe in the wonder of nature and to enjoy the simple magic found within every moment of every day.

I was raised in the arms of a multi-generational family. My parents were

Kathy and Anne Murphy with their father Francis at his college graduation from Western New England College, June 1953.

a quintessential part of Tom Brokaw's "Greatest Generation." My father was a self-made man who had survived the Great Depression by picking raspberries and working for the Civilian Conservation Corps. Francis Murphy served his country valiantly in World War II and returned home to marry the love of his life, Eileen Casey. The youngest child of elderly parents, my mother felt that she could not abandon her parents, and so the newlyweds moved into my mother's family home. Their plan was for my mother to work while my father attended college, but when my sister was conceived during their honeymoon, they were forced to make adjustments to those arrangements. Instead of merrily matriculating in academia on a full-time basis while my mother continued her wartime employment at the American Bosh, my father attended college at night and worked full-time since an "enceinte" secretary was not accepted in the post-war office environment. The endearing photograph of my five-year-old sister and myself posing with my beaming father, attired in his cap and gown, is a prideful testament to that hard-earned scholastic accomplishment.

The middle child of a middle-class family born in the mid-size city of Springfield, MA, I was a typical baby boomer of the 1950s. My sister and I walked over a mile to school and never gave it a second thought. We would meet our neighbors along the way and section off into clusters of older and younger classmates. The more mature groups would practice their spelling on the way, while my friends and I would take out our thread-bare jump ropes and very carefully skip on our polished saddle shoes over the cracks in the sidewalks so as not to "break our mother's back." My mother did not learn to drive until I was almost seven, but it really didn't matter as we owned only one car. Material expectations were low and therefore satisfaction came relatively easily. The competitive subliminal messages of advertising had not yet been ingrained into the psyche of my peers and their parents. On Saturday afternoons my sister and I were given dance lessons although my mother complains that mine were somewhat of a waste since I generally sat on her lap for the majority of the hour. Come recital time, my mother, along with all the other would-be Rockette

Kathy and Anne Murphy in their home sewn tap dancing outfits.

mothers, created our elaborate costumes by hand.

Eventually my sister and I both progressed from tapping our feet to twirling the baton. I acutely remember the pain associated with banging my baton into the black-and-blue bruises on the inside of my elbows while practicing to the sounds of John Philip Sousa's "Stars and Stripes Forever." My older sister seemed to excel in every endeavor she attempted, and soon, while I continued to perfect catching the baton while spinning in a circle, she was selected to twirl the menacing-looking fire baton, whose ends were covered with fabric and dipped into a vat of kerosene. Of course, this necessitated my father joining us at every parade and exhibition with his trusty fire extinguisher in hand. When hula hoops rolled into our lives, I creatively incorporated the soft-plastic spinning device into my twirling routine for what I can imagine was a supremely strange sight to behold.

My paltry physical prowess propelled me eventually to place my baton down and pick up a tennis racket. For two summers my friends and I would ride our bikes over to Forest Park and engage in round-robin double-tour-

Sunday dinner with my cousins, celebrating my fifth birthday, May 1953.

naments until the blisters on our palms forced us to stop. And then, just as I was starting to finally gain some strength in my weak backhand, the younger siblings of my friends began to consistently embarrass me on the court, and I found it necessary to attempt yet another athletic endeavor. I finally found my niche in cheerleading.

I began my cheerleading career in fifth grade and continued on at Cathedral High School and into my college years at Regis College. Hitting the tape measure at only five feet, I was short in stature but loud in lung power. I felt totally in command as I screamed out "Give me a C," and the entire bleacher section would belt the letter back at me. I do, however, remember one colossally embarrassing wardrobe malfunction when the clasp on my ten-year-old cheerleading skirt popped open and my kilt fell to the ground as my body catapulted upward. Luckily, the point guard made an incredible play at the time, and the focus of the crowd was tuned in more to the exhibition on the court than to my unintended exhibitionist predicament. In the late 1960s, most Catholic colleges in the Northeast were either all-male or all-female and so, the women's colleges would take turns cheering for the neighboring men's sports teams. While I was banned from conversations in the classrooms at the College of the Holy Cross, I was welcome to run up and down the perimeter of their basketball court and root for their victorious Crusaders. My Regis squad even spent one afternoon cheering for the Boston Patriots although my soccer-playing daughters cringe at the thought. Little did I realize at the time how often my cheerleading credentials would be employed during my association with major league baseball.

Mother's Day on Tiffany Street, May 1955. Mary and Bill Murphy, Kathy and Anne Murphy, Mary Ellen, Jim, Tim and Sheila Rooney.

As mentioned before, my maternal grandparents lived with us, and every Sunday my mother's two sisters and their families would join us for Sunday dinner. Roast beef, carrots, and mashed potatoes were served around the large circular dining room table, as the men in attendance were loath to eat chicken, associating it with Herbert Hoover's promise to put a chicken in every pot. I can't quite comprehend the logistics of seating eight adults and nine toddlers from the age of eight weeks to eight years on a weekly basis, but somehow my mother always seemed to have it under control. I can still picture the adults relaxing around the table playing cards after the meal while my cousins and I laughingly dared each other to "cross over" playing Red Rover in the back yard in good weather or learned how to bounce back from random adversity as we sat inside challenging each other in *Chutes and Ladders* or *Sorry* on rainy afternoons. It didn't matter that my grandfather had fled Ireland during the potato famine to forge a new life in the United States only to find discriminating signs. It didn't matter that their meager savings accounts had been wiped out during the Depression. It didn't matter that my mother and her sisters had spent sleepless nights worrying over the fates of their fiancés while rationing meat and butter during the war. That was all in the past. Their future was filled with endless possibilities. The adults were ready to bury their former problems and anxious to enjoy the fruits of the promised prosperity. The joyous ruckus emanating from our play was a living embodiment of that great future. Life was safe and predictable on Tiffany Street in the 1950s.

Unlike the uncomplicated fictional family situations that appeared weekly on *The Donna Reed Show*, life, unfortunately, did not stay seamlessly serene for very long. First, my kindly old grandfather died, followed a few years later by my more demanding grandmother. My uncle was stricken by Parkinson's disease and left a young widow and two young children behind. The same year my cousin started first grade, my aunt returned to the workforce and inserted a totally unfamiliar model into our way of life—a mother who worked outside of the home. Toddlers eventually turned into teenagers, fetching the ball was replaced by organized ball games, and life simply became more complicated. With the birth of my brother, our home became a little too small for our growing family. The second time our house on the top of a steep hill was struck by lightning, my parents decided to sell and move closer to the high school my sister and I would be attending. Extended family Sunday dinners continued, but on a tighter schedule and with a smaller number in attendance.

Early into the new decade of the '60s, I graduated from eighth grade and thought my world was coming to an end when we ventured away from my familiar neighborhood and moved into a new home on the other side of town. Somehow the total upheaval to my life that I had tearfully envisioned stemming from my five-mile move never occurred as our house became a central meeting place for my friends, partially due to its location, right around the corner from the high school, but largely due to the warm brownies that greeted us when we walked through the door after school.

Be True to Your School

My high school years flew by as I participated in school plays, the school chorus, student government, and the varsity cheerleading squad. Most weekends our family could be found attending my younger brother's sporting events. Life could get a little adventuresome on the sidelines on afternoons when an obnoxious mother of an opposing team member menacingly screamed at her oversized offspring to "kill the quarterback," and my shocked pacifist mother retaliated with "Don't you dare lay a hand on my precious son!" Having a room of my own was a concept that never even entered my mind. My sister and I had always shared a room, and I remember feeling a little lost when she left for college and I was left with no one to rehash the day's events after the lights were turned off. I looked forward to vacation weekends when

Anne was home for a few days and we could resume our darkness-inspired introspective dialogues.

Excessive school spirit in the sixties routinely spilled over to the entire family units of the school community. Since I spent years yelling my lungs out on the sidelines of our school gymnasium, it went without saying my parents and my younger brother Dan would be there at every game to cheer their cheerleader's team on. With the competitive competency of our basketball squad, post-season play was almost always a given, and my family's station wagon joined a caravan of other fully packed cars in a community effort to support the team in tournament play. My first encounter with my future husband occurred during my sophomore year in high school and was less than romantically memorable. Our two schools met in the finals of the Massachusetts Catholic League State Basketball Championship in 1964 where I was a boisterous and bouncy cheerleader and Skip was doing an annoyingly effective job of keeping our leading player, and my best friend's brother, from scoring. As the game ended, his Catholic Memorial High School from West Roxbury just barely defeated my Cathedral of Springfield team, and everyone in my family agreed on the long, heartbreaking car ride home that had it not been for that infuriatingly competitive nameless guard, our team would have easily won.

A highly involved and conscientious student, in the fall of 1965 I applied to, and was accepted as an early decision candidate, by Regis College, a small Catholic women's liberal arts college in a western suburb of Boston. At this point in our country's cultural history, career options for women were generally limited to teaching, nursing, or working in an office as a secretary. I enrolled in Regis as a psychology major, assuming I would minor in education and eventually teach English.

Early in my freshman year, my psychology professor, Dr. Warren Gibbons, approached me to ask if I would consider a part-time position typing his research study, and suddenly my world was opened up to excitingly new and unimagined career paths. Within a few months of delving into this fascinating project, I was certain that I would be seeking a PhD after graduation rather than the commonly sought-after "Mrs." degree. With the absolute assurance that only an eighteen-year-old college freshman can assume, I was certain that I had found my niche in life and was fully focused on following this innovative and inspiring new dream.

DO YOU BELIEVE IN MAGIC?

Just because I had decided to dedicate myself to the field of psychology didn't mean I intended to spend my college years sequestered in my dorm room scrutinizing the works of Sigmund Freud and Eric Erickson. On weekends my friends and I would attend a "mixer" hosted at one of the various men's colleges in the greater Boston area. As mentioned before, the majority of Catholic New England colleges were single-sex. Boston College, the College of the Holy Cross, and Providence College were all-male while Regis, Emmanuel and Salve Regina educated only the female segment of polite society. In an attempt to keep its students focused on their studies rather than on the surrounding social life, freshman students at Regis were scheduled for 9 o'clock classes on Saturday mornings, resulting in a 10 o'clock curfew on Friday night—unless you happened to be safely seated on the school bus returning from a night of dancing at a neighboring men's college mixer.

Occasionally the social committee of Regis would send out flyers to the brother colleges (never to the sister schools) announcing that a Friday night dance would be held at a certain time on a specific date, downstairs in the Student Union in Weston, Massachusetts. Midway through the second semester of my freshman year, our college sponsored a multi-school mixer on a Saturday night during a special Sister's Weekend. Considering the close bond that Anne and I shared, there was no question that my sister would be joining me at Regis for this Sister's Weekend.

Skip had turned down a full college scholarship to the College of the Holy Cross when he decided to sign directly out of high school, but he vowed that he would complete his education during the off-season. Luckily for the course of my life, this educational resolution brought him back to the Boston area during the winter. After living on his own for three summers, one of which was spent enjoying the life of a major league ballplayer in Kansas City, moving back into his boyhood bedroom under his parents' roof must have been just a little bit boring for this off-season athlete. In an attempt to reconnect with his best friend from high school, Skip would occasionally placate his pal's whims and join him for some rather unusual weekend outings. On the day of the Regis College Sister's Mixer, Skip was back in Norwood working on an accounting assignment and fending off annoying interruptions from his friend Louie to join him in attending a college dance. Skip finally relented and agreed to accompany Louie to Regis, as long as Louie agreed not to call again before 7 o'clock.

Around 7:30 in the evening, Anne and I were taking the electric rollers out of our hair and searching around for the right shades of lipstick to go with the pink Pandora sweater I had chosen and her pale blue selection. At about the same time, Skip was jumping out of the shower and jumping into his car to drive across town and pick up his friend and having serious doubts about his decision to humor his old high school buddy and join him on his scouting expedition

At about 8:15, Anne and I left Domitilla Hall and strolled across campus with a group of my friends and their sisters to the lower level of the Student Center where the lights had been turned down and the music was blaring. A few busloads of young men from neighboring male colleges had already arrived and, as was generally the case during the first half-hour of a mixer, groups of girls were ogling and being ogled back by would-be suitors. A method to the madness of the music was always apparent during the early stages of a mixer. Three or four fast songs would be followed by one slow melody, which was, in turn, followed by a short soda break. This tuneful timing allowed the co-ed a reasonable time to get to meet a young man, say a few words during a slow dance and then rush off to the ladies' room to reassess that young man in the company of her friends. Anne and I had each met, and subsequently rejected, a possible dance partner during the opening set of the evening. While we were returning to the mixer on the opposite side of the hall, strategically avoiding our initial dancing partners, we bumped into Skip and his six-foot-four friend Louie scoping out the scene. We were just beginning polite introductions when the music started up again, effectively discouraging any further conversation until break time. Still trying to avoid a second dance sequence with an overbearing boring brute from BC, I accepted Louie's invitation to join him on the dance floor, even though I was hoping his slightly shorter and considerably more handsome friend had asked first. Gentleman that he was, Skip asked my sister if she would care to follow us onto the parquet.

It's important to note here that my sister already had a boyfriend and was not looking to replace him any time in the near future. With that in mind, I felt free to flirt with her dancing partner. As we twisted and bugalooed side by side, Skip and I began making more eye contact with each other than with our dancing partners. As was the custom at the end of the set, we broke up and reconvened in the appropriate rest stations to evaluate our next moves. Anne had observed the initial attraction between Skip and myself and suggested that we go back to get to know these friends a little better, only this time she would try to engage the taller one in conversation so I would be free to dance with Skip. Unbeknownst to us, a similar conversation was taking place between Skip and Louie. Skip insisted that, due to the discrepancies in our heights, he should dance with the shorter sister and Louie should partner up with the taller one. Echoing the words of an old song, we changed partners and then, we would never want to change partners again.

A recent survey stated that the odds of becoming a major league baseball player are less than 1 in 16,000. Given that there are more females than males in this country and that not all players choose to get married, the odds of marrying a professional baseball player become significantly less. I would venture an educated guess that the odds of meeting a professional baseball player at a woman's college mixer are infinitesimally small. This odds-breaking chance encounter changed the course of my life. Skip and I spent the rest of the evening together as we shared limited bits and pieces of personal information during the short musical reprieves. We got along great although I did find it a little strange that Skip and Louie both knew all the words to "Kansas City."

The first inkling I had that Skip had more going on in his life than merely matriculating at Boston College for the semester was when he pulled out his Professional Baseball Players Association identification card to write my number on the back. Naturally I thought he was bluffing, but decided I liked him well enough to give him the benefit of the doubt. After all, here was an entirely new pickup line I had never heard before and, being fascinated with the field of psychology, I was curious to see where it might lead. My curiosity was heightened when he stopped by his car (a 1966 blue-and-white Thunderbird convertible) as he walked me back to my dorm. While not exactly love at first sight, a significant amount of intriguing interest was definitely in the air. I was ecstatic to have my sister staying over in the next bed as I trusted her to share with me her honest assessment of the evening. Over the next few hours we replayed the night's events amidst suppressed giggles and open speculation as to whether or not Skip would call the next day.

Life is full of random encounters that intertwine with other chance coincidences. One of my best friends at Regis was the daughter of a professional baseball umpire. By nine o'clock the next morning, Anerie had her father, Ed Hurley, on the phone and was pumping him for information about my dashing dancing partner. Reassured about the veracity of his seemingly outrageous claim to fame, I was even more impressed by the personal seal of approval my friend's dad relayed to her regarding the reputation for integrity of this new "person of interest" in my life. "He's one of the good guys in the game," umpire/father figure Hurley related. And his initial assessment was right on target. It was time for my sister to get ready for her return trip to West Hartford and for me to stop pacing the hallway. A loud ringing sound emanated from the phone booth down the end of the corridor. (Not only did we not have a personal cell phone, we did not even have the luxury of a phone in our individual room.) With a smug "I told you he'd call" grin, my sister relayed the message that a certain Mr. Lockwood was on the phone for a Miss Murphy. The rest, as they say, is history.

Soon after this magical meeting, Skip was inducted into the Army Reserves and went north to fulfill his military obligation in Fort Dix, New Jersey, rather than south to join the Athletics for spring training in Arizona. As much as I was enamored by my dancing partner, I was first and foremost a serious student and continued to immerse myself in my liberal arts education. While pretending to myself that I didn't care for Skip all that much, I still wrote letters to him every week and conscientiously checked my own postal cubby for incoming mail. I received a phone call on the Wednesday night before Mother's Day of 1967. Skip was being handed an unexpected leave and planned to come home to surprise his mother for the weekend, and he cordially requested the pleasure of my company for that upcoming Saturday evening. Despite the fact that I had already secured a ride home after class on Saturday from one of my friends to visit my own mother, I answered in the affirmative to the date and then called Greyhound to check out the bus schedule to Springfield on Sunday morning.

Speaking with Skip on Saturday morning, I knew he was due to arrive around seven that coming evening, however, I had no idea where we were going and so consequently had no clue what to wear. For someone who was not all that interested in courting, I was putting an awful lot of effort into getting ready for this date. My heart seemed to skip just a little too excitedly for my own taste when I spied Skip's blue Thunderbird slowing down and pulling up in front of the dorm. In 1967, men were never allowed past the front desk of a woman's dorm and so a few moments after I had closed the curtains, I heard my name paged over the intercom to inform me that I had a "visitor in the lobby." By now I had my breathing under control and was ready to resume our friendship on a gracious basis.

Unbeknownst to me, our destination for the evening was a downtown Boston theater's special screening of *Un Homme et une Femme (A Man and a Woman)*, perhaps one of the most romantic movies ever made. The soundtrack alone could soften even the most hardened heart. Even though I continued my conversational French studies in college, I was still thankful for the English sub-titles to augment my more literal translations. As the movie ended, Jean-Louis raced his car along side the train tracks to reunite with Anne because their love was beginning to grow. I could completely connect with that same sensation that somehow our love was beginning to grow greater than the two of us also. As Skip walked me to my dorm just before the doors were locked at the bewitching hour of my midnight curfew, I mentioned that I would be leaving at seven the next day to board the bus for Springfield. To my immense delight, Skip's Thunderbird pulled up outside my building at 6:45 the following morning, ready to transport me in style to my parents' home. We reenacted last night's romantic movie scene as Skip raced down the highway to Springfield. An hour-and-a-half later (it would have taken me 4 or 5 on the bus), I was sitting in my childhood kitchen introducing my "new boyfriend" to my parents. After a quick cup of coffee, he was back on the Mass Pike, returning to take his own mother out to brunch while I sat starry-eyed in my living room unsuccessfully trying to decipher the Olde English dialogue of Chaucer's *Canterbury Tales*.

Despite my best intentions of not getting serious with anyone of the opposite sex, including a letter to that effect sent to Skip while he was in basic training a few months later, my emotional heart trumped my rational head, and I fell hopelessly in love. Over the next three years we composed countless correspondences to each other as Skip criss-crossed the country and I continued my undergraduate education at Regis. His military commitment put the brakes on his baseball career as he skidded in and out of minor league teams in between basic training and his monthly weekend warrior requirement. He spent time in Elmira, NY, Newport News, VA, and Phoenix, AZ, under the Athletics' tutelage and enjoyed a short-lived hiatus with the Houston Astros in the spring of '68 before being drafted by the Seattle Pilots in the expansion draft. Through it all, he continued to return to Boson to matriculate in the off-season and rekindle our romance. I accepted Skip's proposal of marriage during the Christmas break of my junior year in college. I also accepted the fact that obtaining the necessary doctorate in psychology in order to conduct useful research was no longer a reasonably attainable goal, and so I switched my major to English to procure a teaching degree I could take with me on the road. As I was planning my wedding in the Summer of '69, Skip was splitting his time between the Pilots' AAA club in Portland, OR, and the major league team in Seattle, WA.

Just a few minutes before my 10 o'clock curfew on a cold and windy night in early February 1970, I said a warm goodbye to my fiancé with little hope of seeing him again before our wedding in June. The following blustery morning Skip squeezed into his sensible Volvo (my practical suggestion that replaced his problem-ridden Thunderbird) that had been thoroughly stuffed with his worn-in cleats, his favorite gloves, and his lucky bats along with boxes packed with delicate crystal and china. A large chunk of available space in the car was taken up by my carefully packed hope chest. This large wooden piece was securely squashed into the back seat and surrounded by blankets and towels as I had reminded Skip countless times to be extremely careful of the chest due to the fragile nature of its contents. Four days later, he arrived in Tempe, Arizona, thankful to have made it halfway across the country with our engagement gifts still intact and eagerly anticipating the opportunity to pitch himself into a permanent position in the starting rotation of the Seattle Pilots baseball club.

Rumors begat rumors throughout the winter and continued on into the spring. The owners of the Seattle club had not received the anticipated local support during the first year of the franchise, and the much-rumored financial struggles of the organization appeared to have a base in reality. Paired up with last year's disappointing fiscal picture was the fact that the aviation industry in Seattle was suffering an enormous loss in productivity, and the anticipated gate revenue for the financially strapped Pilots painted a pretty dismal picture. Rumors concerning a buyout of the franchise had surfaced during the off-season, but we had not been privy to any inside information. (The Boston papers were a lot more enamored with their "Impossible Dream" team to care much about what was transpiring on the opposite coast.) Concrete details were tough to come by. The daily speculation during the spring as to whether or not the team would be moving away from Seattle triggered a lot of tension. There appeared to be a lot more to manage than merely deciding what players would be playing which position. Anyone familiar with Jim Bouton's, book *Ball Four*, can imagine the ingenious atmosphere that existed inside the clubhouse. The new manager, Dave Bristol, appeared to be taking his time assessing last year's core pitching talent before giving the fringe pitchers (in which group Skip was included) a serious look-see. Listening attentively between Skip's words during our bi-weekly phone calls, I could tell that Skip was a lot more pleased with how he was pitching than with how often.

The 1970 spring training season of the Seattle Pilots/Milwaukee Brewers ended in a mass of confusion. Who was in charge of the team? What city would the franchise be located in? Where would Skip be playing? When would this speculation end? Why didn't we have any control over all these important decisions in our lives? And most importantly: How was I going to deal with this insecurity for the rest of my life? The equipment van had already left for Seattle, but it was taking a hiatus in Las Vegas, awaiting the final decision to be made regarding the future of the franchise and its subsequent move to Milwaukee. I admit to being clueless at the time as to the enormous impact this logistical upheaval was going to play in my life. I was far more concerned about studying for my "comps" (one comprehensive exam spread out over two days that would test all the English material covered in the past four years) than I was in worrying about where in the United States I would be moving to in June. Despite my 94-year-old great aunt's frantic warning from her nursing home bed to stay far away from the Suquamish Indians on the outskirts of Seattle, I was more than ready to forge ahead into the Northwest. And then, just as the new season was about to start, the Seattle Pilots franchise filed for bankruptcy, and the league quickly and reluctantly okayed Bud Selig's offer to purchase the team and move it to Milwaukee. In the midst of this chaos, Skip was unceremoniously left off the major league roster and assigned to the AAA affiliate that would stay put in last year's Pacific Coast League location, Portland, Oregon.

In a rare move of generosity, Skip was given permission by the new Brewers organization management to leave spring training a day early to drive his household-goods-laden car north and join the team in Portland. Naturally the hope chest was carefully repositioned and secured in the back seat along with a number of other boxes marked "IMPORTANT FRAGILE." I was tenderly told "not to worry, things are going to work out just fine" by my husband-to-be from his motel room somewhere in the middle of nowhere on his way to who knew where. "You're going to love Oregon," Skip warmly relayed, and besides, "Who wants to live in Milwaukee, anyway?"

The next morning, on a wet and winding road somewhere north of Sacramento, CA, Skip's sensibly safe Volvo refused to climb the steep incline and sputtered to a stop on the side of the highway. More than just a little frustrated with the situation, Skip locked the car and started walking in the breakdown lane to find help. As he glanced behind him, he could see his brand new car filled with all our worldly possessions staring to roll backwards down the hill. Leaving his common sense behind, Skip ran towards the vehicle, unlocked the door, and jumped into the driver's seat as the car continued to slide off the road and get caught in a guardrail overhanging a deep ravine. After extracting himself from the Volvo's precariously perched position, he hailed down a good samaritan to call AAA (the American Automobile Association, not the minor league affiliate) for him as he agonized over his predicament. An hour later, the vacant vehicle had been extricated from the embankment and towed to the nearest repair shop that had a technician with at least a working knowledge of foreign autos. The semi-literate mechanic assessed the damage to the car and determined it would take at least two weeks for him to order the necessary parts and complete the necessary repairs. With the nearest car rental agency over an hour away, Skip had no reasonable choice other than to place his trust, and my hope chest, in the care of total strangers, and hop on the local Greyhound bus heading towards Portland. Throwing his baseball equipment bag in the overhead compartment and carefully placing two randomly selected large fragile boxes on his lap, he headed towards Portland with high hopes for the coming season and deep misgivings about leaving my cherished china behind.

An endless afternoon was spent bumping along the winding highway with the awkward cardboard boxes carefully arranged on the adjoining seat before my fiancé and my home furnishings safely arrived in Portland, Oregon. It took a few more days for Skip to settle in. Finally, after renting a car for the home stand and securing a furnished apartment for the season, Skip moved in and began to unpack my precious possessions. His relief at the excellent condition of the china was countered by his astonishment with the limited contents: a four-piece place setting of strawberry embossed china with matching serving pieces, garnet red wine goblets with matching water and juice glasses and the *coup de grâce*, a large ceramic cookie jar. Later that evening, he "calmly" shared his consternation over the fact that he could have easily purchased similar stoneware in Oregon at a fraction of the frustrating cost of transporting said boxes all across the country. What do men know of the emotional connection of dining off dishes that were thoughtfully purchased by well-meaning relatives?

Two weeks into the new season, Skip's pitching career was on a forward roll while his car was standing still in the repair shop. On a scheduled off-day in Milwaukee, the new team in town, the Milwaukee Brewers, scheduled an exhibition game with the Atlanta Braves, formerly known and loved in Wisconsin as the Milwaukee Braves. Not wanting to waste a valuable start from one of the few competent starting pitchers, Dave Bristol called Skip up from Portland's AAA team to pitch for the Brewers. Timing is everything in life, and Skip chose the perfect time to perform at the apex of his ability. Skip not only pitched a one-hit shutout, striking out Hank Aaron in the process, but he also drove in the winning run to win the game. What I wouldn't have given to be at that game! Unfortunately, since the game was considered an exhibition match, no official statistics were recorded, but the fans and the coaches sat up and took notice. The new manager was impressed. Skip was instructed to cancel his plane reservation back to Portland the following day and instead make a reservation at the local hotel for the next few days. He would be staying with the big club for the time being. His great jubilation was mixed with just a small amount of my uncertainty as to what impact this might have on our wedding plans in Massachusetts. Of lesser concern was the question of what to do with his car that was still being repaired in California.

One of my close college friend's favorite expressions was: "Don't worry, God will provide." I guess I had to agree. God had provided the opportunity for Skip to showcase his talent, and Skip used that opportunity wisely. The little details of our life quietly fell into place. Skip continued to throw the ball hard and remained in Milwaukee for the next four years. His Volvo was finally fixed and shipped to Wisconsin although it continued to balk at taking left-hand turns until we traded it in a year later. And Skip, with the aid of his commanding officer of the Army Reserve Unit in Quincy, MA, made it home in early June to meet me at the altar at the appointed time and place. Who said dreams only come true in fairy tales?

2

Take Me Out to the Ballgame

WE'VE ONLY JUST BEGUN

According to Hindu tradition, rain on your wedding day is a sign of good luck as it signifies a strong marriage. The premise behind this belief is that a wet knot is harder to untie. The skies showered us with torrential downpours on June 6, 1970, the morning I became Mrs. Claude Edward "Skip" Lockwood and vowed to be true for better or for worse, in sickness and in health, in good times and in bad, for long as we both should live. Over the years there has been a lot of tugging on that sodden knot, but the bond of love that was cemented on that delightfully damp day has continued to hold strong.

Naïve cannot begin to describe my view of reality on the eve of my marriage. My sheltered upbringing, as previously described, assured me that as long as I put forward my best effort, God would always provide. Skip and I became engaged during the Christmas break of my junior year of college and spent over a year planning an elaborate wedding to be held the weekend after I graduated. Throughout the sultry summer prior to my senior year, my mother, sister, and I journeyed from Springfield to Boston to Hartford, previewing the packages of function halls and florists as we concentrated on the countless intricate details of wedding planning. Pale pink pastel tablecloths with matching napkins were selected from a rainbow of colors to coordinate with the bridesmaids' gowns. Pink and white roses were chosen to grace the center of each table, and the favorite local five-piece wedding band, reminiscent of *The Wedding Singer's* ensemble, was reserved for the reception. Lovely white satin bows adorned with seasonal flowers would line the church aisles and, after agonizing over all the inspired options, cascading baskets of ivy-lined flowers won out for the bridesmaids. My own bridal bouquet would be sculpted out of white roses and ivy. To depict this day in pictures, we scrutinized the portfolio of several photographers and agreed upon the most unpretentious ego to capture our love for posterity.

Everything was falling into place. Skip had completed his active duty with the Army National Guard and was back to being a full-time professional baseball player and a part time "weekend warrior." Never once did it occur to us that it was ludicrous to plan a June wedding in the middle of the baseball season or that Skip would have any problem making it home to participate in the ceremony. As the year progressed and more and more last-minute decisions had to be made, I think my mother was secretly pleased that I was so engrossed in my studies I did not have time to interfere with her meticulous arrangements. The fact that Skip left for spring training in February and would only randomly return for weekend reserve meetings did create a few minor logistical problems. Massachusetts bureaucracy required the bride and groom to go together to city hall the week before the wedding to register for their marriage certificate. With Skip being a thousand miles away in Milwaukee, this was virtually impossible, so my younger

Mr. and Mrs. Skip Lockwood on their wedding day, June 6, 1970.

brother posed as my future husband while I quickly and competently filled out the necessary paperwork. In an amazing stroke of timing combined with a large scale of sheer luck, Skip was scheduled to pitch at home in Milwaukee on Wednesday, June 3, and then fly back to Boston for his monthly reserve duty. He flew into Boston Thursday morning and, with the blessing of his commanding officer, cut his Boston military obligation short and arrived in Springfield, MA, just in time for the 6:00 wedding rehearsal Friday night. No problem.

Bridesmaids adorned in pale pink pique dresses and carrying white wicker baskets filled with ivy and roses made a dash for the limo as the heavens opened and the rain poured down. My father's big black golf umbrella sheltered my own antique white lace gown as we joined my friends in the waiting limousine. Laughter squelched any jitters as we all took off our satin pumps and raced barefoot into the back of the church to avoid ruining our delicate satin shoes. I recognized that morning that no matter how organized you are or how many plans you have made, it is impossible to maintain complete control of events. My own carefully orchestrated daughter's wedding this past February started with an impromptu romantic candlelight rehearsal dinner, due to a power outage, and ended with a blizzard that forced all the guests to spend the night at the hotel. As I glided down the aisle on my father's arm to the strains of Pachelbel's "Canon," I felt comforted by my parents' love and confident in pledging that same devotion to my husband. Gazing into each other's eyes, we vowed to love, honor, and respect each other. Aside from the uncooperative weather, the day was perfect. The classical music set the mood for a beautiful ceremony and, despite the few giggles that could be heard from my college friends when the priest asked: "Do you, Kathleen, take this Claude?" our lives were forever joined together. Although life has presented considerable challenges since that time, I have learned over the years that love does not come easy, but with constant effort and attention it can survive. Forty years later, we are still very much in love and committed to honoring those sacred vows.

Bright and early, as the sun rose on a beautiful summer morn the following Monday, Skip and I boarded a flight from Hartford, Connecticut. A very prophetic photograph, taken on the tarmac outside the plane that was to transport me to a whole new world, captures me in custody of the burdensome briefcase. We landed in Milwaukee, Wisconsin, with just enough of a layover to collect the plethora of packages that had accompanied us on the plane and cram them into the little white Volvo Skip had left at the airport the previous week. With all our earthly belongings safely stored in the Governor Mitchell Airport parking garage, we headed to the other end of the airport in time to catch the team flight to Detroit.

Wives rarely accompanied their husbands on road trips at this time, partially due to the high cost of air travel in relation to players' low salaries, and partially because other players did not really care to have their traveling escapades reported back home. "What happened on road trips, stayed on road trips." Being a new bride, I did not fully appreciate this unspoken code of conduct and wondered why I was getting such curious stares from the team. Later I discovered that the majority of the players assumed I was Skip's girlfriend, which would have been fine, but when they realized I was his new wife, the curious stares turned into suspicious glares. We had followed the "If you do not ask, you cannot get "no" for an answer" approach when neglecting to discuss our wedding plans with the Brewers management. Skip merely flew home for his monthly Army Reserve meeting and returned with a new bride. Thankfully, Tommy Ferguson, the team traveling secretary and a fellow Bostonian, became a willing accomplice. Not only did he give Skip advance notice of the Detroit/Cleveland itinerary so I could arrange a seat for myself on the same flight, he secretly secured the bridal suite for us in Detroit. Despite his penchant for chewing tobacco, Tommy was a rare gentleman and in a class by himself when it came to caring about the players and their families.

Word of our nuptials spread quickly, and a handful of players came over to congratulate us and warn me about the "crazy world I was entering." How prophetic. The world of baseball turned out to be wild, wonderful, perplexing, passionate, fanatical, frustrating, exciting, extreme, and most definitely, certifiably crazy. I was beginning to feel a little overwhelmed at the inquisition by Skip's teammates, and so we discretely settled ourselves into the back of the plane to avoid further scrutiny. Thus began my journey into the unknown and unpredictable world of baseball life outside of the ballpark.

MOTOR CITY MADNESS

I had always dreamed of spending my honeymoon in Australia, strolling through the rain forests, touring the outback while watching baby kangaroos jump by, snapping photos of little koala bears munching on eucalyptus leaves, and taking leisurely strolls along pristine beaches. Strangely enough, Detroit and Cleveland never figured into my honeymoon dreams, but I learned early in our engagement the need to be flexible so: Goodbye, Sydney; hello, Detroit! It did not take long to realize that my honeymoon would differ significantly from those featured in most issues of *Brides' Magazine*. Upon arrival in Detroit, the reality of life on the road on my own set in. Everyday traveling hassles do not exist for a professional athlete. Care is taken not to stress out any of Peter's lost boys, and so all the little details of this nomadic lifestyle had been arranged in advance by a responsible adult, the traveling secretary. A bus was waiting at the terminal to pick up the team and dash them away to their next game. With a quick kiss and a promise to leave me tickets to the game, Skip boarded the bus with the rest of his team and headed straight for the ballpark. His luggage had been specially tagged, taken off the plane and sent to the hotel. I was left alone in the airport to retrieve my suitcase at baggage and secure my own transportation into the Motor City. Having made a copy of Skip's itinerary, I knew the name and location of the hotel, so I flagged down a cab and bravely proceeded to find my own way in a strange city.

The Mario Andretti clone of a cab driver wove his way in and out of traffic jams, and I was delivered to downtown Detroit in record time with my heart beating as fast as the tires skidding across the pavement. Entering the grand lobby of the hotel, I deftly pushed my suitcase with the tip of my toe to the front desk and attempted to register. The portly assistant manager was pompously polite but reluctant at first to give me the keys to the room since my driver's license still reflected my maiden name. His arrogant attitude changed drastically after conferring with the hotel manager. The Brewers' traveling secretary had personally spoken to the hotel manager and advised him of our recent nuptials. Suddenly I found myself being warmly welcomed to the Motor City, escorted up to the top floor, and ushered into the bridal suite (unfortunately, by the bellhop). Talk about a whirlwind romance. After a quick shower to revive my spirits, I returned to the lobby an hour later equipped with a new sense of confidence and ready to attend my first game as a professional ballplayer's wife.

The cab ride to Detroit's baseball stadium was an education in itself. Graduating as an English major, I thought I understood what the word slum meant, but my conception of a slum differed drastically from the bombed-out ghetto the cab driver drove through on the way to Tiger Stadium. On a hot summer evening, scantily dressed children were jumping through puddles on streets flooded by fire hydrants. Tightly clad pre-pubescent girls were hanging out with studly wannabe thugs while "Summer in the City" blasted through the airwaves on a portable radio. Gangs of angry teenagers huddled on street corners while the police made their presence very apparent, breaking up crowds and casually swinging their intimidating billy clubs. Every time the cab stopped for a red light, I held my breath until it started moving again. I arrived at the stadium more than a little unnerved and with a new appreciation for the blessings I had been given in life.

The surly cab driver let me out at the dark corner across the street to avoid his getting caught in the pre-game traffic. I had been instructed to pick up my tickets at Will Call. Regrettably for my throbbing feet, squeezed into my new high heel sandals, it took circling the stadium two times before I could find an attendant who knew where that window was located. After finally securing my admittance to "the show," I located my seat just behind the dugout and sat down, emotionally exhausted. Heaving a heavy sigh, I attempted to gather myself together, put the unnerving cab ride behind me, and enjoy the present moment. Assuming that everyone in my row was somehow connected to a Milwaukee Brewers team member, I readily engaged in conversation with the strangers sitting next to me.

The Paul Bunyan look-alike to my right turned out to be a divorced ex-ballplayer. After congratulating me on my marriage, he proceeded to give me some unsolicited marital advice. This giant egomaniac was a pitcher himself, and so he took it upon himself to explain the inner psyche of an athlete to me, in particular, how frustrated a pitcher can get after a bad outing. His ex-wife simply did not understand his need to come home after a game and smash the lamps or break the legs of the kitchen chairs to release his anger. I was not totally familiar with the majority of his colorful "expletive deleted" vocabulary, but I did manage to nod at the appropriate times as his described his destructive behavior. He really hoped that I would take his well-meaning advice and be more understanding and forgiving of boyish temper tantrums so my marriage could last. Wow! Afraid to find out what other little quirks I should try to overlook, I decided to focus my conversation on the six-months' pregnant young lady to my left. Communication was difficult at first because there did appear to be a bit of a language barrier between my slight Boston accent and her heavy southern drawl. While I was perhaps a little overdressed for a ball game in a demure pastel linen sundress with matching sandals, she obviously had selected her wardrobe from the Fredrick's of

Hollywood catalog, intent on attracting lots of attention. Her response to my inquiry of to whom on the team she was married caused me to question my decision to marry a professional ballplayer. She haughtily replied that she was not yet married, "but the s.o.b. who impregnated her better make good on his promise to marry her quickly before her baby was born a bastard." Double wow! Welcome to baseball life. How in the world was a sheltered, Catholic young lady from Massachusetts ever going to survive in such an environment? Taking a long, deep breath, I regained my composure and concentrated on my present predicament. Like Wendy, I had just left the safe confines of home and flown off to follow Peter Pan on a great adventure. I was determined not to be dismayed by this first encounter in baseball land but to continue to keep thinking happy thoughts and enjoy the ride.

If America's National Pastime was going to govern my life, I decided to become a student of the game so I could appreciate its complexities. Up until this point, my life had been ruled by time constraints. Classes were held on a specific day at a specific time. Exams were scheduled in four-hour time slots. Papers were due by 10:00 A.M. or not accepted for full credit. My day was totally structured and my watch was my most precious possession. I quickly discovered that time is a relative concept in baseball.

The rules of baseball are simple. The pitcher stands on the mound and throws the ball to the batter, who attempts to hit the ball past the opposing players, who are trying to catch the ball. It's a team sport dictated and controlled by individual performances. Physics teaches us that for every action there is a reaction. This theory can be vividly witnessed during a baseball game. Ultimately the pitcher controls all the action. Nothing happens until the pitcher decides to let loose of the ball. Once that ball is thrown, the focus now is on the reactions of the batter. He might react quickly, make great contact with the ball, and get a hit. A slightly slower reaction could result in fouling the ball off, and an even slower reaction would most likely end up with a swing and miss. If and when the batter does manage to hit the ball, his fate is now in the hands of the opposing players on the field who are perched in anticipatory positions ready to react as the ball comes their way. Infielders need to react very quickly to decide if the ball is going to the left or the right or if it might be necessary to jump up at just the right moment to snag the ball. Outfielders have slightly more time to react, but must cover more ground to capture the ball. Physical and mental errors often come into play during this confrontation, and "lady luck" contributes greatly to the outcome of this game of inches. The game is scheduled to be played in nine innings with each team getting three outs per inning, but if the game is tied after the suggested time period, play continues indefinitely. Occasionally a game is suspended due to local curfews, but if this happens, the game continues the following day until a victor is established.

The basic rules are simple, but it's the people who follow these rules that make it interesting. I could already identify a few of the more colorful players before the final out of my first road trip game. Some players thrive on being the center of attention, making ordinary plays look spectacular, sliding into bases just for the fun of it and leading the constant chatter on and off the field. Others display the quiet confidence of superior talent, making the impossible look routine and approaching the plate with a smug grin and a defiant swagger. Whatever their outward appearance suggests, almost all professional ballplayers are first-time Little League all-stars at heart. The pitchers simply want to throw the ball past the batter, and the batters want to hit that ball out of the park. Everyone wants to play all the time, but the rules only allow nine players on the field at a time. The remaining players participate in the game from either the bullpen or the dugout.

Relief pitchers and the second-string catcher reside in the bullpen. An unspoken chain of command rules the bullpen, but in this "you're only as good as your last outing" world, the top reliever can change on a weekly basis. Due to the outfield location of most bullpens, it is challenging for the players to keep centered on the contest, and so the talented athletes creatively find ways to stay caught up in the competition: Effortless juggling exercises, makeshift empty-bottle bands, junior-high hot foots, and other childish shenanigans frequently find their way inside the bullpen fences. Players in the dugout have a better view of the action and thus are more involved with the play on the field. They scrutinize the opposing pitcher's style in anticipation of getting a chance to hit later in the game. Veteran bench-sitters perform a pivotal role in mentoring the younger players with encouragement and creative criticism. Between bags of sunflower seeds and gallons of Gatorade, the reserve players analyze everything from the pitcher's curveball to the blonde in the second row. Good-natured mischievous ribbing helps to relieve the monotony and moodiness of these bench-sitting backup players.

Flamboyant ballpark vendors add character to the action. Selling trays of hot dogs, soda, peanuts, and popcorn, these personable peddlers compete with each other for the fans' admiration. One will capture attention with a baritone rendition of "get your hot dogs here," another might deftly swing his soda tray in a seesaw manner and never spill a drop, but the peanut pushers are usually the most proficient in artistic expression. With amazing skill, one can locate the fan yelling for "peanuts," toss the requested number of bags up ten rows with an assortment of overhand, underhand, and behind-the-back throws, keep an eye on the money being passed down to him, and send the correct change back, all while spotting his next challenge. Talent comes in all shapes and forms at the ballpark.

To the delight of the hometown baseball fans that balmy June evening, the game ended with a victory for Detroit. It would be just one of many losses that year for the Milwaukee Brewers. As the Tiger fans joyfully whooped and hollered after the last out, I sat quietly in my seat waiting for the commotion to end before leaving the shelter of the stands. Jostling through the rowdy crowds, all streaming towards the exits at Indy 500 speed, I was definitely more than a little intimidated. Up to this point in my life, my multicultural interactions consisted of my Irish friends and myself sampling cannoli at the St. Anthony's Italian church festival. The concrete hallway at the end of the runway was far from inviting as I paced, alert and alone, for Skip to emerge from the clubhouse. Finally my solitary sojourn was over, and I was reunited with the reason I left the safety of my home and traveled on to Neverland.

Finally we were going to have dinner! The lifestyle of a professional athlete does not readily promote healthy eating habits. A late breakfast followed by frequent snacks keeps the body fueled until after the game. Evening dining choices are limited by which restaurants are still serving after the game. These meager meal options are further limited by the restaurants that were considered "off limits" to a player accompanied by his wife. Being a classic, clueless newlywed, I did not question why Skip insisted that I stay in the restaurant foyer while he went inside to check out the menu at the dark little steak house near the hotel. I had no idea that Skip was scoping out the restaurant to see if it was safe to enter (i.e., it was clear of any overwrought outfielders drowning their sorrows with sympathetic sycophants). After a few late night dinners where we had run into only a handful of players, I did question why so few players seemed to be dining out after the game. My inquiry was answered with an honest retort that, after the first night of almost stumbling in on an embarrassing encounter, Skip was announcing our repast destination in advance, and those players who might have a "wandering eye" were given fair warning.

If I thought my trip from Milwaukee to Detroit was a challenge, it was nothing compared to my excursion from Detroit to Cleveland. The new owners of the Milwaukee Brewers organization did not have deep pockets. Consequently, travel arrangements were made with more concern for cost than for convenience. The chartering of a private plane to whisk the team away after the game was never seriously considered. Instead, a "comfortable" bus would charter the major league players from Detroit to Cleveland after the game. Obtaining a seat on the team bus was out of the question, so I again set my sights on the second star to the right and ventured out on my own.

My sheltered upbringing had certainly not prepared me for city life. About an hour after the team left for the ballpark, I went down to the lobby to wait for the shuttle bus that would transport me to the airport. Not being a seasoned traveler, I was almost half an hour early for the scheduled departure time, afraid that it might leave without me. After sitting on the tapestry couch for approximately 15 minutes, frequently glancing out the window for the bus, I grew uncomfortable by the intense inquiry of a creepy-looking man sitting across from me. Not wanting to be rude, I politely smiled back and became unnerved by his dark disconcerting demeanor. Listening to my gut feeling that "something was just not right," I got up and moved to the other side of the lobby. This sketchy-looking man followed me across the parquet floor and proceeded to sit down in the chair closest to mine. A slight feeling of panic overtook me. It was more than the stale air in the lobby that caused my palms to sweat and my heart to race. I was filled with relief when I spotted the airport shuttle bus slowing down. My emotional reprieve was short-lived. My would-be assailant casually bumped into my shoulder, whisked open his jacket, and exposed himself to me. To say I was shocked could not begin to describe my traumatized feelings. I tried to scream, but words would not come out of my mouth. Self-preservation took over, and I forced my rubbery legs onto the bus. I slid into the seat directly behind the bus driver and prayed that this sleazy character would not follow me onto the bus.

As I tried to regain my composure and catch my breath, I disintegrated into an emotional mess, partially frightened to death by the experience but more aptly extremely upset with myself for not standing up and reporting the incident to the proper authorities. Was it really only a few months ago that I was vehemently arguing against the "excuse" of rationalization? My convictions had seemed to be so clear during my ethics seminar, as I stared out the stained glass windows of the ivy-covered, brick, rotund classroom and argued forcefully that a woman should always stand up for herself and never be intimidated by an aggressive male. Reality had certainly shaken those ivory tower convictions. After all, what could I have done? I knew no one who lived in Detroit and had no idea how to contact Skip at the ballpark. I did not even have a credit card with my new name embossed on it. If I missed my plane, I would be totally stranded. As I sat staring out the grime-stained window of the airport shuttle bus, my pulse was calming down, but my mind was racing full forward. Here it was only Week One of my new life as a baseball bride and I was already struggling to maintain my core beliefs. While I was still convinced that life was going to be a great adventure, I was starting to redefine what kind of an adventure that would be.

Thankfully, the rest of my solo trip to Cleveland was uneventful. My luggage had been tagged with the teams and was heading to the Indians' ballpark along with the rest of the Brewers paraphernalia via the highways, and so, I only had one small carry-on to contend with. Recent experience had taught me to be a little more cautious about smiling at strangers, so I kept my eyes focused forward and found an engaging elderly woman to sit next to while waiting to board the plane. Clouds were both floating by in the sky and covering my mind during the short flight to Cleveland. I realized that I was going to need to become a little less open and a little more street-savvy. Upon landing, I guardedly scurried to the exit of the terminal and hailed a taxi cab to downtown Cleveland. Once again I arrived at the hotel before the team, but this time I was prepared for the front desk clerk's interrogation. I flashed my most endearing smile along with my glimmering wedding ring as I registered as Mrs. Skip Lockwood. Collecting the key to my room and double checking that I was not being followed, I avoided the lobby and strode directly to the elevator and up to the safety of the hotel room. Securing the dead lock bolt, I physically collapsed on the bed, but I did not mentally relax until I heard my husband's reassuring knock on the hotel door a few hours later.

Mercifully, Municipal Stadium was only a short ride through a safe industrial area from the hotel. To my untrained stadium-calculating eye, the Indians' stomping grounds had to be the biggest ballpark ever constructed. With seating for over 70,000, the place was enormous. Unfortunately, a combination of unfavorable economic conditions combined with unspectacular play from the home team resulted in the majority of seats being vacant. There were no streaming crowds to fight, and it was relatively easy for me to obtain my ticket and find my seat behind the visitor's dugout. In only a few days Tommy Ferguson, the Brewers' traveling secretary, had become my new best friend and would randomly drop by my seat at the ballpark to check on my well-being. No other wives were on the trip, but he did introduce me to a few extended family members who were seated in my section. As I struck up casual conversations with my fellow visiting team fans, including a radiant redhead and a brilliant brunette, I was cognizant of not asking any questions I did not really want to know the answers to.

It quickly became clear that the characters in this new chapter of my life were going to differ vastly from my previous peer relationships. My brief initiation into the athlete's life on the road helped me to appreciate the many different levels of competition that exist in baseball, both on and off the field. Although I had never been one to bury my head in the sand, I also did not want to be in the position of compromising my relationships with the small group of wives I would be meeting in Milwaukee. For the time being, I was willing to assume that all the gorgeous groupies were only goggling the gregarious single players. Life experiences have reinforced my initial belief that most people are worthy of the benefit of the doubt. Over the years I have come to realize that not every situation is as unseemly as it might first appear. I have probably witnessed more ballplayers fending off advances as surrendering to them. In fact, it is my unscientific personal observation that the more talented the player is, the less likely he is to succumb to a meaningless encounter at a bar. A player with true talent is generally secure enough in his own accomplishments that he does not require the constant reassurance of his athletic proficiency as much as the marginally talented, self-centered egomaniac. In true Peter Pan fashion, many gifted athletes are not seeking an emotional encounter as they fly across the country. Most are content to merely rehash the game over a beer and crow about their accomplishments.

My so-called honeymoon was coming to an end. After only two nights in Cleveland, it was time to move on. We were up early and had our bags down in the lobby before 10:00 A.M. The welcoming smell of freshly brewed coffee greeted us as we waited in line to be seated at the hotel restaurant. Quiet team members sat scattered around the restaurant, hunched over the crossword puzzle and dining on plates heaped full of bacon, eggs, and pancakes. This was my first indication that we were actually staying at the same hotel as the Milwaukee Brewers team. I received a few polite smiles, but there seemed to be a "no talking allowed" rule in place as the players mentally readied themselves for the upcoming day game.

From the Brewers' perspective, the game was a total disaster. A few errors, a few hit batsmen (including my husband), a smattering of hits, and a home run resulted in a significant win for the Cleveland Indians. After my traumatic experience in Detroit, I was certainly not anxious to take another solitary trip to the airport. Thankfully, my husband concurred. Skip and I procured a cab and headed towards the airport after the rather difficult final game in Cleveland. Once there, Skip would meet up with the Brewers at the terminal and continue on to the West Coast with the team. I would board another plane and fly back to Milwaukee. The logical side of my brain tried to remind the emotional side of my mind that I had no reason to be getting so upset. I ought to be accustomed to Skip leaving; after all, we had spent more than half of the past three years writing letters to each other from various locations all over the country. But my egocentric emotions took over, arguing that, in the past, I was left behind either in the comfort of my parents' home or amidst the chaos and camaraderie of my college co-eds. As I watched my husband turn his back and disappear down the long corridor of the Cleveland Hopkins International Airport, the reality of my new baseball widow existence set in. Skip was off to the other end of the terminal to join his teammates for a week full of scheduled games and late night get-togethers out west; I was heading "home" to Milwaukee to an empty apartment with only a car full of unopened boxes to keep me company for the next week. This solitary scenario was not quite the glamorous lifestyle that had filled my dreams for the past year.

Okay, enough self-pity. Time to regroup and forge forward. I pulled my boarding pass out of my pocketbook and headed for the gate. No sooner had we taken off than it was time to land. I could feel my heart skip a beat as the landing gear opened on our descent into General Mitchell Airport in Milwaukee, Wisconsin. It was a beautiful Sunday evening as the plane taxied into the terminal. Every new adventure must start with the first step, and so I embarked on this journey by descending the exterior stairway of the plane one step at a time. If Mary Richards could make it in Minneapolis, I could certainly learn how to thrive in Milwaukee. I would just have to turn on my biggest smile and look for the love that was all around me.

It was that all-surrounding love that placed such a strain on my determined smile. The dispiriting state of my present solitary situation hit me the minute I entered the concourse. The airport was filled with families welcoming loved ones to Milwaukee, Wisconsin: fathers hugging darling daughters; mothers cuddling sticky sons; children reuniting with long-lost grandparents, and husbands enthusiastically embracing their wives. An overpowering sensation of isolation hit me. Feeling more than just a little overwhelmed and out of place, I passed by all the friends and lovers waiting anxiously at the gate. I knew better than to scan the crowd for a familiar face in this unfamiliar concourse. Instead, I mustered up all my remaining courage and headed directly to the baggage claim area to retrieve my luggage. I reached over and grabbed my outdated *KEM*-monogrammed luggage from the carousel and left the happily reunited couples behind. Suitcases with wheels were not in vogue in 1970, so with a slow and steady gait I pushed and pulled my unwieldy suitcase through the terminal and across the parking garage to retrieve our car. Despite my best effort to keep it all together, my stoic demeanor began to disintegrate, and my eyes began to water as I read the bright blue neon sign: Welcome to Milwaukee, Home of the Milwaukee Brewers! Some welcome.

I had just enough strength left to heave my navy blue leather bag up onto the passenger seat and squeeze the matching valise onto the front floor. Inside the confines of my fully packed car, I weakly smiled into the rear view mirror and sighed: "Welcome home and welcome to the next unpredictable adventure in this new chapter of your life." Somewhere deep down in my subconscious I heard the following strains echo: Remember you are in love and with that love "you're going to make it after all."

So began my initiation into the amazing world of major league baseball. For the next twelve years we shared countless new horizons. Like the song lyrics, we started out walking and learned to run as we drove down the many roads chosen for us by the powers that be and worked hard to maintain our individual sanity along with our marriage—together we had just begun.

HAPPY DAYS

I had read about the gregarious nature of Midwesterners, but reading about that warmth could not compare to experiencing the kindness and generosity of the staff at Milwaukee's County Stadium. Marian Cunningham's double from *Happy Days* beamed from behind the Will Call ticket window, congratulated me on my recent marriage, and welcomed me to my new home. The gate attendant glowed with enthusiasm as he pulled open the barrier and offered a sincere "Welcome to County Stadium!" As an elderly usher meticulously wiped off my seat, he winked and whispered that he recognized me from my wedding photo in last week's sports page. He then proceeded to introduce me to the other players' wives sitting in his section. What a delightful difference from my first honeymoon ballpark experience in Detroit.

Upon entering the friendly confines of County Stadium, I was struck by both the charm and the immaculate cleanliness of the old ballpark. While the Brewers were a brand new team in town, they were playing in a stadium that was steeped in tradition and history. The largely German and Polish population had embraced the likes of Hank Aaron and Warren Spahn as their native sons, and they were now gearing up to welcome a new generation of would-be heroes. Freshly painted seats were anchored on smooth concrete aisles. Seating sections were partitioned by metal banisters that gleamed in the sunlight. Ushers rushed to wipe the imaginary dust off the wooden chairs. "Please" and "Thank You" seemed to be the catch words of the day. Organ music escorted the fans to their seats. Sure, the concession stands sold the required hot dogs and popcorn throughout the stadium, but it was the smell of beer and bratwurst smothered in barbeque sauce that permeated the stands. First impressions can be lasting, and my first impression was extremely positive. I knew I was going to like it here.

There was an undercurrent of enthusiasm and expectation in the crowd on this lovely late June evening. Summer had finally come to Wisconsin. Fans stood for the National Anthem and celebrated every word. The Brewers had just come off a two-week road trip, and the local fans were eager to welcome them back. The players were given a standing ovation just for running out on the field and assuming their designated positions. When the larger-than-life Gene Brabender took the mound that night, he took the hopes of the fans with him. They cheered with every strike and groaned with every hit. The umpires were only right when they made calls favoring the home team.

I thought I had left the stressful aspect of my life behind when I graduated from college in June. It did not take long to learn that the stress of completing assignments over which I had been given specific guidelines and was in total control of my own effort was nothing compared to the stress associated with being the wife of a major league baseball pitcher where I had absolutely no control over anything. I could yell as loud as my vocal chords would allow, but my cheering had no impact on the speed or location of Skip's fastball. The narrow line between the "thrill of victory" and "the agony of defeat" became apparent to me the first game I watched Skip pitch in Detroit. He had come in with bases loaded and struck out the first two batters he faced (thrill) and then, with two strikes on the last batter, he gave up a game-winning home run (agony). I was instantaneously initiated into the highs and lows I would be encountering over the next dozen years. No wonder so many baseball wives color their hair. A few too many hits for the Minnesota Twins and a few too many runners left on base for the Milwaukee Brewers along with a few misplayed balls on both sides made for an exciting game. Unfortunately, the Brewers lost that game, as they would so many others that season, but I fell in love with the ballpark and its fabulously forgiving fans.

When the game ends, the waiting begins. As the fans head for the exits, baseball wives head for the waiting room. The new owners of the Milwaukee Brewers had a million details to work out in the six short days between being given the final approval on April 1, 1970, to purchase the Seattle Pilots and opening the season at County Stadium as the Milwaukee Brewers. Most of the team's baseball equipment had already left Arizona and was on a truck on its way to Seattle. Basic necessities, such as bats and balls, had to be purchased. Administrative staff, gate attendants, ushers, and concession workers had to be hired. There was not enough time to order new uniforms, so tailors were engaged to remove the Pilots logo from the front of the team shirts and replace it with the Brewers logo. The blue-and-yellow stripes from Seattle remained on the sleeves for the time being. We are lucky enough to have Skip's original shirt, a true collector' item, hanging on our family room wall.

With the plethora of problems weighing heavily on the minds of the new Brewers' management, embellishing a waiting room for the players' wives was not high on the priority list. An old storage room was given more of a *Design on a Dime* cleaning rather than a *Divine Design* makeover. The long rectangular shape of the freshly painted ecru room was furnished with assorted, discarded, multi-colored, vinyl chairs randomly lined up in groups of three or four against the walls, creating an antiseptic, hospital-waiting-room atmosphere. Perhaps the management wanted to insure the privacy of the wives, and so no sign denoted the location of this room. More likely no one had time to even consider this omission. Luckily I was able to follow my fellow box mates after the game to this hidden room.

Professional baseball is an all–American game played by athletes of all ages and maturity levels who hail from small towns and large cities all over the country. The wives of these players are even more diverse. Between the very young high school sweetheart and the almost over-the-hill thirty-some-thing veteran wives, there exists a myriad of life expectations and experi-ences. There are gorgeous Southern blondes and Texas beauty queens, down-home Southern country girls and Midwestern models, Bible-belt con-servatives and Northern liberals, stewardesses and seamstresses, black, white and Hispanic, along with trustworthy first wives ready to overlook almost everything and pragmatic second wives who rarely miss anything.

Being brought up in an Irish-American community, my association with diversity was extremely limited; a wedding between an Irish Roman Catholic and an Italian Roman Catholic was considered a "mixed marriage." Intellec-tually I did not harbor any deep-seeded biases, but I had never casually social-ized with anyone from the minority segment of our society. During my first week with the Brewers, I had engaged in conversations with women whose ethnicity would mirror that of the United Nations. My cohorts were racially diverse and spanned a broad spectrum of ages. I was an extremely naïve 22 year old who had just graduated from college and had never lived on my own. I had never cooked a meal—from concept, to shopping, to preparation to presentation—by myself. Suddenly I was thrust into the company of experi-enced women who appeared to know everything about raising a family and voiced stories and shared histories with almost everyone on the opposing teams.

Disneyland welcomes visitors to the park and tunefully reminds them that it's truly a small world. It did not take me long to discover that despite all the apparent differences among the spouses, there were many more similarities. Every baseball wife's first love and loyalty is to her husband, and the psychological demands on this relationship can become overwhelming. Often an outward appearance of confidence masked a gnawing insecurity. The Brewers were enjoying their first year in Milwaukee, and so everyone on the team was new to the town. The franchise itself was in its freshman year and had just taken over a failed first-year expansion team. Half of the team had been traded during the off-season, and a new manager was on board. My perception of being an outsider trying to fit into an established sodality was shifting; everyone on the team hovered in some state of transformation, and we all were learning how to cope with the constant changes. Long before "been there and done that" became a t-shirt cliché, the all-knowing reassurance offered to me from the eyes of a fellow wife helped to ease my transition into the sisterhood of the traveling baseball spouses.

Players' paths often intersect in major league baseball. Tito Francona was a veteran teammate of Skip's our first season in Milwaukee, and his son, Terry, was an affable ten year old who would shag balls in the outfield before the game and intensely scrutinize the action on the field from the family section once the game began. Many a cold night would find Terry returning from the concession stands with a cardboard tray full of steaming hot chocolate to warm the hands of his mother and the other freezing Brewers wives, myself included. Twelve seasons later, Skip was the veteran player, and Terry was the up-and-coming youngster in Denver, Colorado. Now that he is the manager of the Boston Red Sox, I'm sure Terry has no trouble finding a helpful hand to procure a piping-hot chocolate for him on a cold playoff night.

While hot chocolate might have been popular in the family section of the ballpark, it was not the preferred beverage of the majority of the fans. Legend has it that every time two roads cross in Milwaukee, four corner bars formed. While this might be a slight exaggeration, beer drinking definitely played a prominent part in the city's culture. Even the name of the team, the Milwaukee Brewers Baseball Club, gives credence to the impact spirits spin in the life of the town. In the early '70s, Milwaukee was home to the Big Four Breweries: the Blatz, Pabst, Schlitz, and Miller brewing companies. The opening joke delivered with the incomparable dead-pan panache by Bob Uecker at baseball banquets in Milwaukee related to the antics of Milt Famey, the fictitious relief pitcher who had a bad habit of sipping beer in between pitches. As the story went, the more beer Milt Famey sipped, the less control he had of his pitches. During one ineffective outing on the mound Milt took quite a few swallows in the process of loading the bases with complimentary trips. After walking in the winning run, Milt crushed his beer can and threw it behind the mound. The opposing manager rushed onto the filed to discover what foreign object had just been ejected from Milt's back pocket. Retrieving the tangled tin after the game, he quipped: "This is the beer that made Milt Famey walk us!"

THE BEER BARREL POLKA

Perhaps it was the ethnic influence of the predominantly German and Polish population combined with the constantly inclement weather that triggered this "love of the suds." Whatever the cause, the result was some very bizarre behavior from some very eccentric athletic supporters. One such baseball buff always sat in the front row near the visiting dugout. This six-foot-two, two-hundred-and-fifty-plus-pound gentle giant would enter the stadium every night carrying a beer in each hand and balancing a large paper megaphone filled with popcorn. Watching him carefully weaving his way down the aisle, I was impressed at how skillful this woozy man could juggle his wares. By the second inning the popcorn would be empty, some of it eaten, but more of it spilled on the field or on top of his fellow rooters. Throughout the stadium, beer vendors strove to boost their sales by yelling "get your ice cold beer here," but this particular patron needed no encouragement and kept these vendors busy. This excessive enthusiast reveled in cheering for the Brewers and taunting the opposing team's on-deck circle. Despite his semi-inebriated state, his cheering was always family-friendly and he became an integral part of the Brewers' curious culture. In the wives' section, a bet was always in place as to when the overzealous (and overweight) fan would fall onto the field. This face-planting event generally occurred sometime between the sixth and seventh inning. At that time a strategically placed security guard would kindheartedly help this woozy fan back into his seat and inform him he was cut off from drinking for the remainder of the game. Sporting a huge smile and giving an appreciative wave to the cheering crowd, the beer meister would fall into his seat and remain relatively rational until the next base hit. While his antics in the stadium were harmless, the thought of this liquor-impaired individual getting behind the wheel of a car was pretty scary. I was thankful that he was imbued with a modicum of common sense and always took a cab home from the game.

Major league baseball had finally come back to Milwaukee, but the National League town of Milwaukee was slow to connect with American League players. Sold-out games had been commonplace when the Braves inhabited County Stadium, but full capacity crowds existed only in the imaginations of the owners of this new franchise. In an effort to stimulate more support for the franchise, the promotions department came up with an inventive idea. "Bernie Brewer," the ultimate baseball fan, would set up camp in center field and stay there until the Brewers fans filled the stadium. On a sultry summer day at the beginning of a long home stand, Bernie Brewer was hoisted up to the top of the scoreboard in center field and settled into a Winnebago camper for his self-imposed incarceration. It was assumed that it would take less than a week for the local fans of Milwaukee to sympathize with Bernie's plight and arrive in hoards to the ballpark to release Bernie from his camped captivity. Unfortunately for Milt Mason, the 69-year-old baseball aficionado who agreed to don the lederhosen of Bernie Brewer, the stadium did not sell out. The home stand came to a close and Bernie was still wallowing in his Winnebago over center field.

The promotion was successful in raising the community's awareness of the Brewers, but not in the way the team's management had hoped for. Instead of generating enthusiasm for the new and exciting team, the promotion highlighted the lack of interest many local baseball fans had for an American League franchise. The failure of the fans to free Bernie Brewer became the lead story on the 6:00 news. The pitiful plight of Bernie got more attention than the players' performance on the baseball field. There was a slight increase in ticket sales as curious customers came to observe the home that Bernie was hovering in, but attendance did not come close to the 40,000 needed for Bernie's freedom. Baked casseroles and cookies from the kitchens of fellow friendly fanatics were hoisted up the scoreboard for Bernie, along with abundant amounts of liquid libations, as Bernie continued his captivity through another home stand.

Trying to entice more fans to enter the stadium, the club orchestrated several promotions to "Get Bernie Down." Banner Night, Bat Day and Team Picture Night did little to bolster attendance. After the team failed to draw support with generic giveaways, some genius in the promotions department came up with the misguided idea to broaden the fan base and appeal to the pub population with a ten cent beer night. Thankfully, Skip was not on the mound this particular out-of-control evening. A significant number of fans flocked to the park and bombarded the beer vendors as soon as the gates opened. A great many of these enthusiastic attendees appeared trashed halfway through batting practice. The National Anthem was sung with quite a bit more gusto and the lyrics were a little less recognizable.

Before the first ball was plucked from the pitcher's glove, there were punches being thrown in the bleachers. By the second inning, the scuffles in the stands were taking precedence over the action on the field. The outfielders were impeded from running after routine fly balls by the empty beer cups and half-filled popcorn containers being thrown from the stands. Copious containers of "suds" were consumed by the brew crew. The roar of the crowd took on a whole new meaning as the boisterous boosters got louder and louder. Obnoxious, overzealous, and overbearing baseball addicts stumbled out of their seats and fell onto the field. 1970 was a year that had already seen its share of mob-related riots, and this crowd was definitely spinning out of control. Midway through the game, the umpires assessed this potentially dangerous situation, took control, and suspended the game. Bernie Brewer watched over this mayhem from the confines of his camper on top of center field. The beer had flowed generously and steadily, but the required number of fans had not flooded the stadium quite as freely. Bernie would have to wait a while longer for his freedom.

Forty days and forty nights later, and with the aid of some inventive attendance accounting, Milt Mason was mercifully released. Bernie Brewer's role evolved during that first year of the franchise. The people of Milwaukee identified with this loyal fan and valued his show of unconditional support. Milt Mason returned daily, under the guise of Bernie, to the stadium to watch the game from center field, knowing that he could leave his perch and return home at the end of the game. A new twist was added to his repertoire. Whenever a Milwaukee Brewer batter hit a home run, Bernie would slide down a chute into a gigantic mug of beer. The crowd would cheer loudly and raise a toast to their beloved Bernie. The crowd support for major league baseball in Milwaukee has improved quite a bit over the past four decades, partially as the result of some exciting teams and partially due to the unusual realignment of teams in 1998 that brought Milwaukee back into the beloved National League, but some of the original, endearing, symbolic practices survived. Bernie Brewer still slides down from center field after a home run, but he is no longer a lonely camper. Bernie has been joined by Bonnie Brewer, who assists the ground crew in smoothing out the base paths and keeping the wonderful fans of Milwaukee reminded of their connection to the breweries of the past.

Throughout our early years with the Milwaukee Brewers, Skip's career was shadowed more by a cloud than by a halo. Something always seemed to go wrong on the days that he pitched. The papers had tagged him as the "hard luck" pitcher. There was no such thing as a routine fly ball or a given double play. More than a handful of opponents reached first base after being called out on strike three and incredibly, during one of his pitching appearances, the right fielder caught the ball in the outfield, stumbled and dropped the ball over the fence—for a home run to lose the game. The season ticket holder sitting near the wives' section even suggested the organist play "Send in the Clowns" when the team took the field. On one particular afternoon in Milwaukee, our second baseman ran to the mound before the first pitch and whispered to Skip, "Hey, big guy, I had a really rough night last night. Please don't let any balls come my way." He then proceeded to take his place at second base and give Skip the thumbs up sign. Unbelievable.

It was hard to block out all the negativity that was surrounding Skip's appearances on the mound. Frustration became a force to be dealt with on a daily basis. The minimum salary in 1970 was only $10,000, and the majority of the Brewers, ourselves included, lingered near the bottom of the pay scale. Bargain hunting was not merely something to do, it was the only way of making ends meet. It was hard not to laugh at the notion the outside world held that we lived such a "glamorous" life when the only thrilling events in our life concerned the ineptitude of the play in the infield.

Midway through our first season in Milwaukee, Skip was pitching another tough game on the road. He had walked the first batter and the next had reached on an error. Anxiously perched on the sticky black naugahyde sofa in our small apartment, I watched Dave Bristol, the Brewers' manager, run out to the mound. The hometown announcers theorized about the conversation taking place on the mound. "Looks like another tough break for Skip. Obviously Dave is saying something to calm his young pitcher down," they surmised. The parlay on the mound was anything but calming. Dave Bristol stood nose to nose with Skip and let him know, in no uncertain terms, that he was tired of hearing about all the hard luck Skip was having. "Son, you have to make your own luck in this game. If you don't get out of this inning without giving up a run and win this G.D. ballgame," Bristol yelled, "I'll have your northern butt on the next bus to the minor leagues the first thing tomorrow morning." I guess motivation can come in all forms. Skip won both the game and the respect of his southern manager, but the team continued to struggle.

Towards the end of the season, I drove the short distance of ninety miles to Chicago to prolong my first year as a major league rookie wife and hopefully celebrate one last victorious outing with my husband during the final weekend series in the Windy City. The added opportunity to spend another memorable night listening to the up-and-coming folk singers, such as Jim Croce, who frequented the small coffee houses on Rush Street, before the team left for its final road trip of the year in Oakland added to the allure. For a few hours I was transported back to my carefree college days, appreciating the artistic finger picking of a tuneful poet who was telling our lives with his songs.

The bone chilling winds, combined with the cold bats of both teams lingering at the bottom of the standings, led to a pathetic number of fans supporting the players on the field at Comiskey Park. The scoreboard listed a paid crowd of 1600, but the actual body count was significantly smaller. From my vantage point, it was obvious that both Illinois and Wisconsin fans had switched their loyalty from baseball to their respective football teams, leaving their physical support of the White Sox and the Brewers behind to cheer for the Chicago Bears and the Green Bay Packers. I had become accustomed to seeing sparsely-filled sections at County Stadium, but the scattered sets of blanketed frozen fans shivering in the park, lent an eerie feeling to an already icy day. As a cloud cover came in during the mid-afternoon to block the small glimmer of warmth radiating over the park, even the staunchest supporters folded up their woolen tartan blankets and called it a wrap for the season. Other than a few of the questionably sane die-heart loyal fans, it was only the players' families, the concession stand workers, and the ushers who remained until the final out. The local paper surmised the next day that fewer than four hundred faithful followers were left after the fifth inning.

Bundled up in my late season "summer game" attire of a long, woolen, camel's hair coat, a much more functional than fashionable ski hat, and fur-lined gloves, I felt that I could last one more hour before frostbite set in on my tingling toes. The few other Brewers wives who had journeyed to Chicago for the weekend had sensibly headed back to Milwaukee before the game began, but being the ever enthusiastic former cheerleader who had not missed a home game since my wedding in June, I was determined to see the season through to its mid-western conclusion. Tommy Ferguson, the Brewers' traveling secretary, also braved the arctic elements that afternoon and would occasionally stop by my seat with a fresh cup of piping hot chocolate to warm up my frozen fingers. Tommy was impressed with my rugged determination and took it upon himself to reward me for my season long-loyalty.

I CAN FLY

Following the game, the team was scheduled to depart for Oakland on a chartered flight. I planned to take Skip to the airport myself and drop him off at the terminal on my way home. During the seventh inning stretch, Tommy stopped by to tell me that arrangements had changed and I would not be able to drive my husband to O'Hare as planned. I sensed a mischievous twinkle in his eyes and before the final stanza of "Take Me Out to the Ballgame" was sung, Tommy informed me that he had cleared it with the management to include my name on the passenger list of the final trip. With the seasoned skills of a superlative secretary, Tommy had it all figured out. We would surprise Skip at the airport where he would find me comfortably seated on the team plane. He had even found a college-bound clubhouse attendant to chauffeur my car back to County Stadium. The fact that I had only a small suitcase packed with winter clothes was inconsequential. The Wendys of the world must always be ready to take off on new adventures with only the clothes on their backs. My husband was duly impressed by Tommy's adept alteration of the agenda and thrilled that we would be flying off to California together. "Consider it a delayed wedding gift and enjoy yourselves," the magnanimous Mr. Ferguson whispered. "Use your meal money and take your wife shopping in San Francisco," he continued, aware that my winter wardrobe was ill-suited for the Indian summer of Oakland.

After an early morning check-in at the team hotel, we slept until mid-afternoon. When we awoke, there was a message in Skip's box from Joe Rudi, Oakland's premier outfielder, inviting him to dinner that evening. Skip had been Joe's AA roommate in Modesto, California, early in both their careers, and Skip had served as Joe's best man when he married Sharon in the middle of that season. I had the pleasure of meeting Joe earlier in the year when he had come out to our apartment for dinner after a late game and spent what I am sure was a rather uncomfortable night sleeping on our rented sofa, and I looked forward to meeting his wife.

The Rudis picked us up at the team hotel. Sharon and I stopped by the front desk on the way out while our husbands waited outside. Leisurely lounging around the lobby was an ensemble of eager women waiting to pounce on the not-so-unsuspecting ballplayers staying at the hotel. Clueless as I was at the time to the brash boldness of such bleach-blonde hussies, I passed by this group on my way to the ladies' lounge to take one final check on my appearance. When I returned to the lobby, I noticed a stunned look of disbelief on this cast of made-up characters and a self-satisfied smile of gratification shining through Sharon's grin. It seemed that while I was out of the room, it had been suggested to Sharon that "this territory was taken" and we "should look elsewhere to pick up our own ballplayers." Deciding that there was no time like the present to vent her outrage at such an outrageous suggestion, Sharon informed these "groupies" that they should have a little more respect for themselves and for the families of these married players. "Where is your self-esteem?" she questioned. "The majority of players are all married men. They have wives and children they love back home. Don't you realize that they're only using you for a one-night stand?" Concluding with a condescending glare, she turned around and stormed out the front door. "Please don't discuss this incident tonight at dinner," Sharon softly whispered. "Joe would be shocked to think that I had the courage to confront that group, but I just felt I had an obligation to all the wives out there to tell those low-life ladies off." As shocked as I was by the encounter, my admiration for the fortitude of this fabulous woman far outweighed my disgust with the dawdling dolls. At times during the course of my baseball life, I must admit to not-so-quite respectfully relaying this same advice to other clusters of would-be home wreckers.

What an inauguration into baseball bliss! In less than fifteen weeks I had traveled ten times more than I had in my previous twenty-two years. Between my initial encounter with an ex-pitcher anger-management candidate to this most recent run in with the sultry suggestive sirens, I had been introduced to an entire segment of society I never realized existed. The liberal arts education I thought I had received at Regis College could not compare to the hands-on liberal education I had gained throughout the course of the season. Little did I know at the time how much more my education would be enhanced in Mayaguez, Puerto Rico, over the winter.

MARGARITAVILLE

The "suggestion" from the general manager of a major league team to a player that he spend the off-season fine-tuning his pitching repertoire playing winter ball south of the border is not so much of a suggestion as it is an ultimatum—if you want to be back in the majors the following year, you go. The Dominican Republic, Puerto Rico, and Venezuela all field competitive winter baseball leagues. Each local team is allowed to have a handful of American players on its roster. Many American major league baseball teams have arrangements with Caribbean teams to send up-and-coming young players south for the winter to acquire a little more experience. In 1970 the Milwaukee Brewers and the Boston Red Sox had such a joint arrangement with the Los Indios baseball team based in Mayaguez, Puerto Rico.

Like most premier high school pitchers, Skip also excelled at the plate. Days after graduating from Catholic Memorial High School in West Roxbury, Massachusetts, Skip Lockwood signed a professional baseball contract with the Kansas City Athletics as a heavy hitter. Four years later, the A's hands-on owner, Charlie Finley, realized his investment in Skip's bat was not paying off and switched Skip back to pitching. It was decided for us by the Brewers management (who had inherited my husband from Seattle, who had drafted him from the Athletics) that we would spend our first marital off-season in Mayaguez, Puerto Rico, where Skip was to work on controlling his unpredictable curveball. We had no objections to this arrangement. Spending the winter in a tropical island sounded pretty exciting to a newly married couple from cosmopolitan Boston currently residing in the bowling capital of the country. Although I had overheard some disconcerting stories about the living conditions in winter ball, I assumed they were extreme exaggerations made by disgruntled pampered princesses. I, myself, was looking forward to experiencing a new culture and perhaps even becoming fluent in a new language. To this end I purchased a paperback copy of Spanish translations that did not include the colorful slang employed in taunting the players' wives.

The day after the season ended, Skip and I drove back to the Boston area for a week's R & R with both of our families and then we were off to an imagined island adventure in a tropical wonderland. All the travel and housing arrangements had been prearranged for us by the team in Mayaguez. Our itinerary indicated that we would be living at the La Palma Hotel in downtown Mayaguez. My father recalled staying at The Palms in Palm Beach, and vividly described the posh rooms and the luxurious surrounding landscape. I envisioned an enchanted paradise.

Leaving Boston on a cold October morning, we had anticipated lounging around a pool, relaxing with a rum punch later that afternoon. The exhausting expedition of our southern excursion should have clued us into lowering our expectations. Our plane took off from Logan Airport at 7 A.M., made one stop at New York, and landed in San Juan about 3 P.M. No food or drinks were provided at any time. At the San Juan airport we were led across the tarmac and onto a pre–World War II propeller plane where seats were assigned according to the numbers registered on the mandatory step-on scale. We were not allowed to sit together because the weight load on the small plane had to be distributed evenly throughout the plane. After flying over mountainous territory that caused the cabin to careen in constant dives and leaps, I was glad that we had not gotten a chance to eat anything. As the plane began to descend, I kept frantically searching the ground for an asphalt airstrip when suddenly the plane lurched, banged and bumped up and down a few times and finally touched down in the middle of a cow field. This dilapidated runway was a far cry from the luxurious landing strip at Fantasy Island. There would no tuxedoed midget excitedly pointing out "the plane, the plane," and no line of lavish limousines waiting to transport us to our island paradise. Instead there were only a few dusty pickup trucks and a pair of tired-looking taxis awaiting our arrival in Mayaguez.

We piled our meager belongings into a 1950s taxicab and headed towards town. Nothing in my liberal arts degree from Regis College in Weston, Massachusetts, prepared me for life in Mayaguez, Puerto Rico. The five-mile trip into town took almost half an hour as we were required to make frequent stops to allow herds of animals to cross the dirt road. The "downtown" area was centered around a semi-deserted central plaza featuring bronze statues of Christopher Columbus and other early explorers. The surrounding business district consisted of two or three blocks of old buildings, a couple of corner bars, a few liquor stores, a movie theater showing X-rated films, and a laundromat. It appeared as though the 20th century had yet to reach this end of the island. The run-down cab pulled up in front of a run-down hotel named, you guessed it, La Palma. After the initial shock of our slum-like surroundings wore off, we staggered inside to register. This proved to be quite a challenge because the receptionist at the hotel pretended that he spoke only Spanish, and I could not figure out how to communicate effectively using my paperback translator. (It is a curious coincidence that many times during the winter I could hear this same receptionist laugh out loud while listening in on my English lamentations.) We were handed the key to a room on the second floor and proceeded to lug our bags up the steep stairway located on the back perimeter of the property.

To say the apartment was not quite what the owner of the team had led us to expect would be a gross understatement. Our "luxurious" apartment consisted of one room with a sagging bed in one corner, a vinyl love seat in another and an aluminum table with four mismatched chairs to the left of the door. The walls were a dingy shade of yellow that gave the appearance of never having had the benefit of a Spic and Span bath. The "kitchen area" was equipped with the smallest sink I had ever seen and a refrigerator straight out of the twilight zone. While we felt relieved to discover that the apartment was equipped with indoor plumbing, we would later find out that you could get hot water only about two hours a day although one never knew exactly what hours that would be, and at times, even the entire water supply would mysteriously disappear. Relying on my "always be prepared" motto from my days as a second-grade Brownie, I kept a back-up supply of water in a pot on the stove at all times. Illumination consisted of a single light bulb handing from the ceiling, which for us presented a huge problem since my husband's sensitive eyes were really bothered by overhead lighting.

While the bad news was this was going to be our apartment for the next four months, the good news was it was going to be our apartment for *only* the next four months. I was madly in love and could live anywhere for a few months as long as we were together. It is said that misery loves company, and we were not alone in our housing headache. All the American ballplayers were staying in the same hotel, and all were enjoying the same austere accommodations.

The town of Mayaguez is located at the far end of the island, miles and light years away from San Juan. Baseball in Mayaguez exists not only as a form of entertainment but also as venue for gambling. Betting appeared to be an integral part of the culture. The local fans would bet not only on wins and loses, but also on the number of hits, the number of strikeouts, or the run spread of the game. Some fans bet their entire week's salary on a single game. All the American wives became acutely aware of whether or not the fans were upset with our husbands for not supporting their bets. On most nights there were only five pale-faced women in attendance at the stadium, and this faint group could usually be found sitting together behind the screen at the ballpark. It was not that difficult to identify the ballplayers' wives. A few baseball fanatics felt that the wives were personally responsible for any failings of their husbands and so it was not all that uncommon for said fans to fill up balloons with beer and target them at the American wives when our husbands were not living up to the expectations of the gaming fans. On such nights the wives often played a game of musical chairs, moving to a different viewing section after each inning to outsmart the bloated balloons.

As a child of the '60s, I was socially active and strongly opinionated. Growing up in Massachusetts, I felt connected to the Kennedys' altruistic ideals, and ingrained in my inner core was the belief that it was my duty to make a difference in this world. The civil rights movement was heading in the right direction and, although I fully agreed with the anti-war consensus that America had no reason to be fighting in Vietnam, I supported the troops. Small-minded, prejudicial stereotypes were anathema to my concept of reality and I smugly felt that I was way above the racist mentality. The season we spent living in Puerto Rico punctured my idealistic bubble and jolted my parochial belief system. It is the first time I had ever experienced prejudice, and that prejudice was targeted at the American wives. The one theater in town showed mainly X-rated American films, and consequently the local male population viewed all American women as easy marks. As long as the American wives were in the company of our husbands, we were treated with respect, but try to go to grocery store alone and catcalls and whistles were omnipresent. As a brunette, I could almost blend into the crowd, but this constant harassment caused two of my blonde friends to dye their hair brown. Fortunately, most ballparks were within a few hours driving distance from Mayaguez and the local Puerto Rican team owners were loath to spend the money to house the players in a hotel for the night unless absolutely necessary, so road trips were never that frequent.

As much as we American wives all disliked the hotel, we were very content to seek refuge there whenever the team was out of town. Gathering in one room, we would listen to the radio broadcast of the game. Delivered entirely in Spanish, the radio announcer was not physically at the ballpark. Instead he was sitting next to a ticker-tape machine in a small office in Mayaguez. The announcer was fed limited information, such as hits and runs, over the ticker tape and would employ his imagination to vividly recreate the game over the radio, crafting record-breaking fastballs and heroic catches at the wall in the mind of the listener. Whenever the announcer mentioned that Skip was warming up, I was pretty certain that he would soon be put into the game. To add to the confusion of trying to understand the Spanish broadcast was the fact that two of the sponsors of the team inserted subliminal commercials throughout the broadcast. If a batter got a base hit, it was called a Zapatta (which was the name of the shoe company that sponsored the team), and a home run was referred to as Cervesa Indios (the beer sponsor). Trying to decipher the announcer's Spanish commentary through the scratchy radio waves, we were never sure if our husbands were hitting the ball, giving up a home run, or merely waiting on the sidelines while a commercial aired. Despite my personal frustration trying to comprehend what was truly happening on the field, one had to appreciate the talent and enthusiasm of this resourceful broadcaster.

Growing up I never really concerned myself with the logistics of laundry. At home I usually placed my dirty laundry in the hamper, and it would magically show up the next day on my bed, clean and folded. At college the laundry service would deliver clean sheets and towels every Monday, and while there was a washer and dryer on our floor for a fashion emergency, I usually waited until I went home for vacations to avail myself of the magic hamper. Unfortunately my five children have followed in this time-honored tradition. Our first apartment in Milwaukee was equipped with a washer and dryer, and so I naively assumed that such machines would be standard equipment in every home. Our little room did not have a washing facility, there was not one on the floor, and one did not exist in the entire hotel. Jane Decker, the trainer's wife who lived next door, had spent three winters in Mayaguez and was my source for all practical information and emotional support. She directed me to the laundromat around the corner and kindly suggested that doing the laundry in town was a couple's experience "not to be missed." Truer words were never spoken.

On a hot humid afternoon, my husband and I entered the dingy laundry facility, well aware that we were the only English-speaking Americans in the building. In spite of the fact that all the instructions were in Spanish, we did manage to get the machine loaded and were figuring out how to turn on the antiquated appliance when a mysterious loud noise disturbed our concentration. A goat was being led into the laundromat and was not at all pleased to be there. The other patrons in the facility appeared non-plussed by this intrusion. I vaguely recalled visiting a petting zoo as a child, but I had never seen a full-grown goat before up close and personal. I asked myself for the umpteenth time that week: What in the world was I doing here? The answer, of course, was that I was with the man that I loved. It was apparent to the native clientele that I was not integrating easily into my new surroundings. We completed the task of washing, drying, and folding our laundry amidst the curious overt ogling of *los amigos* as quickly as humanly possible and vowed to find an alternative for cleansing our clothes. That night, when Skip went to the ballpark, he enlisted the help (bribed) of one of the clubhouse attendants to do our personal laundry after he finished with the team uniforms. Once again my laundry problem was solved by a magic hamper.

Bill and Mary Lou Lee lived in the apartment above us. Whatever stories you might have heard about Bill "Spaceman" Lee, including the implausible hemp-high pancake topping that surfaced during his brief run for president in 1988 on the Rhinoceros Party ticket, cannot begin to match the riotous reality of his larger-than-life personality. Suffice it to say that if Bill were one of Peter Pan's lost boys, he would have never opted to return to London. I thought Bill's eccentricities were extremely inventive and creatively comical, but then I was not the one married to this perennial little leaguer. Mary Lou Lee was an extraordinary woman. Voted Miss Congeniality in an Alaskan beauty pageant, she was as kind and grounded as Bill was fun-loving and crazy. The Lees had brought with them a beautiful new baby boy. God must have spent a little more time on Mary Lou's basic demeanor because I cannot remember her ever complaining about the lack of creature comforts of home. I do, however, recall smiling every morning, overhearing Bill upstairs simultaneously rocking the baby and counting the sit-ups for his wife as she strove to get back into her pre-pregnant profile. I seriously doubt that I would have found very much humor in the scenario if I had been the one working out on the hard, out-dated, linoleum floor.

Public transportation was virtually non-existent, and the exorbitant cost of renting a car was way out of our budget. Since both the Lees' and our financial situations were similarly stretched, we decided to pool our pecuniary resources and purchase a second-hand car with our upstairs neighbors. Admittedly the vintage VW bug we bought had a few problems. One door opened only from the inside and the other only from the outside. The paint was peeling off both the hood and the roof of the car, but we reasoned that could easily be remedied. Mary Lou was a very gifted artist and painted flowers, birds, and bumblebees on the hood of the car and a large peace sign of the roof— after all this was 1970. We definitely had the most identifiable car in the village of Mayaguez. I am convinced the car ran on fumes. We filled the car up the day we bought it and never again put any gas in the tank. Somehow the car got us all back and forth to the beach and the ballpark daily and never broke down. This was truly an amazing automobile. Only when we went to sell the car as we were leaving Puerto Rico did we discover that the sticker on the windshield signified a rejection, not an inspection.

Located at the far end of the island of Puerto Rico, the town of Mayaguez should have been a tourist designation for its beautiful beaches. I say "should have" because swimming was not allowed off the beaches of Mayaguez in 1970. Although "Charlie the Tuna" was never chosen by the Starkist canning and processing factory, his friends and family were, and schools of sharks patrolled the waters right off the coast, most likely unable to distinguish the leg of a human being from the tail of a tuna. About an hour north of town lay the stunning surfing mecca of Rincon (where my college son caught great waves during his spring break 35 years later), and on rare days off we went snorkeling at Boquerón Beach to the south. Most days we would travel about 30 minutes to a sheltered local beach. The team trainer, Nelson Decker, gave us what appeared to be rather bizarre directions to this beach on our first free day. We were instructed to follow Route 2 (a partially paved country road) through four intersections, to listen for the coqui frogs, and then to take a left at the pig sitting under the giant palm tree. Singing frogs who chirped "coqui, coqui"? Left at the pig? As wacky as it might sound, we heard the frogs calling out to us, and the pig sat in the same shaded spot for the entire winter.

At the time I did not appreciate how lucky the Lees were to have such an adaptable baby. I naively assumed that all infants simply ate, slept, and smiled at will with utter contentment. Mary Lou and I would create an oasis in the shade for the baby's port-a-crib where he would contentedly coo for an hour or two. We would then unpack our picnic lunch and relax and revel in the quiet solitude of our private paradise. Jane Decker, the trainer's enlightening wife, informed us that this beach was generally crowded during the summer months, but the locals felt the seventy-degree winter weather was way too brisk for body surfing.

All the American players and management were housed at the La Palma Hotel, but we were not the only residents of the hotel. The apartment to the left of ours was occupied by the team trainer, Nelson Decker, and his wife, Jane. The Deckers had spent a number of years in minor league cities and in various winter ball locations, and Jane's insights and compassion gave tremendous support to this new baseball bride. Six months before, I had been struggling with hypothetical psychological coping theories, and now I was in a semi-civilized country, dealing with anti–American prejudice with a husband struggling to find his curveball. Jane offered me invaluable, unsolicited, emotional sustenance.

I never did converse with the woman who lived in the apartment to the right, but she did leave an indelible mark on our Mayaguez experience. As I mentioned before, Skip absolutely hated overhead lighting, and the only illumination in our apartment came from the single light bulb hanging form the ceiling. The day we moved in, we had requested, in a combination of sign language and broken English, a table lamp from the front desk. We had been told the only lamp they had was being repaired and they would bring it up as soon as it was fixed. Every day I would go to the desk and inquire about the lamp and every day it was going to be ready "*mañana.*"

Getting a good night's sleep is essential to a professional athlete. Sleeping through the night was quite a challenge in Mayaguez. The mattress was so bad we had taken it off the bed and placed it on the floor to try to get some support, but it was still dreadfully far from comfortable. The main somnolent setback sprang from the constant commotion from the apartment next door. You see, the woman next door had the exact same one-room layout in her adjacent abode as we did, which she shared with a Saint Bernard dog and a six-month-old baby. As close as we could decipher, her occupation appeared to be that of a "lady of the evening." At odd hours throughout the night, loud knocking could occur on her door, followed by the dog barking, which in turn would wake up the baby and, since Lolita was otherwise occupied, the poor baby would cry uncontrollably. We had periodically complained to the front desk, but since little Lola was apparently a legendary fixture at the hotel, the desk clerk again pretended not to understand our complaint. One evening, when this sultry senorita had entertained so many clients coming in and out in two-hour intervals that it was impossible to get any sleep at all, we called the desk and complained four times. Finally at about three in the morning, there was a knock on our door. It was the hotel manager with a big smile handing us the repaired table lamp, assuming that it would make up for our loss of sleep. I quickly grabbed the proffered lamp before Skip had the opportunity to pound it over the manager's head.

I felt very fortunate to be living on the second floor of the hotel. The other baseball wives living on the first and third floors were constantly complaining about the cockroaches in the bathrooms of their apartments. One small bug did appear on the day after we arrived, and I must admit I was not a particularly good sport about this uninvited pet. Screams and tears quickly come to mind. Skip calmly offered to take care of the problem, and he did so with great success. It was not until after we had left the island that he admitted to getting up very early every morning and killing the ugly black bugs before I woke up. I'm pretty sure that the incentive for his pre-dawn bug patrol was based more on his need to avoid a repeat of my hysterics than on altruistic true love, but whatever the motivation, I totally appreciated the results.

For the past twelve years, I have run the Christmas pageant at St. Theresa's parish in Rye Beach, New Hampshire. The inspiration for this involvement undoubtedly came from the pageant I witnessed our first Christmas together in Mayaguez. I'm a firm believer in the role that faith plays in a person's life. In the words of Rod McKuen, "It doesn't matter what you believe, or how you believe, but that you believe." Personally I believe that faith, hope, and love are an integral part of life. Being brought up in a very close-knit family, it was hard to be so far away from home that first Christmas, and so I sought solace in the local church.

Our Lady of the Candelaria of Mayaguez is an old and magnificent Roman Catholic cathedral. Stepping inside this building for the first time, I felt transported back into seventeenth-century Spain. Light streaming in past the medieval, stained-glass windows fell on dark wooden pews and illuminated priceless, hand-carved statues surrounding the altar. Life was pretty unpredictable on the outside, but a sense of peace permeated inside the confines of the Church. With the exception of the human-hair wig on the exquisite marble statue of Mary, it appeared that life had stood still in this part of the country since the Middle Ages.

The "Best Christmas Pageant Ever" staged in 1970 at the Christmas Eve mass in Mayaguez almost defies description. Obviously a yearly tradition, the angel costumes were constructed out of permanently wrinkled satin that had not seen an iron in over a decade. The angel wings must have been tightly wrapped in tinsel at one time, but the huge smiles on the faces of the participants more than made up for the lack of sparkle left on their wings. Almost tripping on their fathers' bathrobes, the shepherds schlepped into the church as the sounds of authentic mooing and bleating could be heard from the neighboring farm. The crowns of the Wise Men appeared to come from some long-lost relatives stop at a San Juan Burger King, and their robes were woven from limp and lifeless felt fabric. Joseph must have been chosen for his piety, not his size. Being vertically challenged, he only came up to Mary's shoulder. Saving the best for last, Mary slowly walked down the center aisle, smiling her "all I want for Christmas is my two-front teeth" smile and carrying a Betsy-Wetsy doll. An open, blue, taffeta robe showcased a tattered, lace mini-skirt. Three, large, black, bobby pins held her white mantilla in place. The high point of the outfit came from the white, patent leather go-go boots on her feet. Try as I may, my own Christmas pageant productions have never quite compared to the one I witnessed in Puerto Rico on that inspirational evening.

In 1970 Mayaguez had no provisions for housing the mentally challenged. There was an old man, Animo, who lived in the doorway of our hotel. From day one, Mary Lou and I took pity on this homeless man and would often leave dinner in a paper bag for him by his blanket. The arrival of our antiquated VW sparked life into Animo. He moved into our car the first night we parked it in front of the hotel. During the day we had full use of the vehicle, but after midnight Animo slept inside and protected it against vandals. The car received a daily washing and, all in all, it was a great arrangement for everyone concerned. As mentioned before, when we went to sell the car at the end of the winter, we discovered that it had come fully equipped with a rejection sticker, and therefore it would be impossible to legally sell it. Despite this tiny technical drawback, there were a lot of local fans who seemed very interested in purchasing it. Skip and I assumed it was for Mary Lou's fantastic artwork, but in reality the interest was not in the car, but in the license plate. We held an auction for the car the day we were leaving. People kept yelling at us in Spanish, which, unfortunately, even after four months of deciphering with my trusty dictionary, we could not understand.

Finally, Skip held out his hand, and one man put $50 in it, and another handed the money back to his friend and put $100 in Skip's hand. At the close of the auction, we had gotten back the $250 we had paid for the car. You can imagine our surprise when the high bidder went over and took the license plates off the car and left the VW. As we prepared to depart the town of Mayaguez, we deftly positioned our pillows and blankets in the backseat of the VW and verbally deeded the vacant Volkswagen to Animo. I took comfort in that fact that at least one person's living condition was improved by our presence on the island.

Growing up in a family that started preparing for Christmas the day after Thanksgiving, I was discouraged by the lack of decorating options available in Mayaguez. With all the self-confidence of a 22-year-old, self-appointed interior decorator, I created my own Christmas decorations. With the limited raw material options available, I covered the living room wall with a Nativity scene constructed out of felt. There was the stable housing Mary, Joseph, and the baby Jesus, surrounded by cattle, visited by the Wise Men and their camels and the shepherds and their sheep. While the artwork was rather primitive, it gave a festive mood to our surroundings. A post-beach Christmas party was hosted at our holiday-inspired apartment to compensate for the loneliness we all felt being so far away from home at Christmas.

The American players and their families never did quite understand the obsessive-compulsive connection the local communities in Puerto Rico attached to their hometown team. There was a definite link between the final score of the baseball game and the bragging rites of the townies until the next athletic contest. As previously mentioned, gambling had a lot to do with this phenomenon, but a fierce Puerto Rican pride was also painfully prevalent. One particular American pitcher for our Mayaguez team and the co-owner of our VW vehicle learned a very vindictive lesson in exactly how much pride mattered to the native Puerto Rican.

Bill Lee adhered to the same theory on pitching that the majority of successful major league pitchers espoused: The pitcher owns the plate, and if the batter chooses to lean over and crowd that plate, he does so at his own risk. On a hot and humid night in early January at the Mayaguez Stadium, a player on the visiting team from San Juan hovered over the plate in an aggressively deliberate attempt to take away the inside corner from the starting pitcher who, on this sultry evening, was none other than the flamboyant Bill Lee. Bill, never one to be intimidated by this type of aggressive action, threw a nasty fastball on the inside part of the plate to brush the batter back. This native, favorite-son, free-swinger jumped back a little and then stood up and yelled something in Spanish at Mr. Lee. The batter then swung his bat around a few times in angry defiance and returned to his batting position, this time crowding the plate even more. As you might expect, Bill was totally up to the challenge and hurled the next pitched inside even more, this time drilling the blatantly bold batter in the ribs. Mere words cannot do justice to the scene that unfolded in the infield. In a fit of temper, the prideful player dropped his bat and charged the mound with his fists moving wildly in the air. Bill Lee just stood on the mound, saying nothing and making no movement until his opponent came within two feet of the rubber. Bill then calmly stuck out his fist and knocked the would-be warrior out cold. In the wives' section, we were all doubled over in laughter over the incredible sucker punch delivered with such deadpan panache.

Unfortunately for Bill, the popular, passed-out player was a former Golden Glove boxer, and his Ponce teammates and their faithful followers were not the least bit amused with Bill's audacious antics. The following week, the Mayaguez team bus arrived at the San Juan Stadium and was greeted with an exceptionally hostile welcoming committee. Bill was waylaid as he walked off of the bus. An angry group of fans and relatives of Bill's knockout victim knocked Bill down and beat him up. His injuries were so extensive and the bad vibes between the two teams so evident that "the powers that be" decided it would be the best for all concerned for the Lees to leave the island and return to the mainland ASAP. Sometimes even the most daring of Peter's lost boys cannot avoid being ambushed by those who refuse to play by the rules of decency.

Towards the end of January, Skip pulled a muscle in his arm. Since the owners of the Mayaguez Indios team saw no reason to keep (or pay) an injured athlete on the roster, we were "allowed" to leave early and recuperate back home before spring training resumed in February. Within a day we had sold our car (at the aforementioned hotel steps auction), packed our belongings, and geared ourselves up for the gut-wrenching plane trip back over the mountains. In a rush to leave the island, I neglected to take down my Christmas murals. Two years later one of my baseball friends was staying at the same winter ball hotel and told me that the hotel was charging extra for the "decorated" apartment on the second floor.

Many years have come and gone and conceivably I have chosen to forget the sharp edges of our stay, but nevertheless, my water-colored memories will always warmly include the laughter shared and the life lessons learned that first winter season of our married life in Mayaguez.

3

Life Is a Ballgame

MOMENTS TO REMEMBER

With a new appreciation for our native land, we left our alien athletic adventures of Puerto Rico behind and returned to the familiar chaos of our extended families. My sister's wedding was fast approaching, and I relished the opportunity to share my newly acquired marital advice. Looking back I can't imagine how my parents adjusted to the dramatic change in our family dynamics. We had always been a very stable and stationary family. The biggest upheaval in my life came the summer before my freshman year in high school when my parents purchased a new home closer to that high school. That necessitated a move from Holy Name Parish to Holy Cross Parish. Within this past year, I had graduated from college, married, and relocated to Milwaukee, and my younger brother had graduated from high school and moved into his college dorm. Now my only other sibling was getting married and following her recently drafted fiancé to a far off naval base in San Diego, with the prayerful hope he would not be deployed to Viet Nam. The winds of change were blowing a little too briskly. My father was financing his second spectacular nuptial within the year. My sister and I have differing opinions as to whose wedding took the cake. While we could leave it up to the panel of judges on *Top Chef* as to whether the presentation of the prime rib at my reception topped the filet mignon plating at hers, I reluctantly concede that the shimmering, soft snow surrounding her service topped the heavy rain pouring down on mine. My mother was losing her two daughters to opposite ends of the country and, if that wasn't bad enough, the family dog had died the month before. Thankfully my brother, Dan, "her pride and joy," would at least be home for the summer months.

Only five days came between the last dance at my sister's service in Springfield, MA, to the first sit-ups of spring training. Valentine's Day found us flying over the freeway towards Tempe, AZ. Other than the constant drone of the highway and the annoying glare of the oncoming traffic headlights, I don't remember much of our sprint across country. I do, however, recall getting up at dawn on day four and driving over eleven hours through the barren plains of Texas to arrive in Phoenix at dusk, only to learn that there were no rooms available at the team hotel. In fact, after checking with the local chamber of commerce, the desk clerk informed us that there were no rooms available in the entire city. We were weighing the options of spending the night in the car or driving back 50 miles to the nearest vacancy when two of the Brewers minor league coaches entered the lobby. Overhearing our plight they conferred with each other and considerately concluded they could share their accommodations for one night. I could have kissed (and probably did) Del Crandall when he offered us his room. A little over a year later, on the night Del took over as the field manager for the Brewers, Skip pitched a one-hitter against the Yankees and presented the new manager with his first win. One good turn deserves another.

To a co-ed who had matriculated at a small women's college and had spent last February shoveling two feet of snow off a friend's car in the cold suburbs of Boston to skid over to my practice teaching assignment, the blazing sun beating down on the terra cotta baseball diamond on the ASU campus seemed heavenly. I seriously questioned how anyone could get any homework done in this fun-loving environment. Could one really contemplate the meaning of life while reading Descartes in a skimpy white bikini? We had rented an apartment near some of the other Brewers, and impromptu barbeque parties occurred nightly. Halfway through the spring training season of 1971, I woke up one morning and marveled at how my world resembled a whirlwind roller coaster ride from the day I voiced my vows last June. Last summer I learned to adjust to the incessant traveling schedule of my husband and the ensuing loneliness of being left behind. Empathetic baseball wives had taken me under their wings and taught me, if not how to fly, then at least how to flap my wings and survive. I was now happily reconnecting with some of these wives and passing my own advice on to other new brides. I had become part of a very select sorority. There would be no initiation hazing or hoops to jump through in this sisterhood. Instead, emotional support would be offered from other women dealing with their own anxieties and trying to keep up the confidence and spirit of their husbands. I was no longer a speculative college student; I was now the tried-and-true supportive wife of a major league baseball player.

Our sojourn in Arizona flew by and it was time to pack up our belongings and head north. A clubhouse attendant talked us into letting him drive our car up north to Milwaukee for the home opener (I must admit it was an easy sell), and so I joined Skip and his teammates to open the season in Minneapolis. After spending the winter in Mayaguez and spring training in Arizona, the bone-chilling temperatures and face-biting wind gusts dealt a forceful blow to my pampered body. Copious quantities of snow had been bulldozed off the playing field and onto the perimeters of the parking lot, cutting in half the available parking spaces; the frozen grass was spray-painted a verdant emerald so the infield would appear a vibrant green on the televised opener.

I was not the only one who had a tough time dealing with the local meteorological elements. As previously mentioned, wives did not usually accompany their husbands on the road. The majority of the team wives were in a caravan following each other along highway 40 towards Milwaukee as their husbands hung out at the hotel and tried to adjust to the freezing climate. Skip and I had been given a hotel room a few floors above the rest of the team to preserve everyone's privacy. One particular California-born player seemed to be having an extremely tough time adjusting to the constraints of the weather. It had been almost two months since the man/boy in question had been hanging ten on his surfboard. Obviously there was no ocean nor waves to surf in downtown Minneapolis, but this did not present a problem for this ingenious wave ripper. Stripping himself of all clothing that might restrict his styling moves, and convincing a fellow teammate to do the same, he jumped upon a waiter's cart and surfed down the hall while his "au naturel" compatriot pushed the trolley. As luck would have it, this naked duo was just heading past the elevators as the doors opened upon this unlikely scenario. I looked at Skip, he looked at me, and we both remarked at the same time: "We really didn't just see X surfing with Y creating the wind, did we?" When we finally regained our composure after a fit of laughing, we decided not to share this bizarre behavior with their conservative spouses. I was pretty sure that these two wives, who were struggling to keep both a whiney child and a yippy dog content on the long drive north, would fail to see the humor in this encounter.

The socio-economic climate that emerged during the early '70s produced a period of intense cultural change throughout America. Long gone was the complacency of the Eisenhower era, and the altruistic idealism of the Kennedys' Camelot died along with our youthful president. The "flower power" of the sixties lost its innocence at Kent State as the media gained mind control of the masses. On April 24, 1971, over 500,000 anti-war demonstrators marched on the Capitol in Washington, DC, in protest of our involvement in Viet Nam. Popular music reflected this discontent through anti-war folk lyrics and angry rock rhythms. The musical *Hair* packed theaters, reflecting the frustration and discontent of the country's youth. With "harmony and understanding, sympathy and trust abounding," the cast cried out for "no more falsehoods or derisions" and pleaded for "mystic, crystal revelation, and the mind's true liberation." Popular novelists such as Taylor Caldwell worried about the careless affluence that was engulfing America. The characters in her books depicted the struggle that was going on within families and the tension embedded in the conflict between the materialistic desire for power and money and the traditional values of love and family. Jerzy Kosinski's *Being There* rose to the top of the book charts as it farcically examined the hypocrisies inherent in our self-serving society; style over substance was taking over our culture. Judy Blume voiced the concerns of the urban adolescent striving to find some meaning in this world with her book, *Are You There God? It's Me, Margaret.* People were pushing the limits, and it became harder to decipher the boundaries. The number of intact families throughout our country was on the decline while the divorce rate was increasing at an alarmingly rapid rate. Dee Brown's *Bury My Heart at Wounded Knee* deeply influenced my own vision of American history. I grew up assuming that the good guys always wore white hats and was shocked by the utter injustice our society had dispensed on the Native American Indians. What chance did our government have of granting civil liberties to all if this shameful sabotage was the basis of our "civil" society? Even the Indians co-existing with the lost boys in Neverland were given an equal opportunity to win.

The civil rights movement had made significant advances, but society was far from embracing equal rights for all. Major league baseball was making some progress in this field, but deep-seated prejudices still remained. On February 9, 1971, Satchel Paige was granted the recognition he deserved when he was the first Negro Leagues player voted into the Baseball Hall of Fame. We took a personal interest in this induction since Skip and Satchel Paige had been teammates for a brief time in Kansas City. Charles O. Finley, the pioneer of promotions, set aside a night to honor the Negro Leagues players at Municipal Stadium in late September of 1965. What better way to pay tribute than to have the most dominant pitcher of the Negro Leagues start the game? Twelve years after his retirement from professional baseball, which included stellar stints across the USA, Cuba, the Dominican Republic, Puerto Rico, and Mexico before being signed (at age 42) as the first black major league pitcher by Bill Veeck in Cleveland, Satchel Page joined the Kansas City Athletics. As the legendary Negro Leagues veterans were introduced before the game, Satchel Paige was "warming up" in a rocking chair. Skip, the youngest player on the 1965 Athletics roster at the age of 18, was astonished at the command the larger-than-life, 59-year-old Mr. Paige brought to the mound. Satchel shut down the Red Sox sluggers, including Carl Yastrzemski and Tony Conigliaro for three innings. Following a prepared script, Paige strode to the mound to start the fourth. Before the first pitch of the fourth inning was fired, Haywood Sullivan, the A's manager, joined Satchel at the mound, retrieved the game ball, and signaled to the press box. The lights dimmed, the fans lit cigarette lighters and Satchel Paige walked off to a standing ovation and a boisterous rendition of "The Old Gray Mare." Politically correct baseball organizations today lack the outright audacity of the fabulous Charlie O.

It was difficult for me to accept all of the stories Skip had told me about his early days in the minor leagues, unnerved at his account of the many times, when he was playing minor league ball in the mid–1960s in Alabama, that the team would eat on the bus because the black players were not allowed to sit at the counter of certain restaurants. As hard as it was for me to conceive that prejudice such as this could exist in our country, my northern bias chalked it up to a Confederate mindset. You cannot imagine my indignity the night a group of the Brewers' wives met at one of the nicer restaurants in Milwaukee that summer when, despite having accepted our reservations over the phone, were informed that, "Sorry, but we just do not have a table available" by the arrogant maitre da' when he observed that our party consisted of a multi-ethnic group of wives! Not wanting to cause further embarrassment to the two wives in question, we left the pompous French restaurant that night and, in a valiant effort to diffuse a potentially divisive bonding experience, shared a wonderful meal at the welcoming German establishment down the street. Never again would any of the 1971 Brewers ever step inside that racist establishment.

That same year I encountered prejudice head-on in the housing market. One of my new friends was a stunning young woman of Alaskan Eskimo heritage. She met her Dominican Republic soulmate in Oregon while she was attending school, and he was playing minor league ball. For some unknown reason, Phyllis was having a terrible time renting an apartment. Every time the couple went to view a unit that was listed in the newspaper, they would be told, "Sorry, it is no longer available." One Saturday, when the team was out of town, I accompanied Phyllis to look at an open apartment. Assuming that I was interested in the rental, we were given a grand tour of the building and presented a lease on the spot. The sudden transformation on the face of the rental agent from an ingratiating smile to a sinister scowl when I handed the lease for Phyllis to sign remains etched in my memory. Still, there was nothing he could do, short of being taken to court for discrimination. I'm not sure if this beautiful person, both inside and out, ever confided to her prideful husband all the details of her house-hunting dilemma. However, my own assumption of the basic goodness of human behavior in business was tainted by this particular two-faced real estate agent.

Fortunately these two particular low-life individuals did not reflect the spirit of the general population of Milwaukee. The majority of the Wisconsinites we encountered during our four years in Milwaukee were down to earth, wonderful, warm and welcoming. Still, finding short-term housing for the season was not that easy a task in a city that valued long-term relationships. As the second season of the franchise was just beginning, one new apartment complex was nearing completion, and half of the team was lucky enough to reel in a rental. As the season progressed, it became almost a weekly occurrence for a one-bedroom apartment occupied by player A to be subleased to player B and sometimes on to player C in response to the constant shuffling of the major league roster. This physical proximity to the other ballplayer families made for a very close-knit team. There was a large common room adjacent to the pool and at least once a month there would be a BYOB team potluck party held there. The thought of having a party catered never entered anyone's mind. We were all pinching pennies, and this low cost socialization suited both our entertainment needs and our budgets. An added benefit to this housing situation was the fact that, long before carpooling became the environmentally friendly thing to do, the players would hitch rides with one another and alleviate the need for their wives to make multiple trips to the ballpark.

Safety is always a concern for any woman who spends a lot of time home alone. We had agreed to buy a small renter's insurance policy from an Air National Guard acquaintance of Skip's as soon as John returned from his two-week summer camp, but the motivation to purchase this policy had more to do with giving the struggling agent some business than any concern for our meager possessions. The thought that someone might break into my apartment never entered my mind until I came home one day to find our residence in a total state of disarray. While Skip was away, I flew home to be with my mother as she was recovering from surgery. On my return, one of my fellow Piccadilly Place tenants picked me up at the airport. I sensed that something was amiss as soon as we pulled up to the building. The drapes that I always left opened were shut tight. I opened the door to my apartment to find the couch pillows thrown all over the floor. As I cautiously moved on into the bedroom, I was met with a disastrous sight—the closet door was open and piles of clothes were tossed everywhere. Clearly this had not been a quick hit-and-run operation. Whoever had broken into our apartment recognized our photographs and realized that the team was out of town for the week. These bold vandals took their time enjoying our provisions as well as our accommodations. There were beer cans, cookie crumbs and popcorn scattered all over the living area. Upon further inspection, I realized that both our television and stereo were missing from the cabinet. Before we left for winter ball the previous October, I had taken the advice of former expatriates and copied a number of record albums onto tapes to bring with us. All our rock tapes were gone while my James Taylor and Rod McKuen recordings were left behind. This manner of selective stealing permeated into the bedroom. Skip's leather jacket was missing, but his suede coat was carelessly flung in a heap on the floor. My beloved lace, butterfly dress, reminiscent of one worn by Goldie Hawn during a cocktail party skit on *Laugh In*, was no where to be found. Also missing was my favorite *faux* fur pinto coat. However, my stylishly sedate linen "going away" ensemble was ruthlessly thrown on the bed. As I sorted through the mess, I began to wonder what was wrong the clothes that these thieves had so carelessly discarded.

This was the first, but unfortunately, far from the last time that we were burglarized. It was, however, the last time we waited for a friend to return to town to sign up for an insurance policy. An eerie sense of sadness and disillusionment occurs when your personal space is violated. I became suspicious of anyone I hadn't seen around the complex before and started bolt-locking my door whenever my husband was not home. I was not comfortable with my new cautious cynicism, but found it hard to go back to my totally trusting view of life. On the first evening of the next road trip, our paper boy arrived at my door accompanied by two friends—a teen age girl just about my size and a fullback-looking fellow close to Skip's height. They all appeared surprised to find me home, and they mumbled some excuse about making sure the paper was arriving on time. Soon after they left, I called the police to report this strange visit, but the break-in was never solved. A few days later the paper boy arrived at an hour when he knew Skip would not be at home and angrily announced that he was "sorry I thought he was a thief." Needless to say, we cancelled our paper subscription and although I kept my eye out in the high school corridors for my one-of-a-kind coat during my seasonal substituting days, I never did recover my special coat or my naively innocent outlook on life.

THE TIMES THEY ARE A-CHANGING

Hope springs eternal at the start of each new baseball season. Leaving the sub-zero temperatures of Milwaukee in February of 1972 and heading to Arizona for spring training, optimism reigned supreme. The Brewers had made a huge trade during the off-season, acquiring Jim Lonborg, George Scott, Ken Brett, Billy Conigliaro, Joe Lahoud, and Don Pavletich. This welcomed addition of power hitting and experienced pitching brought a new sense of anticipation that Milwaukee would finally field a competitive team. Skip and I had adopted Milwaukee as our surrogate home. Skip transferred his college credits to Carroll College and transferred his reserve unit from Boston to the General Mitchell 128 Air Refueling Unit of Wisconsin's Air National Guard. I was substitute teaching at the local high school and becoming involved with the volunteer spirit of our church community.

Due to the transient nature of the game, very few ballplayers live year round in the city for which they play. Many southern players have no desire to spend the winter in such a cold climate as Wisconsin, and for these cold-blooded players the decision to return home at the end of the season is an easy one. Both Skip and I were native New Englanders and therefore were not put off by the frigid temperatures. It was not our love of the cold climate but our appreciation of the warmth of the people of Wisconsin that moved us to settle in for the winter. At the end of the 1971 baseball season we took a leap of faith, and planning a long stay in Milwaukee, purchased a condominium. This would be our first home, and we spent many a sleepless night agonizing over the exorbitant $24,000 purchase price. The concept of condominium living was relatively new to Wisconsin in the early '70s, and many questions were raised by our concerned friends and families over the security of our investment. How much of the facility did you actually own? Where did all the money for the association dues go? And what would be the logistics of selling this property if we ever were traded? The emotional pull of the complex far outweighed all these logical concerns. The Twelve Bridges West development was gracefully nestled into the woods and included a stone-lined outdoor pool. There were twelve bridges (hence, the name) that served

The calm before the "striking" storm—Kathy and Skip enjoying the sunshine in
Tempe, Arizona, March 1972.

as walkways over the underground parking lot that led from the asphalt circular driveways to the main entrances of the buildings. Each underground
parking space was equipped with an electrical outlet into which a car could
be plugged during the frigid winter months. Our particular condo unit boasted
a thirty-foot open living space with a cathedral ceiling and a separate kitchen
and dining area. A lofted balcony opened up on two bedrooms. Looking back,
it's hard to believe such a magnificent complex came with such a minuscule
price tag. Today's ballplayer pays more for his first car than we did for our
first home.

As an architectural design, the twelve bridges that spanned the property gave a serene storybook feel of Sleeping Beauty's cottage. On the day
we moved, the twenty-mile-per-hour wind gusts that greeted our movers
seemed to have a closer resemblance to a scene from *Doctor Zhivago*. With
a-5 degree temperature and frost-bite wind warnings of-23, we hastily moved
all our belongings into our first "permanent" home in the beginning of
December 1971. The rest of the winter was spent delighting in our domicile,
arranging and rearranging the furniture, and connecting with our neighbors.
The Hegans and the Sanders had also relocated to Milwaukee, and we spent
many an evening planning menus for the night and strategies for the upcoming season at each other's homes. While contract negotiations were discussed
in generalities, individual salaries were closely guarded secrets, and players
never disclosed the actual compensation found on the bottom line of their

contract. At the beginning of February, we rearranged the couch from one end of the room to the other for the final time, cleaned out our refrigerator, set the timers on the lights, and set out towards the warm training fields of Arizona.

This was only my second spring training season, but already I appreciated the luxury of being married to an established player. When you're assured a spot on the team, spring training is "almost" like a vacation. Scottsdale, Arizona, in February is breathtaking, a mystical desert with painted mountains, cactus gardens, and fabulous sunsets. For the first few weeks of spring training, Skip would work out in the morning, and we would play golf in the afternoon and go out to dinner at night, free of the daily pressure of constantly performing to the best of your ability. The veteran player knows what it takes to get himself in shape for the season and slowly eases into that midseason form. The single players usually all stay in the same team-sponsored hotel, while the married players are left to their own devices to find housing. That spring we were lucky to find a new complex in the Tempe area just finishing up construction that allowed players to rent on a short-term basis (not an easy task). Spring training also affords the wives a chance to get to know one another before the demands of the season interfere with social life.

Friendships form fast in baseball. In this "here today, gone tomorrow" world, the opportunity to foster long-term relationships is a luxury few can afford. Jim and Rosemary Lonborg lived in our apartment complex, and we quickly formed a common bond. We were relatively newly-wed, unencumbered by family responsibilities. Frequently on late February afternoons the four of us could be found on a desert fairway (or in a sand trap). While Rosie was a more skillful golfer, we did have a lot of laughs on the course and shared the same philosophy of enjoying the playing of the game more than the outcome. Of course, our husbands shared a more intense philosophy of life and had to be competitive at any sport. Sinking that final putt could make the difference between dining out on king crab legs at The Bombay Bicycle Club or grilling burgers at home. Both our husbands were pitchers and many dinner conversations centered around the necessity of "owning the plate" and the importance of pitching inside. Competitors at heart, Skip and Jim were anxious for the season to start while Rosemary and I were very content to enjoy the quiet solitude of the desert. Morning walks through valleys filled with blooming cactus and evening strolls through rainbow lined skies transported us to a magical world of blissful perfection. We were both accustomed to the constantly changing inclement weather in the east coast, and so it was hard to believe that every day could be this magnificently warm and sunny. Life appeared to be almost too perfect. One morning Rosie came running into my apartment excited that she could spot a rare cloud in the sky. Although it never rained that particular day, we should have braced ourselves for the coming storm.

FREEDOM

I think, therefore, I am (words of Nietzsche). *I think I should be free, therefore I am willing to stand up for my rights* (actions of Curt Flood). "Free agency" refers to the ability of a player to sell his services on the open market. When a player's contract with his team expires, he becomes a free agent and is awarded the liberty to sign with any team of his choosing. This is free enterprise in action. Many people might not be aware that this professional freedom was not always available to professional baseball players. Let me share with you the nerve-wrenchingly challenging adventure of living through that history.

Before the advent of free agency in major league baseball, legally individual baseball players were the exclusive property of team owners. The players were owned outright by the team and devalued on tax returns. A system known as the "reserve clause" gave owners exclusive rights to re-sign their players to contracts on a "take it or leave it" basis with little room for negotiation. Exempt from anti-trust regulations thanks to a 1922 Supreme Court decision, baseball organizations ruled "benevolently" with an iron fist. For years, the players' union, the Major League Baseball Players Association, exerted little influence in the hard-core basic agreement negotiations and existed mainly as a back office function administering a modest pension fund.

In 1966, the players union hired veteran United Steelworkers organizer Marvin Miller to improve the lot of the players and to seek a piece of the growing television revenues for their pension fund. At that time, the minimum baseball player salary was about $6,000 a year. Marvin Miller brought a new approach to player negotiations. Instead of accepting the paternalistic system that had prevailed in the past, Miller employed the traditional trade union approach, confronting the owners with demands and threatening to back those demands up with power.

In 1970, with the backing of Marvin Miller, Curt Flood challenged the reserve clause after he was traded from the St. Louis Cardinals to the Philadelphia Phillies. Curt refused to report to Philadelphia. Instead he filed a lawsuit against Major League Baseball on antitrust grounds, claiming that his freedom in the labor market was restricted by the reserve clause. Buoyed by the advances made in civil rights, Curt decided that, as a 31-year-old free man, he possessed the lawful right to be free.

Curt Flood was as crucial to changing the economic rights of ballplayers as Jackie Robinson was to breaking the color barrier. An outstanding center fielder and an All-Star-caliber hitter, Curt was fully aware of the social relevance of his rebellion against the baseball establishment. Curt Flood grew up a child of the sixties and matured into a man during that defiant decade. Men were dying in Southeast Asia. Activists were marching for civil rights. John Kennedy, Dr. Martin Luther King, and Bobby Kennedy had all been ruthlessly assassinated. Our country appeared to be coming apart at the seams. Mr. Flood believed that he could not ignore what was going on outside the walls of baseball stadiums. He felt it was hypocritical that the basic human rights heroic Americans were dying for abroad were not available to the common man participating in our National Pastime.

In challenging the reserve clause, Curt Flood petitioned the courts to insist that Major League Baseball uphold the traditional American value of individual freedom and, with the help of Marvin Miller, brought his case all the way to the Supreme Court. Rumors suggested that many of the Supreme Court justices personally sided with Curt Flood, but in the final ruling the judges upheld the 1922 legal precedent. At first the media, fueled by innuendoes from the owners, portrayed the valiant Mr. Flood as a greedy, ungrateful egotist who did not appreciate his benevolent owner. Popular opinion gradually shifted sides when members of other labor unions recognized how imprisoned the ballplayers were by their teams. Curt Flood lost his legal suit, but his heroic stand enabled generations of future ballplayers to eventually achieve this freedom.

Skip was the player representative from Milwaukee during this time. Traditionally, the player "rep" was more or less an honorary position. He was chosen by his teammates for his ability to communicate effectively and his availability to attend the yearly winter meeting, reporting back to his team on any small changes made to their pension plan. The Curt Flood controversy dramatically changed the role of the player rep. He was now the lifeline to the players union.

Change was in the air during the major league baseball players winter meeting held in the Arizona desert prior to the 1972 season. Marvin Miller, though short in stature, had a giant personality. His enthusiasm for challenging the archaic system of baseball was infectious. All the player reps were updated on the status of Curt Flood and informed about the vast amounts of revenue the owners would be making from television rights—none of which was intended to be passed along to the players. After every rousing session Skip would come back to our hotel room in Scottsdale with an intense fervor and fill me in on the proposed action. The player reps and their wives swarmed into the hotel cocktail lounge as Marvin Miller held court nightly emphasizing the necessity of firmly standing up for the ballplayers' economic rights. His infectious personality rallied the players together in a call for action. Many players supported Curt Flood in theory, but the reality of taking a stand and refusing to report to a new team was not an appealing option for the majority of athletes living from paycheck to paycheck.

A major league baseball team is far from a homogenous unit. It's economically shaped like a bell curve with a small core group of financially secure, elite players in the middle, surrounded on either end with young rookies earning their first double-digit salary and aging veterans trying to hold on for one or two more years of marginal wealth before they retire. The wives are equally diverse. On the one end, there are financially dependent high school sweethearts who happily follow their husbands' lead without question, and on the opposite edge there are independent professional women who have been accustomed to making their own living and are now dependent on their husband's athletic prowess for financial security. There is usually another group of wives who, for personal or financial reasons, choose not to join their husbands for the season. A small, but vocal group of wives form the central rooting section of every team. These women attend almost every game, understand the nuances of the sport, and rarely keep their opinions to themselves. I would place myself in the last group. While baseball wives have a tendency to emotionally support their husbands' heroics on the field, off the field there was a great deal of anxious discussion going on among the wives as to how to pay the rent or put food on the table if a strike incurred.

Having recently graduated from a Boston area college in 1970, where protest rallies were an everyday occurrence, I was philosophically attuned to the winds of change. Throughout the winter of 1971–1972, Skip and I would discuss the possibility of taking a stand against the owners with other ballplayer families. We all theoretically agreed on the need for change, but no one seriously thought that any definitive action would occur in the near future.

The player reps held their scheduled team meetings at the beginning of spring training, but this year was definitely not business as usual. Marvin Miller personally visited every team to explain his negotiating plan and to generate support for the labor movement. From clubhouse to clubhouse across the country, there came the call to rally together for action. I understand that Marvin Miller was seen as a crusading savior by the disgruntled players inside the clubhouse, but I know for a fact that Mr. Miller was not quite as popular a figure for many of the players' spouses. Who was this man that was causing havoc in their lives? Sure, the system was unfair, but baseball was a game and those were the rules of the game. Many players at that time were only paid during the season, so other than the meager room and meal allowance given weekly in spring training, a lot of families had not received a living salary since last October. No emergency fund existed to support young families. The majority of the wives did not fully appreciate the impact of the reserve clause, so how could the average fan? Popular opinion was not likely to favor the "greedy" players. Anxiety was high and uncertainty ruled.

Peer pressure has always played a large role in boyhood experiences, and I do believe that the executives of the Players Association exerted quite a bit of pressure to sway the unconvinced players. Negotiations to renew the basic agreement continued on throughout the spring to no avail. Finally, a stand and a vote on that stand had to be taken. Despite a clandestine effort by a few selfish superstars to undermine Marvin Miller's efforts, the players voted to strike at the end of spring training that year. There would be no major league baseball played until a new basic agreement was signed.

Professional athletes new to a town usually stay in a hotel for a few days while the players and their families acquaint themselves with the city and locate an apartment that will rent on a short-term basis. Once an apartment is secured, it's necessary to pay upfront with the first and last month's rent, along with a steep security deposit. Next it's time to go out to rent furniture (more deposits), set up a new telephone service ($) and connect the electricity ($$). All this takes time and money. The players and families moving to Milwaukee at the start of the 1972 season were faced with too much time and not enough money. Skip and I felt fortunate to have a home to return to and decided it was only fair to share our home with the other players. Our condo virtually became strike headquarters for almost two weeks. The local papers depicted the owners of the Brewers having lavish dinner meetings at Mader's German Restaurant to lament the money they were losing over the strike; we were serving up low-cost spaghetti dinners and housing homeless players. The Lonborgs enjoyed the comfort of our pull-out couch, Ken Brett had access to the den area, and the Slaytons shared the single bed in our guest room. Talk about luxury! Remembering back, I can hear the constant ringing of the telephone. Marvin Miller was in heated negotiations with the owners and kept in constant touch with the player reps. Player reps from other teams needed to discuss possibilities of compromise. Players called to affirm their solidarity. Players called to vent their frustration. Players called to call the whole thing off.

For a few hours a day, the striking Brewers would hold informal workouts at a local field on their own to stay in shape for whenever the season would hopefully start. This gave the wives a break from "putting on a happy face" and a chance to voice their own opinions. Friendships that had been formed quickly in the spring became solidified during the strike. Wives from New York, California, Missouri, Tennessee, and Massachusetts all had one thing in common—they were all trying hard to handle the daily details of life without placing any more pressure on their husbands. The small group staying in our apartment was very supportive of the strike, but as the strike continued into a second week and we expanded our dinner offerings to those camping out elsewhere, the initial rush of taking a stand was being tempered by the reality of what was being lost and the damage it might be doing to the game we loved.

The 1972 baseball strike was the first major work stoppage in major league baseball history. The strike occurred from April 1, 1972, to April 13, 1972. Baseball resumed when the owners and players agreed on a $500,000 increase in *pension fund* payments and the players won the right to salary arbitration. The games that were missed over the 13-day period were never played. While the owners were complaining about losing thousands of dollars a day, the players were trying to figure out how to pay for a meal at McDonald's. The final agreement did not include compensation for the games lost during the strike, so it was a few months before all the ballplayers' MasterCard bills were back to normal. As a result of the 1972 strike, the financial picture of baseball players changed drastically. Salary arbitration and the eventual granting of free agency set the foundation for unimagined options and opportunities.

In 1971, the average salary hovered around $12,000 per year, forcing most players to hold another job during the off-season. Our teammate Ken Sanders, the *Sporting News* Fireman of the Year in 1971, was offered less than a cost-of-living raise by Frank "Trader" Lane with the advice that "We finished last with you, we can finish last without you." Rumor had it that the entire Milwaukee Brewers team in 1971 made less than Kareem Abdul-Jabbar made, by himself, for the Milwaukee Bucks. If salary arbitration had been in place in 1971, Ken could have tripled his salary rather than settle for the mere pittance he was offered by his "paternalistic" team—that traded him away a year later.

I doubt if the majority of present-day, multi-millionaire ballplayers appreciate the significance of Curt Flood's sacrifice. Curt Flood died quietly in 1997. At his memorial former executive director of the Major League Players Association Marvin Miller said, "At the time Curt Flood decided to challenge baseball's reserve clause, he was perhaps the sport's premier center fielder. And yet he chose to fight an injustice, knowing that even if by some miracle he won, his career as a professional player would be over. At no time did he waver in his commitment and determination. He had experienced something that was inherently unfair and was determined to right the wrong, not so much for himself, but for those who would come after him. Few praised him for this, then or now. There is no Hall of Fame for people like Curt" (baseballreliquary.com). For the thousands of professional ballplayers whose careers ended before the game of baseball evolved into a business, the monthly pension check that was jumpstarted by the baseball strike of 1972 exists as a life saver.

KEEP ON KEEP'N ON

The baseball strike ended and the 1972 season began. Our life returned to its harried version of normalcy. The Milwaukee Brewers' wives had formed a close bond during the work stoppage, and our game-time conversations became much more up-front and personal. During one lengthy rain delay, of which there were far too many that season, the soaked spouses discussed the need to give back to the community that had emotionally supported us through the strike ordeal. For the past two years the wives had modeled at the ballpark in a fashion show that showcased the designs of Jonathan Logan, which coincidentally happened to be the property of one of the owners of the club. It was during one of these shows that I was introduced to the marvels of masking tape and safety pins for last-minute wardrobe repairs. We decided to expand on this showcase concept and organize a charity fashion event featuring the designs of local boutiques, to be modeled by the players' wives. One wife had a sister who had lost a child from sudden infant death syndrome. After researching the problem and recognizing the lack of awareness and resources that existed to support the young families devastated by this syndrome, we became firmly committed to doing all we could to raise awareness about this tragic disorder.

Lucky Scott, the exquisite wife of the affable George, and I co-chaired the event. At the young age of 23, I gained invaluable insight into the perils and pitfalls of delegating responsibility and the necessity of double-, and sometimes triple-checking all the minute details of running an event. In response to the sticker shock of how much of the price of admission was being diverted to the expenses of running the event, we switched our event from a "Luxurious Ladies Luncheon" to a "Bountiful Brunch," saving a significant amount on the cost of the food. It took some negotiations, but we convinced all of the retail boutiques involved that they did not need to receive compensation for the favor of showcasing their designs. Our biggest windfall came when Bob Uecker, the hilarious and immensely popular, self-deprecating color announcer for the Milwaukee Brewers, volunteered to MC the event. I'm certain that it was Bob's comedic role as host, much more than the runway talent of the players' wives, that made the event so enjoyable. To thank the uproariously funny Mr. Uecker for his generosity, I had selected a small jewelry box to be personally engraved by a local jeweler. With so many last-minute details to attend to, I was thrilled that the jeweler had elaborately gift wrapped the present for me. You cannot imagine my dismay when Bob opened up the gift and noticed that his name was misspelled. Naturally I assumed Bob was just reverting back into one of his dead-pan lack-of-respect routines and laughed along with him until I took the item in question in my hand and realized the letter "c" was missing from the name of Uecker. I'm sure the average fan attributed the intense color that suddenly reddened my face to the hot lights on the stage, but I can still remember my intense mortification. From that day forward, my editing skills rose to an entirely new level, and never again would I present a monogrammed memento without first opening it up and checking the inscription. Despite the honorarium *faux pas*, the fashion show was a huge success. The only regret I had was not having the financial resources to purchase the amazing, black, bias-cut one-shouldered evening gown that I had the good fortune to model for the event. Even with the "generous" 10% discount the boutique offered, the dress cost more than I normally spent on groceries for the month. Oh well, at least I felt fabulous for a few hours.

Superstitions play a big role in the life of many ballplayers. My own husband was never all that consumed by superstitious habits—although not even he would ever step on the chalk that designated the first base line on his way to or away from the mound. Some players put much more stock into ritualistic behavior. During the strike, my minimal culinary skills improved with daily practice, and I continued to improvise in the kitchen as the season progressed. The most popular of my creative concoctions was my own authentic Irish-American, Italian spaghetti and meatballs. One day we invited Ken Brett over for a pre-game pasta dinner, and that night Ken pitched better than he had in quite a while. Consequently, every fifth day for the next month-and-a-half I had to prepare my now-famous specialty for this very superstitious single player.

The constant company we enjoyed at the beginning of the season did a lot to move me into an entertaining mode. The Brewers' roster seemed to change weekly as players were released, traded, and moved up and down between Milwaukee and their AAA affiliate in Evansville. Most Sunday evenings after a day game, we would host one or two of the new and/or old couples for dinner. Soon it became apparent that the "times were a changing" at an alarming rate at our house. A strange pattern began to transpire. It seemed that at least one couple who sat at our table on a particular Sunday would be gone by the next. I began to feel that there was some sort of conspiracy going on in the front office of the Brewers' management to trade away all my friends. After a while players who wanted to be traded would beg to come over the following week, whereas players who loved the team and the city became a little skittish about accepting an invitation.

Most major league baseball players are young, talented, and athletic and generally tend to wed women who also strive to maintain a healthy lifestyle. One would assume that major health concerns do not often intrude on their lives, but the reality is that the families of athletes share the same day-to-day medical troubles of all young households; only more often than not, these problems occur when the ballplayer is out of town. I still shudder when I recall my solitary sojourn in the ER of a Milwaukee hospital. Bleeding profusely from what I later realized was an acute urinary track infection, I drove myself to the emergency room in the middle of the night. I was not allowed to pass through the locked door that could alleviate my suffering until I sat down, writhing in pain, and filled out a mound of paperwork. In a society that was espousing the empowerment of women, I felt spurned by the hospital staff. I was treated as an unsavory character for not having anyone accompany me to the hospital. A profound sadness penetrated my psyche. What must it be like to truly have no support? And why are patients treated with care and respect only when they are escorted by a friend or relative who might complain about the mistreatment? At the time I could never begin to anticipate the countless hours I would be spending in the ensuing years waiting in hospitals and emergency rooms advocating the health concerns of my five children, but perhaps that might be the subject of my next book. Back in Milwaukee at three o'clock in the morning, it occurred to me how unfair it was that people often misjudge people merely on outward appearances. Over the many years spent in strange cities, I have tried my best to ease the loneliness of many a scared wife after she was diagnosed with a potentially life-threatening illness, delivered a baby on her own, suffered the disappointment of a miscarriage, or merely agonized over her son's broken bones.

The reaction time of the hospital staff will often change dramatically when the husband/celebrity is around. Mary Lou Lee shared with me her obstetrics ordeal she encountered back in Boston. Going into labor towards the end of a home ballgame that Bill was pitching, Mary Lou waited a little too patiently in the stands until the game was over to summon her husband to drive her to the hospital. As she was wheeled into the hospital doubled over in convulsing contractions, the young nursing student manning the desk recognized Bill's larger-than-life presence and ran over to administer tender loving care to the blister that had forced Bill to leave the game in the seventh inning. I'm sure that even the super supportive Mary Lou must have felt like screaming, "Hey, what about me?" to this clueless co-ed. Thankfully, Bill was in tune enough to the impending delivery that he quickly shifted the attention to his wife's well-being. What she gained in competent nursing care she lost in privacy as a steady influx of medically-oriented Red Sox fans came to check on her and her husband's conditions.

The quality of life, especially for a player's wife, is significantly enhanced when a couple embraces the city where he is playing and chooses to live in that community on a year-round basis. Their tiny social circle widens and a multitude of layered rings are exposed. Skip transferred his military obligation to Milwaukee, enrolled in college on a part-time basis, and became a sought-after banquet speaker (usually getting a $50 honorarium along with a complimentary fried chicken dinner). He also began an internship with an insurance company, while I put my name of the substitute teacher list of the local high school. Being only five feet tall and 95 pounds at the time, for the first few weeks I kept getting asked to leave the faculty dining room. I was an extremely competent English and history substitute, but I must admit to having a few problems on the days I was called in to sub in the home economics department. I recall one week when my culinary knowledge was stretched to its meager limit. The class was covering a unit on vegetables, and the students were discussing all the ways to prepare an avocado (which, at that time, I had never seen). Reading more menus than cookbooks at this time of my life, I explained to the class that I, personally, knew of one method not covered in their book. I instructed them that, far and away, the best way to prepare it was to steam the vegetable in boiling water with lemon and garlic, drain it whole, and then eat it by pulling off the leaves one at a time and dipping them in lemon butter. The next day a very conscientious girl came to me before class and informed me with a shy smile that her mother laughingly told her that I must have gotten avocadoes and artichokes mixed up. In today's media crazy society, I imagine my clueless cooking comments would have made headlines in the morning papers along with an editorial decrying the dreadful incompetence of the substitute teaching system. But back in the

days when a teacher's authority was unquestionably respected, I was still contacted, more often than I would have liked, to sub in a myriad of amazingly
unfamiliar subject matters.

THAT'S WHAT FRIENDS ARE FOR

While we formed many wonderful friendships during our tenure in Milwaukee, a few special relationships stand out. If we could have hand-picked
all the qualities we might hope to find in the neighbors that would be occupying the adjacent unit in our new condominium, we could not have fabri-
cated a more perfect match than the Franks. Jim, an ex–Navy pilot and
basketball star, and Judy, a fine arts graduate, became, and still remain, life-
long friends. We were both childless newlyweds out to change the world. Skip
and Jim would work out together during the winter while Judy and I would
take in whatever limited cultural events descended upon Milwaukee in the
early '70s. Living next door to the Franks, I always felt safe and secure when
Skip was away. A few months later another young newlywed couple, Jim and
Karen Cote, relocated to Milwaukee from Pennsylvania and purchased a
condo in the next building. The six of us quickly formed an impromptu "dinner for six" dining club as we improved upon our cooking skills and tested
out new recipes on each other. Many a cold and rainy night was spent at
County Stadium in the company of these two great couples, and I eventually adjusted to the idea that it was really okay to be a welcomed fifth wheel
as I tagged along on a multitude of group outings during long summer road
trips.

　　Col. Killian and Diane Morkin, the base commander of the Air National
Guard and his wife, took us under their wings and introduced us to the old-
time culture of Wisconsin, including steak tartare and rabbit stew. Wilbur
and Marilyn Scott shared with us their marvelous family and introduced us
to an incredible hands-on, handicapped summer camp sponsored by the
Easter Seal Society. Our close relationship with two doctors, Doug and Jane
Neumann, put some of my supposed life-and-death situations into proper
perspective. One evening Skip, Doug, and I were sitting around the dining
room table waiting for Jane to join us from the hospital where she had been
called in on an emergency case early in the afternoon. The three of us were
lamenting the loss of yet another game caused by a few unearned runs when
an ashen-faced Jane walked in. While we had been obsessing about a lost
game, Jane had just witnessed the loss a young female patient's life at the
hospital. In a matter of seconds, our own irritations vanished as we realized
how minuscule the annoying predicaments we encountered nightly during a
baseball game really mattered compared to the agonizing decisions which can
ultimately result in deadly consequences that occur daily in the game of life.

　　Injuries occur more often than one would hope for in the extremely competitive environment of baseball. Most athletes are able to recover after only a brief stint on the disabled list. Sprained ankles from sliding into second base, minor concussions derived from banging into the outfield wall or colliding with another outfielder, and sore shoulders from poor mechanics or overuse perennially plague professional baseball players. Some injuries require a significantly longer recovery time. Most pitchers spend a great deal more time and effort perfecting their pitching skills rather than concentrating on their potentially life-saving fielding skills. In an effort to put the maximum momentum into the forward movement of the incoming leather-covered round entity, the pitcher grasps the ball, comes to a set position, steps back, lifts his leg high, and rotates his body with a spinning sensation as he propels the ball towards the plate, causing him to lose his balance and land in an awkward position in front of the mound. During pre-game batting practice, the pitcher is protected by a life-preserving screen, but the luxury of such protection does not exist during the actual contest. It's not unusual for a pitcher to take a shot off his shin or to have the sphere swiftly whiz by his face at some point during the season. Occasionally more serious problems arise—a twisted ankle, a pulled groin muscle or a shot off the elbow are all part of the risks involved as grown men continue to participate in a childhood game.

The velocity with which a ball hit off the sweet spot of the bat soars back past the occupant on the mound is directly related to the speed of that incoming pitch. Being a power pitcher with an explosive (albeit erratic) fastball, there were many times when Skip's well-being was put in jeopardy by a line drive zooming past his out-of-position body. I cringe at the thought of one excruciatingly stressful afternoon. Skip had thrown a scorching low fastball which the right-handed batter swung at with deadly determination, resulting in the ball smashing into the center of my husband's chest. With the tunnel vision that lies within the temperament of most professionals, Skip fielded the ball, got the runner out at first, and then collapsed in front of the mound. Time stood still for the next few minutes. Both the catcher and the first baseman ran to the mound, totally blocking my view of the field. My husband did eventually get up and walk off the field on his own five minutes later, but the awful feeling of fear and hopelessness that I experienced in the interim stayed with me throughout his career and returned every time I witnessed a line drive heading back towards the mound. When I visited the Baseball Hall of Fame in Cooperstown with my son a few years ago, this frightening footage was the only video they had on file of Skip's long career. Obviously not appreciating the severity of the scene, my children kept clamoring for me to "show the video of daddy getting smoked" over and over again.

One of our close teammates from the previous year named Al Yates was spending the 1972 season down at the AAA level. After a slow start, his bat was starting to connect with the incoming ball, and the Yates were hopeful they would be moving back up to the big club in the very near future. Excelling at the AAA level can be quite a challenge. The anxious batters are not all that disciplined and will swing at any ball anywhere remotely near the plate. Pitchers are usually held down at this level not because of their velocity but because of their (lack of) control. James Rodney Richards was one such player. JR threw an "extreme heater" but had little control over the ball's location. On a poorly lit field about dusk, Al Yates stepped up to the plate to bat against the fire-throwing, erratic JR Richards. Al was blessed (cursed?) with an aggressive attitude accompanied by a Peter Pan–like ego to match. Al was in the midst of a substantial hitting streak and determined to keep it going on his quest to return to "the show." With utmost confidence Al strutted up to the plate, defiantly glanced out at the mound, non-verbally challenging JR to "hit him with his best shot." JR obliged. Al never saw the ball leave the pitcher's glove. A fast ball moving at over 100 mph left its imprint on the stationary forehead of Albert Yates. Al immediately collapsed to the ground and was taken to the nearest hospital. Diagnosed with a severe concussion, the decision was made by the Brewers management to have Al be examined by the team doctor in Milwaukee. I'll never understand how the local hospital could have released Al and allowed him to fly on to Wisconsin on his own. Karen Yates called me in tears to vent her frustration about not being able to get to Indianapolis before Al left and asked if I could please pick her husband up at the airport and have him stay at our condo. Since the major league team was in the middle of a road trip, I went by myself to pick Al up. I was visibly shaken when I watched Al weaving into the terminal. This six-foot-four, robust young athlete was slowly ambling down the ramp looking as if he had suffered a major stroke. Despite his protestations to the contrary, I insisted on grabbing his suitcase from the baggage claim and carrying it to the car. I had promised Karen I would call as soon as we had settled into my condo, but after witnessing the feeble condition Al was in, I was at a loss for words as for how to assuage her worst fears. After a fruitless attempt at spinning the situation in the best possible light, I suggested to Karen that she might want to drive up the next day and join us for a few days. At dinner that night, the normally ravenous athlete was not even touching the steak I had grilled. Confident that my culinary talent was not the problem, it occurred to me that he did not even have enough strength to cut through the tender beef. Trying my best to turn this awkward situation into a lighthearted dinner, I wordlessly reached over and cut up the food for this proud man. Needless to say, I was relieved when Karen arrived the next day to take over catering to her frustrated husband. Fortunately, Al recovered his equilibrium within the week, but his career never regained its momentum, and a few years later, the Yates left the royal blue-and-gold uniforms of the world of baseball for the navy blue suits of the corporate world of Xerox. Throughout our years in baseball, we witnessed countless careers cut short by fluke accidents. It's frightening to realize how, in an only an instant, a player can turn from a promising prospect to an ex- "would have, could have, should have been" great athlete.

Despite pitching very strong on some very weak teams, Skip never was selected to be part of an All-Star team during his major league career. I, on the other hand, was named to the *Parade Magazine*'s All-Star Wives list in 1972. I couldn't wait for the issue to come out, as I was confident my clever psychological insights into the mind-set of a ballplayer's wife that I had spent over an hour expounding upon with the author of the article would grab headlines. Imagine my bemusement when I opened the paper and found only one little innocuous quote attributed to me underneath my photo. Unlike my husband, I was not familiar with the practices of many sports writers who have a tendency to have their story already written and engage in a lengthy interview merely to obtain a suitable quote to back up their initial theory. Since that time, whenever I read an article depicting an athlete or his wife in a less-than-flattering light, I remember my own inane illusion and give the article about as much weight as the paper it is printed on.

A 93+-miles-per-hour fastball and a deadly curve accompanied Skip as he strode to the mound every fourth day for four years. Unfortunately, weak offensive efforts and fluke defensive plays generally graced the field along with him. One year Skip pitched two one-hitters and still ended up with a losing record. In the rare instances that the team scored a significant number of runs in the early innings, torrential rain had washed out the games before the required five innings could be completed. In one phenomenal game, the right fielder caught the ball and collided with the center fielder as the ball dropped in for a double. Then, with men on first and second, Skip threw a low ball that should have resulted in a routine double play to end the inning, had not the first and second basemen collided and knocked each other out, resulting in another loss. Of course, the fans were free to express their emotions concerning the fielding *faux pas* and boo to their heart's content. Sitting next to the wives, whose husbands had just cost mine another defeat, I had to put on my game face and pretend that it didn't matter. Just another day at the office. We all were well aware that the mental and physical errors were as detrimental to their careers as the impact of their fielding flaws was to Skip's. The words "I'm so sorry he messed up again" were never uttered out loud, but the sympathetic hugs clearly conveyed the intended message.

The early Brewers had last place sewed up by the Fourth of July. Although the team as a whole was not going anywhere, the roster flailed in a state of constant flux. General manager Frank "Trader" Lane lived up to his name. As the third and fourth seasons spun out of control, older, more experienced players were granted their independence (*i.e.*, walking papers) as passionate young rookies were given a chance to shine. This shake-up incited a radical change in the dynamics of our team parties. Sedate family barbeques spiraled into sequels of *Bob & Carol, Ted & Alice*. Skip and I preferred the role of surrogate parents to sultry swingers. We would try to stay at parties until the novice players left with their naiveté still intact. I suspect there were other gatherings that our names were left off of the guest list since it was common knowledge that we preferred to hold on to our own house keys.

After four frustrating years in the starting rotation of the Milwaukee Brewers, Skip had not lived up to performance expectations—neither his own nor the team's. The sportswriters were running out of creative headlines: "Lack of Support Leads to Another Loss for Lockwood"; "Another Bad Break for the Brewers' Hard Luck Starter"; "When Is Skip Lockwood Going to Get Lucky?"; "Rain, Rain Go Away So Skip Can Win!" The self-fulfilling prophecy of misfortune caused by a random series of unfortunate events had to stop.

As another exasperating season came to a close in 1973, Skip met with the Brewers' team management. Something needed to change. Unrealized potential was the topic of the day. All the athletic ability in the world cannot compensate for a loss in confidence. Skip had lost confidence in his teammates' ability to support him, and the team had lost confidence in Skip's ability to win. Success leads to success while failing to succeed only leads to self-doubt. Everyone involved agreed that a trade would benefit all parties. The management thanked Skip for the commitment he had made to the team and to the community. No regrets, no hard feelings, just a subliminal sense of sadness that things had not worked out in Milwaukee accompanied by the anticipation of forging ahead towards a new future. A few weeks later, Skip was traded to the California Angels.

Ever the enthusiastic cheerleader, I supported Skip's decision to move on, even though it meant leaving the adopted town I had come to love. It was going to be hard to say good-bye to my connection with the local community. After subbing in high school on a regular basis for three years, I had figured out how to motivate two of my most challenging students. Impromptu trips to the museum with my next-door neighbor would cease. No longer would we share in the magical mundane pleasures of the Midwest—Friday night fish frys overlooking Mequon Bay, potluck Sunday night suppers with our condo neighbors, Monday night football gatherings with other transplanted ballplayers, and moonlight bowling where Nancy Hegan's striking skills were totally overshadowed by Bonnie Vukevich's skillful appearance in her bowling attire. We never saw the grass peek through the mounds of snow covering the winter landscape as we left Wisconsin, but looking back, the grass roots of our lives were the greenest there.

As previously noted, spirits, both of the emotional and intoxicating variety, flowed freely in Milwaukee. Did I happen to mention that Wisconsinites managed to consume the most brandy in the nation? Two weeks of going-away parties dining on brandy-laced tenderloin, beer-baked bratwurst, and drunken sauerbraten while sipping Brandy Manhattans began to take its toll. My waistline and my splitting headache told us it was time to move on. A final farewell brunch featuring a soufflé with brandy mushroom sauce, brandied cherries flambé, and Brandy Alexanders warmed us all the way to our next adventure in Anaheim. Most of our teammates and friends with whom we shared these special moments have gone, yet some remain. Of all the places I've remembered in our incredible baseball journey, when I stop to think about the people of Milwaukee, "I love you more."

4

California Dreaming

Four Strong Winds

Nothing worthwhile in life comes without sacrifice. After months of soul searching, we reached the conclusion that to revitalize Skip's pitching career we were going to have to leave Milwaukee. Four years in one location might seem like a short sprint to the average American, but four consecutive seasons with a floundering franchise was of marathon proportions to those living in the world of baseball. The average lifespan of a major league ballplayer's career in 1973 was less than 3.5 years (four years of major league service was required to qualify for a pension), and the young Brewers organization appeared to have installed a revolving door at the entrance to the clubhouse. We had lamented the loss of countless teammates to injuries, trades, releases, and reassignments to the minors. Like the ship of Theseus, the Milwaukee Brewers team occupied the same clubhouse, but the individual players had systematically been replaced. Only my husband, Skip Lockwood, and the hard-hitting outfielder, Dave May, remained from the 1970 roster. Despite our resolution, I was having second thoughts when the time came to say good-bye to our friends and neighbors. On a frigid morning in early February, we closed the door on this first chapter of our baseball journey. We could have copied Peter Pan's favorite mode of transportation and flown off on our new adventure, but common sense prevailed as we stepped inside the sedan and took off towards the sirens of surfing mermaids on the West Coast. With happy thoughts of brighter skies, we unplugged our car from its electric starter, pulled out of the underground parking garage, and headed out over the bridge towards Tomorrowland.

Family obligations and educational deadlines had forced us to speed non-stop to spring training in the past. This year we decided to leave ourselves time to take pleasure in the cross-country excursion. With "California Dreamin'" playing on the radio, we merged onto Route 80 and began our inspection of the intriguing landscape lining the highways. For the first few hours we reveled in the peacefulness of the snow-covered countryside. A recent ice storm had left its mark on the barren trees. As the sun broke through the morning haze, the frosty fingers of the branches gaily swayed in the breeze and glistened in a crystal forest, transporting us through the magical, shimmering woods of the White Queen's Narnia. Inevitably, the highway traveled past this enchanted land.

Somewhere on Route 80 between Iowa and Nebraska, we figured out why the Plains States were so named. Miles and miles of plain prairies stretched out as far as the eye could see. No-frills farming framed the highways. No swanky silos decorated the homesteads. Instead there appeared a plethora of haystacks—simplicity at purest form. The glare of the mid-day sun reflecting off the glowing grasslands became blinding. Late in the afternoon I took over the wheel to give Skip's eyes a break, although my driving always seems to keep his heart beating at a more than restful rate.

The first leg of our journey ended with our arrival in Omaha, Nebraska, at dusk: 500 miles down, 1500 miles to go. We were entering a new phase of our lives filled with endless possibilities. I was determined to enjoy the ride. No great adventure would be found inside the confines of a boring chain hotel. Flipping through the pages of our AAA Trip Tik, the advertisement for "a quaint country inn near the stockyards in Omaha" grabbed my attention. Stopping for gas outside of Omaha, I phoned the inn and reserved the Lewis and Clark room for the night. As we veered off the highway and wound our way towards the stockyards, we were pleasantly surprised to find that the exterior of the inn far surpassed our meager expectations. Alas, while the interior accommodations were in the four-star category, the olfactory aromas were off the charts. After ten hours in the car, our legs were a little cramped and the climate-controlled interior of the vehicle was getting a little stale, but that first breath of "fresh" air, sweetly scented by the fragrance emanating from the Omaha slaughterhouses, almost knocked us back down as we opened the doors of our automobile.

Determined to embrace the gastronomical culture of the town, our appetites were tempted by the Omaha beef menu options. Checkered tablecloths and walls filled with maps and mementos of famous western explorers brought to mind the courage it must have taken Meriwether Lewis and William Clark to forge into the unknown territory. Our own journey west was charted on maps based on the information gathered years ago by the Corps of Discovery expedition commissioned by Thomas Jefferson and led by this daring duo. The success of that mission was bolstered by Sacagawea, an original strong and invincible woman, who guided their way, translated their words, and taught them to live off the land. After an artery-clogging meal and some discussion as to what unexpected trails we would have to blaze in the coming year, we collapsed onto the hand-stitched quilts covering the four-posted bed. Early the next morning we awoke to the gentle mooing of the corralled cattle. Perhaps I should have felt a little twinge of guilt for enjoying the remains of the four-legged relatives across the street the previous evening, bur rarely had we relished such sumptuous steaks. A breakfast buffet, served up under the busts of Bossie and her friends, nourished us as we went on our western way.

Leaving the midwestern prairies behind, we hit the trail. Our sedan was packed to capacity with basic provisions for the season as we headed into unknown topography. Blessed by an incredible morning, I found it impossible not to burst out in song. With John Denver playing on the radio, my husband seemed to enjoy (or was it tolerate?) my "Rocky Mountain High" duet. Familiar with the thick evergreens of New Hampshire's White Mountains, we felt at home as our car climbed up the steep mountain roads leading into the dense forestry of the Colorado hills. Little by little the stately spruces appeared to shrink. The towering mountainside trees were gradually replaced by shrub-like foliage, small firs, and pines fighting hard to exist at their elevational limits. As our car climbed up above the tree line, our ears painfully balked at the change in elevation.

Along the crest of the Continental Divide, rock walls built by Native Americans dating back thousands of years stood strong, a testament to the talent of our indigenous ancestors. Mountain men, primarily French, Spanish and American fur traders, roamed the Rocky Mountains in the early 1800s. The Gold Rush miners in the mid-century must have forged out into the wilderness seeking their fortune in this rugged terrain. Here and there we passed deserted mining towns inhabited only by the legends of lost dreams. Hopefully our new-found dreams with the Angels would meet a kinder fate. We covered more ground before lunch than the pioneers did in an entire day. Around 1:00, we pulled into the Covered Wagon Eating Emporium for lunch, a diner with a bigger name than its seating capacity, and ordered the special of the day: "*The Best Chili This Side of the Rio Grande.*" An hour later we were frantically searching for the Rolaids.

Relying on my trusty AAA guide book, we decided to call it a day early and pamper ourselves in the hot tub at a "recently renovated mountain resort." Following the somewhat vague directions in the ad, we took a right turn down a steep-winding road. As the sun started its slow decent into the western horizon, the pavement suddenly stopped and we were now driving on a dirt road. Realizing we were lost, we looked for an opening wide enough to turn around. Soon we came upon a stone-lined driveway that appeared to lead to civilization and decided to follow the smoke. We totally lucked out, landing at a luxurious log cabin complex. This place was phenomenal, a true find tucked away in the woods. The main building, complete with a floor-to-ceiling stone fireplace, housed the reservation desk, library, and lounge. Defying its outwardly rustic appearance, every cabin had its own private bathroom and was heated by a fieldstone fireplace. Meals were served in the "Mining Camp Conservatory" with breathtaking views overlooking a cascading waterfall. This was definitely my idea of camping out. Our fortuitous one-night find turned into two enchanting evenings under the stars.

"The Lodge," we discovered, had changed hands many times in the past seventy-five years and was at this time under the stewardship of a western history buff/hotel management graduate from Cornell. Upon arrival, we were awarded a colorful verbal history of the lodge, including its connection with gambling, prostitution, and bootleg liquor. No wonder this marvelous retreat was hidden in the middle of nowhere. While I at first had my doubts about the Ivy League innkeeper's claim that Jim Croce, Janis Joplin, and Kris Kristofferson had all performed in the lounge, the tremendously skillful finger-picking talent of the folk guitarist commanding the mike that evening made me question my skepticism.

We felt blessed to have stumbled upon this little slice of heaven. Sitting out on the deck of our cabin, staring out at the tie-dyed setting sun, life appeared full of endless possibilities. We were literally and figuratively on top of the world, placing our hopeful wishes on the brightest star. Clearly, magical times would materialize in California. The sunrise was even more spectacular than the sunset. Plan A called for us to move on by noon, but we opted for Plan B and decided to spend the day strolling through the mountain trails. Soon enough the structured schedule of the baseball season would make such impromptu changes in plans impossible. We literally "took time to smell the roses" as the scents of the mountainside foliage far exceeded anything we had sampled in the parfumeries of Paris. Fearful of running into the headgear of a big horn sheep or disturbing the slumber of a giant grizzly bear, we stayed pretty close to the complex. The caution ingrained by my suburban upbringing was not conducive to daring wildlife escapades. As much as we would have loved to spend a few weeks at this heavenly hideaway, the Angels were calling louder than the coyotes, and so we left this little piece of paradise the next day and continued on our westward quest.

Equipped now with meticulous directions from the Cornellian concierge, we turned back onto the gravel path and wound our way through some incredibly scenic shrubbery. Occasionally we would spot a moose or mountain lion enjoying a morning stroll. Soon our hand-drawn map led us out of the woods and back to civilization, but the inner peace and serenity of that restful retreat stayed with us for a long time. Slowly but steadily the miles sped by. The further inland we traveled, the fewer cars we encountered—quite a departure from the hectic pace of Boston's Route 128 or the concrete rumblings on Milwaukee's connecting expressways. It appeared to us that the fast-paced, material-obsessed segment of our civilization had by-passed this part of the country. At the end of a reflective day of "what can we, ourselves, do to make a difference in this materialistic world?" driving discussions, we pulled into a small inn in the middle of Utah. We checked into our immaculate, albeit minimalist, quarters for the evening and headed down to the dining room in anticipation of an equally austere menu selection. The menu offerings were limited, however, we were pleasantly surprised by the quality and presentation of these simple dishes. Julia Child's puff pastry had serious competition from this small-town, chicken pot pie topping. We could not help noticing the homely family lingering in the far corner of the dining room. Three teenage girls dressed in high-neck, long-sleeve, calico dresses, devoid of makeup and coiffed in thick braids and bangs, were sharing a meal with a solemn-looking, bow-tied, middle-age gentleman. Skip and I fantasized at how easy it would be to raise children in such an environment. These three girls shyly giggled their way through dinner, totally absorbed in each other and oblivious to anyone else in the room, so unlike the self-absorbed teenagers we saw at the ball park every day. After the family left, we started a conversation with our waitress. Upon sharing our observances over the sheltered lives of those dining at the corner table with her, she broke into hysterical laughter. It seems that the respectable "father" was one of the leading Mormons in the town and that his "daughters" were actually three of his many wives. Apparently things are not always quite as innocent as they might appear.

Early the next morning we left our shattered illusions behind and moved on our southwestern way. Back at our dining room table in Milwaukee, we had sketched out a tentative itinerary which included an overnight stop in Las Vegas, but when we reached that infamous destination during the early afternoon we both decided that the glitz and glamour of Sin City was not for us. A coffee stop on the strip and a rest stop at the opulent, marble rest rooms at Neiman Marcus on the boulevard provided us with all we needed to see of Las Vegas. The concrete replicas of majestic mountains and cascading waterfalls could not compare with the real thing. We opted to leave Elvis and his impersonators behind and entrust whatever might be happening in Las Vegas to those who chose to stay in Las Vegas. We continued on into the quiet beauty of the desert.

Yesterday's green mountainous scenery transformed into today's earthtone desert terrain. Waves of terra cotta sand stretched as far as the eye could see as the afternoon sun blanked the sky in streaks of pink and purple ribbons. Late in the afternoon we came to a fork in the road. An old wooden sign indicated that one path would lead to the Agua Caliente Indian reservation while the other would bring us directly towards our final destination. Anxious to reach El Centro by the next day, we chose the road more traveled on and undoubtedly missed out on another edifying experience.

Limited lodging choices were listed in my Nevada guide book for the upcoming evening. After rejecting a few strip motels as just a little too native for our semi-sophistication, the glare of the sun shone down on an inviting sign above an adobe structure advertising *The Oasis Motel*. Despite its somewhat ostentatious name, the motel was a mirage in the desert. Pale turquoise walls and sand stone paintings adorned the walls, and an authentic, woven Navaho blanket covered the bed. Long before the current decorating Feng Shui trend took hold, the balance and harmony created in this simple room did wonders to soothe our tired spirits. One more mountain, one more river, one more day, and we'd be joining the pitchers and catchers of the California Angels organization for early spring training workouts in El Centro, California. The silence of the desert lulled us to sleep. The next morning we work up thoroughly rested and ready to complete the final lap of our road trip. The morning regulars at the coffee shop connected to The Oasis voiced their concern about the possible dust storm that threatened the area. Having lived through northeastern hurricanes and midwestern blizzards, Skip and I shrugged off any problem caused by encountering a little dust. We were penalized for our scoffing an hour later when the mesa winds swept across the desert, swirling tiny sand funnels across our path. Gene Autry, the singing cowboy owner of the California Angels, appeared to be subliminally greeting us to his franchise with a visual rendition of his "Rolling Along with the Tumbling Tumbleweeds" as we cautiously motored through the desert roads and arrived at our final, arid destination—El Centro, California.

LONELY TOWN

The California Angels structured their spring training in a physically and logistically demanding manner. Two weeks of intense workouts in a desert boot camp preceded the move to the full team training center at the Palm Springs Stadium in cosmopolitan Palm Springs, California. The area has undoubtedly changed a lot in the past three decades, but in 1974, El Centro was not very central to anything. Set in the middle of a dusty barren region two hours away from the creature comforts of contemporary civilization, it was a perfect location for a player to get in shape, as there was definitely nothing else there to distract from the task at hand. The height of fashion shopping could be found at the J. C. Penny Catalog Store, a significant step up from its competition, Woolworth's 5 & 10 Cent Store. Apart from the two small coffee shops on Main Street, the dining choices consisted of the buffet-style restaurant inside the Ramada Inn or the new addition to the town: Denny's. With all these enticing incentives, it's no wonder that the majority of the California Angels wives stayed home for the first two weeks and waited to join their husbands when the team reached Palm Springs.

The Angels administration did not appear to be quite as family friendly as the Brewers. Upon our arrival in Phoenix a few years before, after driving 10 hours to find that there was no room at the inn, one of the Brewers' coaches gave up his room for us. In contrast, in the process of checking in at the vastly vacant Ramada Inn in El Centro, Skip was politely informed by a member of the management team that wives were not welcome to stay at the team hotel. We could stay there for the night, but then it was strongly suggested we move on in the morning. I later learned that no such restrictions were placed upon girlfriends. Similar to the dearth of dining options, the lodging selections were equally sparse. After passing on the trailer park and the cactus campground, we checked into the totally unpretentious Motel 6 (aptly named because the rooms rented out at $6.00 a night). I'd drive Skip to the ballpark in the morning and head back to the room to plan my own activities for the day. With no old friends to hang out with and no pool to sit around, my options were minimal at best. A quick stroll around town reaffirmed my initial assessment that I could either sit around feeling sorry for myself with a half-empty glass of water, or I could fill up my cup, sit back, enjoy the great weather, and escape into a novel literary adventure. I proceeded to walk outside my patio door, slather myself with sunscreen, and settle into a well-worn, brown-and-white vinyl, striped lounge chair for the day. Fortunately, I had packed a sufficient number of paperbacks to get me through the week; unfortunately, the desert sun was so strong that my pale, white-winter body burned within a few hours. I developed a severe case of sun poisoning which to this day randomly re-appears in extremely hot weather. Suffice it to say, I do not hold fond memories of El Centro, California. Our lengthy two week sojourn at the Motel 6 ended. I was delighted that my husband was bonding with his new team and hopeful that my own solitary situation would improve once we moved on to Palm Springs. At the youthful age of 24, I had been one of the organizers of the Brewers wives for the past three years, planning charity events, to be sure, but also hosting impromptu luncheons for the new wives in town to get acquainted. So far, no such welcoming committee had stepped forward, but I was confident that my social circle would soon expand.

The Angels' itinerary allotted two days for the players to drive the necessary two hours to Palm Springs and acquire accommodations for the next four weeks. By now we were aware of what hotel was off-limits to us, but were given no help by anyone in the organization as to where to find a short-term rental during peak tourist season. A severe case of sticker shock ensued when we started looking at the resort villas a few of the established players were staying at. The majority of the ball players in the Brewers organization were all close to the bottom of the major league pay scale, and so we all lived in similar apartments and shared the same rather modest lifestyles. This was not the case with the Angels. Quite a few players on the Angels roster did not need to rely on their *per diem* voucher to pay for their spring accommodations. While it might have been great to spend the month relaxing in a one-bedroom adobe villa overlooking the sixth green, we settled into a simple, stucco, one-room efficiency on the outskirts of the city with a partial view of the canyons miles away.

I finally started to make some new acquaintances, but they did not include the ballplayers' wives. On October 17, 1973, members of the Organization of Petroleum Exporting Countries (OPEC) voted to use oil as a weapon to punish the West for its support of Israel in the Arab-Israeli war. The oil ministers recommended an embargo against unfriendly states and mandated a cut in exports. Saudi Arabia, Libya, and other Arab states proclaimed an embargo on oil exports to the United States. OPEC forced the oil companies to increase payments drastically. The oil embargo hit the U.S. consumer hard. Plentiful petrol at paltry prices no longer could be found at the pumps. In late November 1973, President Richard Nixon signed the

Emergency Petroleum Allocation Act which authorized price, production, allocation, and marketing controls on the U.S. oil supply. The price of oil quadrupled by 1974, and the availability of this liquid gold took a nose dive.

Throughout the previous winter, a number of op-ed articles ran in the *Milwaukee Sentinel*'s editorial page, theorizing on the havoc to the economy the oil embargo was going to provoke, but other than a slight rise in the cost of gas, none of the doom-and-gloom predictions had come to pass. We had not encountered any apparent fuel shortages on our drive across country and, since there was nowhere to go in El Centro, we never gave the issue another thought until we arrived in Palm Springs. Two diametrically opposed images struck us as we drove into the city of Palm Springs. Immediately struck by the lush green oasis that suddenly emerged in the middle of the barren desert, the palm trees that really captured our attention. These splendid, stately, narrow skyscrapers stretched their trunks to the sky and then gracefully fanned their leaves out as they outlined the sidewalks and bordered the boulevards throughout the entire town. The disparity of this lush Mecca rising out of miles and miles of desert sand was magnificent. In contrast to this elegant, ecological chain of trees framing the city blocks was the procession of gas-guzzling, black sedans blocking these same streets, as drivers lined up waiting for the chance to fill the barren tanks of their thirsty vehicles. From a distance it appeared as if a brigade of black beetles was lining up in an apparent attempt to attack the palm platoon. It was very easy to belittle this incongruous sight as we arrived; it was much harder to appreciate the humor in this situation when I joined the gas queue a few days later. These chauffeurs (a.k.a. men in black) became my first confidants in California, as I spent many a morning standing in the aforementioned line while my husband ran sprints in the outfield. Skip "helpfully" suggested to me that I might want to get myself a Captain & Tennille–style cap to fit in with the attire of choice of my hired compatriots waiting to fuel up, but as much as I was trying to adapt to my new surroundings, I realized I had to draw the line somewhere.

The city of Palm Springs appeared to have been the brainchild of a city planner who had spent time at a Disney design set. It could have very well been designed by Mary Poppins—it was "Practically Perfect" in every way. Picturesque stone walls surrounded pristine, gated communities. Luxurious resorts offering golf, tennis, and spa treatments could be found at every corner. Wonderful little boutiques filled with colorful clothing and shimmering jewels lined the shelves and display cases in the shopping district. Tall, tanned "beautiful people" strolled along the avenues and dined leisurely at trendy sidewalk cafes. The day-to-day concerns of the world at large were nowhere to be found. An invisible barrier seemed to protect the city from reality, forbidding liberal anti-war protesters or crunchy granola environmentalists from disturbing the tranquility of the town. Try as I might, I could not picture myself fitting in this ethereal lifestyle. I left this posh corner of the playground of the stars to the Hollywood hopefuls and drove back to the ball field.

Finally, a new friend! Baseball wives can often recognize the patient presence of another baseball spouse without being formally introduced. She is the one sitting quietly by her car reading a book, writing a letter, or making sandcastles in the tree belt with a toddler to help pass the time. Looking up from my book, I noticed a young mother and child thoroughly engaged in creating a sand-and-stick village behind a vehicle with Texas plates and went over to introduce myself. I was greeted by a wonderfully engaging smile and a handful of dirt—the first by Ruth Ryan and the second by her son, Reed. It was certainly refreshing to witness a genuine mother/son bond in this seemingly superficial city. I was invited to join their construction site as Ruth introduced me to her toddler son and welcomed me to the team. The Ryans had left some good friends back in New York when Nolan was traded from the Mets, and Ruth acknowledged the loss of friendship I must have been feeling. Obviously, even though I was trying my best to be upbeat, someone who had been there and done that could recognize the symptoms of disconnection. Both our husbands happened to be pitchers, and so we had each come to expect somewhat lengthy waits outside the locker rooms. I was almost disappointed when Skip uncharacteristically emerged after only a 15-minute wait—I had forgotten how much I had missed caring female companionship.

My personal perspective on life improved once the games began. Ruth took it upon herself to introduce me to the other wives, and I began to feel a bit more connected to this new group of women. Unlike the Brewers, the Angels did not seem to have many team gatherings during spring training, and so it was going to take a while to get to know the husbands of my new associates. Luckily, a few of the resorts some of the more established players were staying at allowed us access to their facilities, and I was fortunate enough to play some terrible golf on some wonderful courses. By the end of spring training, I was beginning to connect with some of the other new wives, but sadly, two of their husbands were cut from the team just before camp broke, and I had to settle for a small but selective circle of friends.

Roxanne Valentine was the nucleus of that circle. A fellow transplanted New Englander, she and I became friends while endlessly waiting for our husbands to emerge from the clubhouse. Time is a relative concept in baseball, and the time it takes in spring training to run extra laps, tweak a particular pitch, perfect a specific skill, disguise a distinct delivery, ice an injury, or merely just unwind from the game can be monumental. My unscientific observations conclude that a player with small children is able to complete his post-game routine in a much timelier manner than a single or childless ballplayer. Undoubtedly the alacrity in which an athlete exits the stadium is partially due to the patience, or lack there of, of the wife waiting on the outside. Being both young and childless, Roxie and I both had patiently accepted the reality that our husbands would routinely be among the last to leave the confines of the clubhouse, and we spent many a March afternoon getting to know each other in the players' parking lot. After only a few post-workout conversations, I believed that I had found a kindred spirit on the team. We both missed our close New England families and the stimulation of our college dormmates. We recognized that "what in the world am I doing here?" question in each other's eyes. Nothing in either one of our sheltered upbringings had prepared us for the role of chief cheerleader, travel and relocation agent, and emotional support therapist that the baseball wife was required to perform. The Valentines had been traded the previous year, and so Roxie could empathize with my sense of separation from my friends, but not with the logistics of moving. Bobby had only been traded from Los Angeles to Anaheim, and Roxie was lucky enough to keep her rental home. She generously invited my husband and me to share their home until we found a place to rent, and we gratefully took her up on the offer. As the California Angels broke camp, Skip and Bobby flew off with the team to open up the 1974 season in Chicago. I stuffed our suitcases into our car and followed Roxie through the desert and on towards the southern California Pacific coastline.

WELCOME TO THE HOTEL CALIFORNIA

A little more than 2000 miles separate Milwaukee, Wisconsin, from Anaheim, California, but the cultures of the two cities are light years apart. The temporary housing options in Milwaukee were very limited; in contrast, the rental selections in southern California appeared limitless. My initial plan to rent a cozy cottage by the beach had to be revised once I discovered that oceanfront real estate in southern California was extremely pricey. In less than a week of dawn-to-dusk apartment hunting, I located an ideal apartment for the summer at the Vista Del Lago Apartment complex in Costa Mesa, California. One of the many "adults only" complexes in the area (I never could understand how children could be legally discriminated against) this was by far the most intriguing. It was a short, four-freeways, fifteen-minute drive from the ballpark, and the series of man-made rivers that ran through the property gave the tenants of the complex the impression that they were living right next to the beach.

The day we moved in, Skip and I took an evening stroll around the complex. We wandered over wooden planks lined with nautical pillars connected by thick ropes. A string of paddle boats was lined up next to the dock, ours for the taking. While the one-bedroom apartment was on the small side, the central clubhouse included six motel rooms that could be rented out to tenants when out-of-town company came to town—what a fabulous concept. Meticulously landscaped throughout the complex were a series of small pools and hot tubs ensconced among lush shrubbery and tall palm trees. How could we not be confident that Skip's luck was about to change as we relished the vibrant foliage and sublime smells of our new surroundings? As we rounded another path near the far end of the property, we were greeted by a roar of raucous laughter indicating that a party must be going on. A dozen bodies were submerged in steaming bubbles. My preppy attire of patchwork madras shorts and a light blue alligator-embossed polo shirt proclaimed I was not a native surfer girl. Still the group in the hot tub was very hospitable. They welcomed us to California and encouraged us to shed our shirts and join them in the hot tub. At first I could not quite comprehend their invitation, then I spied a pile of randomly scattered clothes upon the table and understood that the hot tub was occupied by bare, naked bodies. "Thanks, but we really need to get back" was our polite, but obviously puritanically-shocked response.

In his book *The Natural*, Bernard Malamud suggested that southern California was formed by tipping the United States on its side and letting everything loose fall into that southwestern corner of the country. It seemed to me, at that moment, his theory was right on target. Yes, I assumed the culture could tend to be a bit more liberal in California, but I didn't understand exactly how dissimilar my core belief system was with my new neighbors until I spent a few afternoons participating in some mind-boggling discussions concerning my lifestyle around the pool. To be fair, people who live in short-term rental communities are generally a little more *avant garde* than the normal population of the area. Be that as it may, the concepts of commitment, fidelity, and family values did not appear to be high on the priority list of this self-indulgent segment of southern California society. Advertisements for plastic surgeons and divorce lawyers filled the papers, while "Just Re-married" banners could often be spotted on late model convertibles. Try as I might, I never was able to convince my native Californian non-baseball "friends" that there was nothing intrinsically wrong with me because I would not even consider cheating on my husband while he was out of town. After all, according to their scheming scenarios, how was he ever going to find out? Clearly I had very little in common with these bizarre brainstorming swingers. How I longed to be back at the art museums or taking underprivileged young girls to the zoo with my old Milwaukee faithful friends. Midway through the second long road trip of the season, I joined a wonderfully committed community of VISTA volunteers and made it through the long, lonely road trips by anonymously helping out in a special education summer program. Giving to others is always a lot more rewarding than gossiping about them.

"Being frustrated is disagreeable, but the real disasters in life begin when you get what you want." Such prophetic words from Irving Kristol. Skip's pitching role on the Angels staff had yet to be defined. With the Brewers he had been very comfortable pitching as the #2 or #3 starter. Free from the pressure of being the #1 starter, he never had to worry about getting bumped from his regular spot in the rotation. Skip had pitched well during spring training, but the split-squad game rotation made it hard to judge what the manager had in mind. Nolan Ryan's fastball placed him firmly in the #1 spot, and

Bill Singer's experience cemented him in #2. An unassuming and extremely talented young lefthander, Frank Tanana (who would win *The Sporting News* AL Rookie of the Year award for the season), had impressed all the coaches during the spring and was a surprising #3 starter. The imposing stature of 6' 5" Andy Hassler seemed to favor him for the #4 spot, and it doesn't take a brain surgeon to deduce that the #5 starter will be spending a lot of time in the bullpen.

The precarious position of a long-relief pitcher was not quite the boost to Skip's career that he had envisioned. Still, the season was just beginning and we were both knew how volatile the velocity of a pitcher's fastball can be early in the season. We had experienced the chaotic first few weeks of the season in the past, plagued with bad weather, game cancellations, and ensuing doubleheaders, which played havoc with the starting rotation. With a little patience (of which Skip possessed very little) his status would surely improve.

LIFE IS A HIGHWAY

The major league baseball season consists of 162 games with only half of the games played at home. Off-days are sprinkled throughout the season, falling on a Monday or a Thursday. Logistically, the teams located on the extremities of either coast need to use those off-days for travel, and consequently the time a player spends at home is decreased and the length of the road trips can seem endless to a player's wife. After leaving our home in Milwaukee in February, driving across country, settling into two different spring training sites, camping out at a friend's house, and finally moving into our own apartment, Skip was home for a whopping five days before the team was scheduled to leave in mid–April on a lengthy road trip that would take him to Oakland, Baltimore, Cleveland, and Boston. To add insult to injury, there were three off-days included in their trip. Envisioning my stimulating conversations with my fellow apartment dwellers for the next two weeks, I was less than thrilled. Roxanne Valentine was also dreading the prospect of starting off another long season of lonely nights by herself and came up with a great idea. She and I would drive up to Oakland, enjoy the weekend (and a precious off-day) with our husbands and then take our time driving back to Anaheim via the Pacific Coast highway. Skip concurred with this plan, especially given that I could shoot some fantastic shots of the Big Sur area for his photo journalism correspondence class.

What a wonderful weekend we enjoyed in the San Francisco Bay area! Our days were spent cheering for our side in the nine-inning contests between the Angels and the Athletics in the cold concrete of the Oakland Coliseum, but at night we ventured over the bridge from Oakland to San Francisco. For a somewhat sheltered New Englander who had spent the last four years in the conservative midwest, the eclectic bohemian sights and sounds of the Haight-Ashbury district in San Francisco was definitely an eye-opener. Perhaps if I had remembered to "put some flowers in my hair," I would have blended in a little better. During my college years I had always enjoyed spending afternoons in the charming old marketplace of Faneuil Hall, but food stalls in this historic Boston landmark paled in comparison to the authentic aromas emanating from the fresh, local seafare being hauled in hourly by the docks at San Francisco's Fisherman's Wharf. The Asian fare we sampled in San Francisco's Chinatown spoiled me for life from appreciating the MSG–laden cuisine found inside cardboard take-out containers. The luminescent drive over the beaming bridge created an enchanted mood for our wonderful weekend.

In his unfamiliar (and at the time unwelcome) role of a relief pitcher, Skip picked up his first win of the season on Sunday afternoon. It looked to us as if the destiny foretold inside the previous evening's Chinese cookie would be coming true-good fortune was finally going to come our way. That night we shared a spectacular dinner at Valhalla's in Sausalito. Sally Stanford herself camped out at our table for a while, charming us with stories of her previous bawdy lifestyle. This seventy-year-old blonde bombshell enchanted us with mind-boggling stories of the background role the living room of her Knob Hill brothel played during the founding of the United Nations. If I didn't know better, I would have thought that she was hitting on my husband. This immensely entertaining dining experience with Sally, one of the most legendary characters in Northern California's contemporary society at that time, alone was worth the trip. Clearly a more forceful gene pool flocked to reinvigorate the northern extremities of the state of California than the narcissist knot that clustered close to the southern tip.

After leaving my heart in San Francisco, it was time for us to part and set out in different directions. Skip took off with his teammates for an East Coast swing as Roxanne and I ventured south along California's scenic coastal Route 1. About an hour later we were lured out of our car by the beckoning beaches of Santa Cruz. We could have easily spent the rest of the week mesmerized by the welcoming waves crashing in against the sand, but our East Coast sensibilities forced us to leave this stunning shoreline after taking a leisurely stroll along the sparkling sand. It was true that we had nothing to do and nowhere to go for over a week, however, our eastern sensibilities would not allow us to stop quite so soon.

Our practicality was rewarded a few hours later when drove into the fascinating village of Carmel-by-the-Sea. We pulled into a parking spot planning to stop for an hour or so. Four hours later, after browsing through only a fraction of the fabulous art galleries and craft shops, we checked into a quaint country inn. Revived by some tea and homemade crumpets, we strolled back to the center of town. By the time we finished our window shopping marathon, the sun was setting over the opal ocean. Neither one of us acknowledged the twilight arrival of that familiar twinge of angst. It's not that we didn't enjoy one another's company, but we each would have preferred partaking in this romantic sojourn with our own soul mate.

The next morning we left this idyllic, little, seaside village and set our sights on a morning photoshoot. The 17 Mile Drive around the Monterey Peninsula was breathtaking. Its natural scenic beauty far exceeded any photographer's wildest imagination. We arrived there on a breezy late spring morning. The sun was shining brightly and its warmth radiated off the tips of the awesome waves. The road was constantly winding to the right and then jetting off to the left, and around every bend there could be found another amazing vista. Pulling over to snap a photo we were rewarded with the astounding sight of sea lions and harbor seals frolicking together near Sea Rock, welcoming each other back to their annual family reunion. My wrist was getting sore from changing the film in the camera so often. The road continued to wind through the dark, forest green Monterey pines and the bristly Cypress tress bracing themselves against the elements. I was confident that I had all the pictures I needed for Skip's project and put away my camera bag, content to relax and simply delight in the day.

Our path led us to the most famous image of the stunning seascape—the Lone Cypress. Standing majestically in its solitary stance, almost as if daring the ocean to challenge its destiny, this graceful tree exuded energy. My own certainty in the wisdom of leaving Milwaukee was beginning to waiver, and so I took comfort in the bravado of this stately tree. Naturally there was no way we could not capture this sight on film. Pulling over to park, once again I retrieved my camera and went to work. With all my little gadgets out of the bag I took a meter reading, figured out what my preferred depth of field should be, set the f-stop and shutter speed, and began to frame my photos. In stark contrast to my meticulous manual adjustments, Roxie took out her automatic camera and carelessly clicked away. As if in an effrontery to my painfully obsessive shooting sequence, a large gust of wind descended upon us and blew my precise instructions all over the place. Upon our return home we had our film developed and were both rewarded with fabulous photos. One certainly had to question if all my precise calculations were really worth the effort (although Skip did receive an A for his project).

Another reason why this drive turned out to be so breathtaking had to do more with the drivers' distractions than with the beautiful sights. The majority of those visiting the 17 Mile Drive were out for an enjoyable relaxing ride along the scenic coast and so excessive speed was not an issue. However, the narrow road along the high cliffs was pretty treacherous due to the lack of attention of so many of the drivers. More than once we were nudged off to the side of the road by a careless convertible driving in the middle of the road with the driver looking at the ocean current rather than at the road straight ahead. I was feeling a little guilty. Since Roxanne was in charge of the car, I was able to thoroughly immerse myself into this environmental marvel. I was certain that if my husband had been behind the wheel, we would have sped through the drive in order to get to the driving range at the Pebble Beach golf course. The concept of what constitutes a natural wonder lies in the eyes of the beholder.

By mid-afternoon we left the Monterey Peninsula and headed south towards San Luis Obispo. "On your way back home you just have to stay at The Madonna Inn. There's nothing else like it in the world," we were told. Truer words were never spoken. The inn is unbelievable: unbelievably garish, unbelievably excessive, and unbelievably pink. Alex Madonna served as the inn's architect and his wife Phyllis its interior designer. With an obvious love for the project and more outlandish creativity than innate good taste, they gathered artisans from all over the world to embellish their unique undertaking. The Madonna Inn was built with stones unearthed during the construction of the Pacific coast highway, and an odd combination of heavy stone and bright pink tones are interspersed throughout the entire complex. Each of the over 100 rooms was ornately decorated in a special theme; there was a Buffalo Room where you could try to sleep with the eyes of an embalmed bison staring into your face, a Jungle Rock suite where Fred Flintstone would have felt very at home and a Caveman Room, one of the most popular, offering a cave-like atmosphere with solid rock floors, walls, and ceilings and even a cascading waterfall shower.

A large, round, postcard display was positioned next to the reception desk in the predominately pink lobby where a traveler could choose her own sleeping adventure for the night. Since we arrived rather late in the day, all the really tacky rooms had already been booked, so we settled on one of the few offerings that was equipped with individual beds. It is rumored that Phyllis Madonna was obsessed with the color pink because she believed that it brought out the best in every woman. We both must have looked resplendent that night because there were more variations on the color pink in the Fabulous Fifties décor than Sandra Dee could ever have envisioned. We finally called it a night after hysterically laughing over the dichotomy of our day. We had woken up at one with nature and, after driving through an impeccably pristine natural setting, ended up going to sleep in a dreadfully artificial, cotton candy pink bedroom. Only in California!

I have often been accused of looking at the world through rose-colored glasses. I certainly did not need any light-illuminating lenses to wake up thinking I had been dropped into a vat of Pepto Bismol as the sun filtered through the fuchsia curtains early the next morning. Somewhat disorientated, having recently spent so many nights in so many different locations, it took a few minutes for me to shake the feeling that I was on the set of *Grease* waking up in Pinky's bedroom. Eventually my foggy mind figured out that the oversized pink poodle in the corner was not a figment of my imagination but a genuine *faux-fur* replica of said dog, intentionally placed there by the imaginative interior designer to flatter her fifties fabrication. The "less is more" concept never graced the imagination of the inn's management. Somehow we controlled our laughter until we reached the car, but this was not an easy task considering the number of overly ostentatious rooms we peaked inside on our way to check out.

Our serendipitous stops became even more surreal. Next up on our southern trek was a visit to the old campgrounds of William Randolph Hearst. All the media hype around the recent kidnapping of Patty Hearst had a lot to do with that decision. That past February, at the same time Skip and I were heart-breakingly saying good-bye to our friends in Milwaukee, Patricia Campbell Hearst was viciously dragged from her apartment in San Francisco by the Symbionese Liberation Army (SLA) and held for ransom. In response to the SLA's demand, Patty's father, Randolph Hearst, donated $6 million of food to the poor in the Bay area, but the self-proclaimed urban guerillas criticized the quality of the food shipment and refused to release the 19-year-old heiress. For over two months, an extensive nationwide search for Patty Hearst had come up empty-handed. And then, at about the same time Roxanne and I were getting ready to drive to northern California, Ms. Hearst was caught on a surveillance camera holding a gun during a bank robbery right in San Francisco. During our weekend stay in the Bay area, the press had a field day prosecuting this poor girl with suppositions and innuendoes. I was astounded at the absurdly ridiculous assertions that were being voiced throughout the media that Patty had become an active participant in that violent underground movement.

While far from an expert in the field, I had majored in psychology at Regis and had studied the compelling drive for self-preservation and the persuasive effects of brainwashing. How any rational adult could think that Patty Hearst would have willingly joined the Symbionese Liberation Army was beyond my comprehension. Perhaps I was a little biased because of the unfair press I had witnessed written about some of our good baseball friends. I was convinced the press was punishing Patty Hearst simply for having been born into a privileged family and not fitting into the stereotypic Junior League mold expected of her. Instead of spending hours in beauty salons, Patty was trying to make her own mark in the world by persuing an education at Berkeley. What a difference a few decades make. Today's press appears to idolize Paris Hilton for being a spoiled little rich girl and the epitome of the self-indulgent generation as represented in the Simple Life. Roxanne shared my sympathies, and so it was with a decided interest in viewing the ancestral country retreat of the Hearst family that we checked out of the Hotel California and drove on until we checked in at the entrance gate to Camp Hill.

As tasteless as the Madonna Inn was tacky, Hearst Castle was the embodiment of elegance. Fashioned after some of the most beautiful castles in Europe that William Randolph Hearst had visited in his youth, this elegant structure regally reigned over the hills of San Simeon. Always an innovator, Mr. Hearst hired a female architect, Julia Morgan, to translate his dream into a reality. For over 28 years, the two collaborated to design, tear down, and redesign a country retreat of monumental proportions. The power of the Hearst press, along with Mr. Hearst's own compelling cosmopolitan persona, had catapulted him into the center of the glamour and glitz of Hollywood in its heyday as well as into the inner circles of politicians. Celebrities from all walks of life hopped aboard Hearst's private railroad car, chugged up the mountain, and converged on the complex to be wined, dined, and coddled by the impeccable staff who presided over Hearst Castle in the 1920s and 1930s.

Over 165 rooms were designed and decorated with priceless art and antiques. Beautifully maintained gardens graced the property along with an amazing array of animals in the private zoo. Hearst Castle was truly the personification of a narcisstic Neverland. Self-indulgent boys from the Hollywood hills would spend weekends with equally needy, flighty, fair-haired girls. The world at large might have been rocked by the Great Depression, but the bright and the beautiful favorites of the gods could be found lounging around the cascading waterfall system at the Neptune pool. Our skittish tour guide informed us that Patty Hearst herself used to play hide and seek with her grandfather behind the marble columns surrounding the pool.

We underestimated the time it would take to tour the castle. A few hours seemed only a few minutes. Had our husbands accompanied us, we would have undoubtedly taken the self-guided portion of the tour at a much faster pace, but Roxie and I were both perfectly content to take our time appreciating the immense effort and exquisite taste taken in furnishing the estate. The mirrored tiles and faux finishes employed to mask design flaws in the model homes of the numerous housing developments in southern California were certainly no match for the magnificent blue-and-gold embellishment on the ceilings and walls of the intricate Romanesque indoor pool.

A self-proclaimed day dreamer, I could envision the excitement I would have felt upon finding my name on that coveted guest list for a politically focused weekend. We both could picture ourselves curled up in one of the comfy leather chairs in the stately study, lost in a forest of mahogany and reading some romantic mystical adventure until the butler informed us it was time to "change for cocktails at seven." Then, dressed in some bedazzling bejeweled creation (that would have been way too fancy for the ballpark), we would gracefully glide down the central staircase and join our engaging contemporaries in the drawing room. The fact that neither one of our budgets could come close to even affording the shoes to match the couture costume never entered our illogical minds. At 25, I was still young enough not to let rational details interfere with my irrational dreams.

While the castle was magnificent, the radio reception was not, and so we left the castle in the clouds and motored down the mountain to catch the late afternoon broadcast of the Angels game on our car radio. Today's wives have the luxury of taping the game and viewing it at their leisure, but in the early '70s very few games were televised and VCRs were still in development. Consequently, when the team was playing on the road, we often had to make the tough choice between sitting down to a relaxing dinner in a restaurant and missing the broadcast of the game or eating take-out in the car. That challenging choice was made a whole lot easier on nights that neither one of our husbands were scheduled to be in the starting lineup. The evening game in Cleveland was broadcast during the late afternoon in California, and so on this particular evening we had the best of both worlds—we were able to listen to the game on the radio while driving and still engage in a decent dining experience when reached our next (as yet unplanned) stop.

Traveling past the materialistic mansions of Orange County to the cosmopolitan city of San Francisco and returning home by way of the charming country near Carmel and the eclectic area around San Louis Obispo, I thought I had seen about all the diversity there was to see regarding the distinct cultures to be found on the California coastline. Of course I was mistaken. Amidst the green grape laden rolling hills of the countryside, a giant white windmill came into sight. Could we already be back at Disneyland?

No, we were nearing the Danish town of Solvang, California. Here was an entire village that appeared to have dropped out of the sky and missed its intended destination of Denmark. A number of working windmills were spinning around, creating the illusion that Don Quixote could be arriving on his trusty steed at any minute. Since we had the liberty of too much time, we opted to continue our journey another day and explore this town. After all, didn't Don Quixote confide in his traveling companion, Sancho, that: "Liberty ... is one of the most precious gifts that Heaven has bestowed on mankind"? Looking at each other in disbelief at stumbling upon yet another great adventure, we circled the small village once and checked into the Royal Copenhagen Inn for the night. In sharp contrast to the incongruous decorating of the Madonna Inn and the upper-class opulence of Hearst's estate, the Copenhagen Inn recreated the ambience of an authentic neighborhood in its mother city. The crisp white linens and hand-stenciled furniture created the illusion that we had traveled halfway across the world in the "old country" rather than only a few miles off the Pacific Coast highway.

The town of Solvang was founded in 1911 by a community of homesick Danes who had fled the cold midwestern winters to form a refuge for themselves and their offspring on the warm west coast. Enormous effort had been taken by all involved in the project to create an authentic recreation of their beloved homeland. The end result of their precise plans was evident in the intricate designs of the architecture on the carved caves, doorways, and roof tops throughout the village. The town transported us back to a simpler time. Automobiles were not allowed on the city streets. Instead horse drawn carriages rambled down the quiet cobblestone roads. Many of the shopkeepers were dressed in authentic Danish attire as they offered their hand-crafted wares and mouth-watering pastries to the appreciative public.

I thought I had spotted one of Peter's mermaid friends, but upon closer inspection I realized she was only a bronze statue created in the image of the Little Mermaid who watches over the Copenhagen harbor. Could it be that the dreams we had hoped to fulfill in California were going to be as misleading as this half-scaled, lifeless representation? After a bountiful breakfast smorgasbord of Danish delicacies, we left the old country life of Scandinavia behind and proceeded to reenter present day Anaheim. By the end of the day we were back to our "normal" existence in southern California, each in our own home planning our days around the broadcasts of the games while waiting for our husband's phone calls.

The following evening I was summoned to the door of my apartment by loud, intense knocking. My heart dropped when I opened the door to find three imposing young men dressed entirely in black informing me that they had come searching our complex looking for Patty Hearst. As the color drained from my face, they broke into side-splitting laughter, obviously satisfied with their prank. They then apologized and insisted that they were really just collecting monetary donations for the local food bank. Unable to think rationally, I gave a generous donation to their cause and breathed a sigh of relief as I slammed the door shut and bolted the door. On retrospect I became incensed with myself for letting my imagination get the better of me and falling for their obvious scam. Why was it that it was so hard to decipher reality from illusion in California?

Over the Rainbow

A circular, concrete baseball stadium loomed up in the midst of an enormous parking lot three miles down the road from Disney's Fantasyland in Anaheim, California. Families flock to the Magic Kingdom to leave their mundane lives behind and embrace their childhood dreams. It is with some of this same hope of reliving their little league glory days that many southern Californians arrived at the Angels ballpark. In the mid-seventies, the California culture was all about acting "cool," and loud cheering and rowdy guffaws had no place in this trendy territory. This venue would never host a ten-cent beer night; Anaheim Stadium offered wine coolers to its fashion-conscious clientele. These paying patrons expect to be entertained and acknowledged their appreciation of an exceptionally fine double play by polite applause. The average Angels fan spent more time on hair and makeup to prepare for his/her arrival at the game than my husband did on warming up for his appearance on the mound. At first I was impressed with the ultra-stylish casual attire donned by the posh patrons until I realized how easy it was to dress with only one climate consideration. Game time temperatures consistently hovered around the seventy degree mark and remained there for the entire contest. Consequently there was no need to pack extra sweaters and jackets in anticipation of a twenty-degree drop in temperature during the game. Rarely was it necessary to seek cover under the rafters for shelter from the cold, driving, bone-chilling rain that had been a staple in Wisconsin. I soon recovered from my awe over their airy attire.

Of course, there were also those who did not feel the need to dress at all. A strange phenomenon called "streaking" took hold during the 1974 baseball season. At least twice a week during the hot summer nights in Anaheim, some exhibitionist would shed all of his/her clothes and sprint across the field, occasionally stopping to say a quick hello to the outfielders before being tackled to the ground, draped in a blanket and led off the field to the welcoming arms of the police force. Ball game action across the country was sidelined by the antics of random streakers. However, this exhibitionist behavior seemed to have caught on with a vengeance in southern California. At first the perpetrators of this bizarre behavior were given their few minutes of fleeting fame in the form of a standing ovation from the fans at the Big A, but as the number of disrobing deviants kept disrupting the action, even the most ardent, freedom-loving aficionados grew tired of this naked appeal for recognition. Eventually, with a combination of tightened security, increased fines and a decision by the press to stop covering the disrobing, the streaking phenomenon slowly faded away. Fame, in this land of make-believe, can be fleeting.

I never did connect closely with the majority of the California Angels wives. The freeway system in the Southern California dispersed the team members in a myriad of different locations throughout Orange County as soon as the game ended. The Angels' ballpark was positioned at the junction of three major freeways and a commute of 20 minutes could take you up towards the mountains, down into the valleys, north towards Los Angeles, south towards San Diego or, my personal favorite, west towards the ocean. The vast discrepancy in monetary compensation resulted in a similar discrepancy in the housing options. The players did not feel the need to cluster into a nearby, moderately-priced apartment complex where they could carpool to the park. Another obstacle was the prejudice that many apartment complex policies seemed to have against renting to families with children. The housing quantity and quality of options for childless couples far outnumbered those of the players "married with children." In spite of a concerted effort, I could not convince the management of our complex to rent to Ken and Maryanne Sanders and their well-behaved children for a few months when they were traded to the Angels midway through the season. These logistical factors, combined with the disjointed spring training arrangement, made it difficult to form a cohesive bond with the team wives.

The seating arrangements at the stadium also contributed to spousal disconnection. While all the wives sat in the same general vicinity, this section was not the sole propriety of the wives and fan-friendly season ticket holders. Our individual seats were spread out in small groupings throughout one large section. As if by some strange and unspoken plan, a segregated design appeared in each evening's seating sketch. While the actual seating chart changed nightly, the white wives always seemed to be seated together, apart from the black wives, who were generally placed far away from the Spanish wives. However, the majority of the younger wives took their assigned seat number more as a suggestion rather than a mandatory placement and moved around the section at will as much as available space would allow.

Many corporations owned season field boxes in our section, and these tickets were handed out to their customers nightly in an effort to reward productivity or entice would-be clients. Most of these clients were oblivious to the fact that they were sitting in the family section and at times would loudly badmouth the father of an impressionable child sitting in the row in front of them. I recall cringing one night when an adorably sensitive five-year-old little girl turned to her mother and asked with tears in her eyes: "Why are these people booing dad while he is walking in from the bullpen?" I don't remember the resourceful response, but I do remember feeling a lump in my own throat in response to this innocent question.

We did share a few memorable times as a group. One road trip night a contingent of California Angels wives attended a taping of the *Tonight Show* with Johnny Carson. Like everything else I had experienced in the Los Angeles area, the actual situation differed greatly from my imagined perceptions. Growing up on the East Coast, I assumed the *Tonight Show* was broadcast live in New York City near the bewitching hour of midnight. While this might have been the case at one time, the *Tonight Show* in 1974 was taped in a Burbank sound studio in front of a live audience around 5:00 P.M. and rebroadcast at 11:30 P.M. Ruth Ryan, Martha Doyle, Marcie Clark and I met at the stadium in the early afternoon and carpooled into Hollywood. Thankfully, my inexperience on the LA freeways took me out of the running as the designated driver. The highways surrounding both Boston and Milwaukee might slow down during the rush hours, but in LA, traffic jams occurred at all hours of the day and night. Perhaps this fear of not flying down the road in a timely fashion is what precipitated the drivers to operate recklessly when they got the chance. Combine this affinity for aggressive driving with the excessive number of gorgeous beauties behind the wheels of magnificent convertible motor machines, who unconsciously distracted the macho men in the passing lanes, and add to that equation the fact that public transportation was virtually non-existent in Tinsel Town, you can imagine the shaky state my nerves were in by the time we arrived at the studio. Our daring driver appeared non-plussed as she pulled into a valet parking area a block away from our final destination and handed her keys to a Kookie look-alike—I felt like I was participating in a remake of *77 Sunset Strip*.

We rendezvoused with other Angels wives who had also navigated their way into the City of Angels and proceeded to join the audience lineup waiting to be seated for the night's show. Barbara Robinson, who meandered over from her nearby Bel Air home, was already in line, holding a place for us along with our VIP tickets. We soon discovered that VIP, in LA terms, stood for vaguely important people, for it appeared that almost every one else in line with us also possessed that impressive nomenclature on their tickets as well.

For an apparently impromptu program, nothing was left entirely to chance. A talent scout was sent out to mingle with the waiting crowd and ultimately determine who would be escorted to the most prominent seating sections. Our seemingly sedate group was dispatched down front, in the first two rows, but discretely off to the side where there would be no danger of the camera catching us acting normal. The seats in the center section, and all along the aisles were reserved for the exuberant audience members who, the talent scout had concluded, would laugh the loudest and clap the longest during the monologue. As we were escorted inside by a socially svelte NBC page, I was struck by the surprisingly small scope of the set. Everything appeared to be manufactured in scale. The backdrop curtain, which looked so large and luxurious on television, was only a compact conglomeration of narrow, bright multi-colored panels. Johnny's desk was not much larger than the one in my cramped college dorm room, and the club chair where the guests sat as they were being interviewed was not much larger than the kitchen chairs in my last apartment. No wonder the guests always seemed to be sitting at the edge of their seats. They might get stuck if they tried to sit back.

About twenty minutes before Johnny Carson was scheduled to deliver his monologue, Ed McMahon came out to warm up the audience. Accompanied by Doc Severinsen's artistically-gifted musical group, Ed told a few jokes and then coached us on our spontaneous responses to Johnny's banter. Whenever the large APPLAUSE sign was held up, we were to clap, and when the LAUGH sign was hoisted we were to break into hilarious laughter. Just in case we forgot that every great monologue deserves a standing ovation, a black-and-white cardboard plaque would remind us it was time to STAND.

Once the *Tonight Show* got underway, the charisma that was quintessentially Johnny Carson showed through, and the response prompts were unnecessary. Johnny's monologue was greeted with genuine laughter, and the appreciative audience stood up without any extra encouragement. Then the first guest, a young semi-inebriated blonde bombshell, who shall remain nameless to protect her lack of innocence, staggered onto the stage. As Johnny struggled to pull a coherent thought out of this plastic personality, I began to see the wisdom behind the cue cards. The rest of the show consisted of the constant ego management of that particular "star," the charismatic chatter of the clairvoyant Carnac the Magnificent, and some unadulterated, unaffected pleasure provided by some four-legged inhabitants of the San Diego Zoo. We raced over to the Brown Derby after the show for a relaxing dinner to allow the immovable, rush-hour traffic the opportunity to slowly start inching forward again around 8 P.M. before we joined the moving parking lot. It was with

Kathy, in the halo of the Big A, suited up for the Angels/Disney Characters softball game in Anaheim, California 1974.

a new appreciation for the magic of television that I viewed that night's episode of the *Tonight Show*, from the comfort of my bedroom when it came on "live" at 11:30 P.M.

THIS MASQUERADE

The close proximity of the ballpark to the Disney amusement park fostered a number of joint promotions from both publicity departments. One Sunday afternoon the wives of the California Angels participated in a softball game against the Disney characters. Needless to say, this was not a very competitive endeavor; still a few of us were petrified about making total fools of ourselves out on the field. We did meet at the stadium for one practice session; however, the focus of the day was more on assessing our correct uniform sizes rather than on assessing our athletic prowess. As was the case with most of the spousal squads I played on during my unspectacular softball career, there were more ex-cheerleaders than exceptional fielders on the team, but considering our competition and our custom-fitting shirts, we managed to render a more than adequate appearance on the diamond. We had a blast on the playing field. I remember reaching first base (on a walk) and playing a hilarious game of cat and mouse with Goofy as he tried to pick me off base. At the conclusion of our exhibition game, the Angels management invited us all up to a private dining room in the stadium for a post-game get-together. I was so looking forward to chatting with the engaging person inside the Goofy costume and remember being totally taken back when I finally met the painfully shy and unassuming man underneath the costume. I had never witnessed such a complete transformation of personality.

By placing the large Goofy disguise upon his head, this young man put on a larger-than-life persona, but as soon as the mask was removed and set down, his exuberant personality was relegated to the ground. The Disney princesses maintained their regal demeanors once their ball gowns were discarded, but their male counterparts appeared less comfortable without their royal attire. I wondered, and not for the first time that summer, why it was so difficult to differentiate fantasy from reality in this fairy-tale state?

"Make love, not war" was the battle cry of the early seventies. The sexual revolution was challenging the basic mores of society. Anti-war protestors were testing the limits of freedom of speech along with their right to freedom of dress and expression. Free love was being espoused by a small segment of our society. Song lyrics such as "If you can't be with the one you love, love the one you're with" reflected this free-spirited behavior. The women's movement had created countless new opportunities for the young women of our country, but at the same time, the concepts of fidelity and life-long commitment were suddenly falling by the wayside.

A strange trend known as "open marriage" increasingly emerged. The male segment of our population appeared to be drawn to this arrangement more readily than the "liberated" females. While living in Milwaukee, I recall being shocked the year before by the (truthful) rumor that two baseball couples on a New York team had taken this open marriage idea to a new level and switched entire families, children and dogs included. This disconcerting exchange was never discussed in the wives' waiting room, but I'm sure this close encounter of the strangest kind also played a part in the lack of team parties that were scheduled during the year.

Skip was thoroughly frustrated with his position as a long reliever and random fifth starter on the team, and so, not wanting to add to his daily stress, I did my best to remain as supportive as possible and tried hard not to voice my own disillusionment with our move. Still, Skip could tell that my social interactions with the outside world while he was on the road were minimal at best. The many tourist attractions in Southern California seemed to bring a constant stream of out-of-town visitors to the homes of my close California Angels friends when the team was away. I longed for the camaraderie of my previous support groups. About a month-and-a-half into the season, Skip emerged from the clubhouse with a big smile on his face holding a small slip of paper in his hand. One of my college friends and her military husband had recently been transferred to the Los Angeles area and had contacted Skip via the clubhouse. In the ensuing months I would frequently forge my way through the traffic jams on the LA freeways and spend a few weekend days in the company of Captain Dave and Jan Herelko.

After a while, the many asphalt roads I traveled over appeared to look alike. On one particularly long road trip I had ventured north to Ventura and got off at the wrong exit on my way home. All of a sudden I became completely disorientated. I pulled off to the side of the road and tried to get my bearings. I could not remember where I was or how I got there. I could read the sign in front of me which indicated that I was driving on Route 1, but it occurred to me that almost every Route 1 in every town looked the same, with identical neon signs indicating the same generic fast-food establishments and chain stores. I had traveled over so many highways in the past year that I was not sure even what state I was driving in. I had no clue where I had come from and had absolutely no idea where I was headed. Distraught and disoriented, I sat there with my heart rapidly beating, trying not to dissolve into tears. Finally I overheard the sportscaster on the radio announce that the broadcast of today's California Angels game would be coming on after the next commercial break. All of a sudden something inside my mind clicked and brought me back to reality. Exhaling very slowly, I turned the ignition on in my car and carefully merged back on the Santa Ana freeway towards Costa Mesa. The prophetic words of Yogi Berra rang in my mind: "If you don't know where you're going, you'll never get there." It occurred to me that with all the time I had in my hands, it was about time I got back to being a little more productive with that time. The next morning I was up early and at my Vista volunteer site with a renewed commitment to make a small impact in one segment of this seemingly silicone section of the country.

To say that our time in California had not lived up to our expectations would be a gross understatement. A giant letter "A" looms over the stadium in Anaheim indicating that here lies the home of the California Angels. After less than a month, I already felt that the imposing letter, from my perspective, stood for Anxiety. The major league baseball season got under way in the beginning of April and, even as the May Day fairies were hiding their tiny flower garden baskets outside little dreamer's door steps at the beginning of May, rumors of an impending trade had already started. Being new to the California culture, I discounted the sportswriters' constant speculations concerning Skip's apparently soon-to-be brief stint with the Angels as merely a Hollywood-hype attempt to create some curiosity among the somewhat apathetic Angels fan base. Try as I might to dismiss the rumors in my mind, Skip's shaky position as a seldomly utilized fifth starter did give a note of credence to their conjectures.

I turned twenty-five in late May amidst rumors that we would be traded for an infielder by the end of the month. We celebrated our fourth wedding anniversary in June, wondering exactly how much longer the reported negotiations with New York were going to take. Around the Fourth of July, weekend I started buying groceries for no more than three days at a time, assuming that a trade was imminent. Every time Skip left on a road trip, he packed enough clothes for an extra week, so he would be prepared if the trade came through while he was on the road. Apprehension was apparent in every phase of our lives. My stomach was in a constant knot from not knowing what was happening behind the closed doors of the general manager's office. Every time the phone rang I jumped, assured that this would be the call to inform me it was time to pack up and move on my own.

On August 8, 1974, Richard Nixon, a native son of Orange County, became the first president in our history to resign. Nixon's resignation jumped out of the headlines of every southern California newspaper, but buried back in the sports section was further speculation that my husband would also be gone by the end of the week. The end result for us was yet another sleepless night, based on more meaningless gossip. Throughout the season many players were traded to and away from the Angels, and Skip's name was mentioned prominently in most of those moves. However, in this "it's never over until it's over" game, Skip remained with the Angels for the entire season.

The apprehension and angst I allowed myself to feel throughout the entire season hampered my ability to appreciate the simple joys of our California experience. I should have taken Carole King's suggestion that I wake up every morning with a smile on my face and show the world all the love in my heart. The miles and miles of warm sandy beaches were unbelievably beautiful, the boats in the Newport marina allowed our imaginations to sail, and I still receive compliments when I wear the hand-forged necklace I purchased from an enormously talented twenty-year-old craftswoman at the Laguna Beach Arts and Crafts festival of 1974. Unfortunately, it took me until halfway through that summer before I realized that compulsive worry was a total waste of time and effort. Never again, I vowed, would I allow the enjoyment of my present situation to be ruined by some supercilious speculations. My "carpe diem" resolve would be sorely tested the following year.

5

Here, There and Everywhere

> It was the best of times, It was the worst of times, ...
> It was the spring of hope, It was the winter of despair,
> We had everything before us...
>
> *A Tale of Two Cities*

We loved living in Wisconsin on a year round basis, but in the words of Ian and Sylvia, our good times had all gone and we're bound for moving on. Financially forced to sell our condo (the rules of the association did not allow subletting) and totally not in tune with the Southern California way of life, we decided to head back to Boston for the 1974–75 off-season. The California Angels season ended with a lengthy road trip, and so I decided to leave (flee?) California and return to Massachusetts and scout out the Boston housing market.

With the autumn leaves of September luring me back, I returned to my parents' home in Springfield and enlisted my mother's help in house hunting. I was on a "mission impossible" to find an affordable property that was within commuting distance to Boston, preferably within walking distance to the MBTA, and that we could rent out in the summer. I contacted real estate agents from Scituate on the South Shore to Marblehead on the North Shore. While I may be mistaken, it appeared to me that the majority of these real estate agents took one look at my youthful demeanor and decided they could deceive me and dump one of their off-beat, over-priced, languishing-on-the-market money pits. In one "stately, old, period colonial" house in Newton, it was impossible to stand up straight in the upstairs bedrooms. A winterized beach cottage, five very long blocks from the ocean in Hingham, was heated by a single wood stove. What was listed as a "quaint carriage house" in Weston was barely large enough to house a baby carriage, but the most bizarre abode was the artist's loft my mother and I were shown in Marblehead.

On our way to view this "unique property," the broker casually mentioned that there was a note on her listing sheet that told her to be careful not to feed, touch, or disturb the owner's precious pet, who slept on the kitchen table. My mother wisely chose to wait outside. I entered the house through a cave-like entrance on the ground floor which led into two rather small bedrooms. This eclectic, open-concept, wooden structure was divided by such a narrow spiral staircase that anyone sporting an extra ten pounds would have found it impossible to access the upstairs kitchen. Halfway up the staircase, I came face to face with the owner's pet—a very large raccoon—sleeping soundly atop the sun-drenched kitchen table. Perhaps I missed a real estate opportunity of a lifetime scrambling down the winding stairs and back into the safety of our car.

Skip thought I was making up the tales I related to him during our nightly cross-country phone calls, but to tell the truth, my daily quest was much more discouraging than my upbeat rendition of those exhausting house hunting horrors. We eventually managed to procure a three-bedroom, ranch-style house in Lynn two blocks from the ocean and four blocks from the commuter train. Initially this property appeared to exceed all our core requirements; we later came to discover there were more problems than perks to this particular property. I'll enlighten you on our Lynn-related lamentations later.

1975 Itinerary

Moved to Boston, MA, to complete college
Traded to the New York Yankees from the California Angels
Attended the National Prayer Breakfast at the White House in Washington, D.C.
Reported to Spring Training in Fort Lauderdale, FL
Released by the Yankees the last week of camp
Acquired by Charlie Finley and the Oakland Athletics organization
Sequestered for a week in a Phoenix, AZ, motel
Assigned to the Tucson Toros (AAA), Tucson, Arizona
Sold to the New York Mets
Assigned to the Tidewater Mets (AAA), Tidewater, Virginia
Brought up to the New York Mets
Returned to Boston for the winter

Skip's parting request to be traded from the California Angels was granted soon after the season ended. We were thrilled when we learned (by a local sports reporter) that Skip would be donning the pinstripes of the New York Yankees during the upcoming season. The anticipation of moving to New York was the focus of our dinner discussions all winter. The Yankees were in desperate need of starting pitchers, and Skip would get to play on a team that had a solid defense and could score runs. His six-year military obligation had finally been completed and would no longer interfere with his baseball career. I was delighted with the prospect of living back on the East Coast where I could visit my family during long road trips. Life was back to being a great adventure.

On a frigid winter morning we awakened to the sound of the wind howling and the sight of snow blanketing the backyard. Could this be the perfect day to leave for spring training or what? Our estimated departure time was delayed to shovel a foot of snow before we set south. By mid-morning we had cleared the driveway and battened down the hatches of the house. Merging onto the menacing traffic of I-95, we joined the convoy of snow birds motoring towards the Sunshine State.

GOD BLESS AMERICA

For a number of years, Skip had been an active participant in the Fellowship of Christian Athletes. In addition to organizing speakers for Sunday morning pre-game services, he had digested more than his fair share of mashed potatoes, mystery beef, and fried chicken as an after-dinner motivational speaker. The anticipated upgrade in the culinary cuisine had nothing to do with our excitement about being invited to attend the 1975 Presidential Prayer Breakfast at the While House to be held in early February. We were thrilled beyond belief at the opportunity and planned our arrival at the New York Yankees training facility in Fort Lauderdale around our attendance at 1600 Pennsylvania Ave. in Washington, D.C. With our sedan stuffed full of dishes, silverware, pots and pans, linens, and clothing for the next six months, we pulled up to the gate of the White House. With a warm "Welcome to the White House, Mr. and Mrs. Lockwood," a security guard checked our name off the guest list without even asking for a picture ID. Following the guard's instructions, we parked our laden-down car on the oval driveway in front of the West Wing. Presidential security in 1975 was dramatically different from today! Leaving our possessions under the watchful eye of the Secret Service, we were welcomed with open arms by a cross section of committed athletes to the most famous home in our country.

President Gerald Ford and First Lady Betty Ford received over 100 athletes at the White House for the annual Presidential Prayer Breakfast. The Watergate scandal that had consumed the country was no longer headline news. A new sense of kindness and civility graced the country. President Nixon had resigned, and Vice President Ford had assumed the role of the leader of the free world. Believing it essential for the country to stop wallowing in negativity and set its sights on the positive possibilities of the future, President Ford, in an altruistic action that most likely caused him to lose the next election, pardoned Nixon and granted limited amnesty to draft dodgers from the questionable Viet Nam war. Rules and rites of passage were slowly shifting. Hank Aaron was the new home run king, breaking Babe Ruth's record in a league he would have been barred from in the Babe's era, and talented young ladies won the right to play Little League Baseball. Faith, hope, and charity ruled the day. Athletes from all walks of life prayed for a spiritual renewal for our country and a greater focus on family values throughout our society. Optimism was the essence of our existence.

The dining room in the east wing of the White House shone resplendent. Platinum-rimmed alabaster china with a silver embossed Presidential seal was set upon white tablecloths with midnight blue napkins. Sterling silver candelabras lit up the circular tables, and every seat was designated with a personalized, presidential, seal-embossed place card. I saw the spirit of Jackie Kennedy's style and grace permeate the room. I agonized over what to wear and settled on a beautiful black velvet suit that I had purchased in the back room of a designer outlet in Paris a few years before on our "Europe on $5 and $10 a day" delayed honeymoon. It was "simple but elegant," and I was elated to finally have an occasion to wear this gorgeous garment (it was decidedly too much for the ball park). Skip's navy suit was spruced up with a muted Brooks Brothers club tie. The ironer in me was shocked to notice a handful of male athletes attired in perma-wrinkle shirts, direct from the dryer. To this day I subconsciously scrutinize the shirt collars of people I meet in deference to the fashion flaws so blatantly apparent at the White House.

I relished the opportunity to get an upfront and personal glimpse into the White House. Having spent the last five years of my life moving from apartment to apartment, I was awed by the comforting sense of permanency that pervaded the First Family's living quarters. One historical crisis after another undoubtedly spurred many sleepless nights for the presidential couples occupying the rooms we were walking through. I could picture the indomitable Dolley Madison organizing the evacuation when she and James had to flee the House during the War of 1812, Eleanor Roosevelt calmly counseling Franklin in the library after Peal Harbor, and the Kennedy children counteracting the pain of the Bay of Pigs catastrophe with a game of hide and seek. There must be some truth to the cliché that behind every successful man is a strong woman. If I was impressed by the largesse of the White House, I was surprised by the small scale of Lincoln's famous four-poster bed. Certainly this minuscule mattress could not be the reason for such a sought-after accommodation? What a privilege to be an invited guest inside this great house. Only in America!

Professional athletes of diverse interests came together to pray they would be worthy of the awesome responsibility that had been thrust upon them as role models for the youth of the country. I was seated next to Olympic bronze medalist Janet Lynn. This painfully shy skater and I commiserated about the loneliness of life on the road. I empathized with her struggle to maintain a personal identity while constantly being scrutinized by the press. The same trials and tribulations seemed to exist at every level of competition, but based on the conversations among the athletes at our table, attitude is everything, and it was easy to detect a pulsing optimism at our table. Athletes appreciate the talent it takes to contend, and those present at this breakfast eagerly interacted with talented individuals from other sports. Team players such as baseball and football athletes sought out solo competitors from the worlds of ice skating, race car driving, and boxing. I've heard it said you can tell a lot about a person by the way he shakes your hand; well, it took almost a week for the imprint of George Foreman's diamond ring on Skip's pitching hand to disappear. It was hard to believe that George had come over to introduce himself to us and to wish Skip good luck for the coming season. Exceptional individuals exude an energy that is contagious, and memories of this breakfast mentored me through the angst I encountered throughout the ensuing year.

We declined the Fellowship of Christian Athletes' offer to organize our itinerary since the White House breakfast coincided with our spring training travel. Relying on my now-trusted AAA guide book, I booked our own arrangements at an affordable hotel on the outskirts of the city. You can imagine our surprise to discover as we checked out that our hotel had already been paid for by an anonymous benefactor. This was 1975, not 1984—was big brother really watching us? Had a government agency checked our backgrounds before we were allowed to park on the oval in front of the White House? Something strange to ponder for sure.

ANTICIPATION

On an emotional high after dining at the White House, we arrived in Florida eager to begin a new season with a new team. The first-class spring training facility that housed the senior New York baseball team epitomized the pride of the Yankees. This was a team that expected to win with an owner willing to spend whatever was needed to produce results. Optimism, talent, and energy ruled. Coastal waterways wound through the city, motor boats outnumbered motorbikes, and the only traffic jams occurred at the scenic drawbridges. Outside cafes and beachfront bistros welcomed spring break guests to town. Fort Lauderdale, FL, was definitely a more happening place than Sun City, AZ, and a huge improvement over El Centro, CA. Could life get any better?

The answered appeared to be "of course" when Skip was reunited with his 1965 Kansas City Athletics roommate, Catfish Hunter. Unforeseen circumstances, including terrible eyesight, night games under bad lighting, and losing a season to active duty in the National Guard had stalled Skip's career. Charlie Finley coercively changed Skip from a power-hitting third baseman to a power-throwing pitcher, now Skip was back on track. If Skip had struggled, Catfish's career had catapulted on its future Hall of Fame track. That fame had not affected the Hunters' country charm as I discovered during some delightful dinners during the spring. Not surprisingly, conversations revolved around some aspect of mechanics and the promising prospect of playing together on a winning team.

The Yankee-pitching staff had undergone a major overhaul over the winter of 1975. At the time Skip was traded to the Yankees to augment their starting pitching staff, Catfish was the property of the Oakland Athletics and had just won the American League Cy Young Award. In a bizarre set of events, insurance mogul Charlie Finley neglected to pay the $50,000 insurance premium that constituted half of Catfish's salary. What rights did Catfish have anyway? Benefiting from the players' new legal options obtained by Curt Flood's sacrifice, Cattish brought his case to the recently-instituted arbitration court. The court ruled that Charlie Finley had breached the contract and thereby nullified the reserve clause that bound Catfish to the A's. Cattish was declared the first modern-day free agent and received over $3.5 million dollars from George Steinbrenner to sign with the Yankees on New Year's Eve, 1974. Unbeknownst to us at the time, Skip's hopes of a future with the Yankees ended with his friend's good fortune.

Math question of the day: A team is in need of a starting pitcher. One player with great potential is being paid $20,000, and another with a proven All-Star record is earning $600,000. Who is the management going to play? No contest!

Over the winter, Skip completed his undergraduate degree in the classrooms of Emerson College and worked on the technical aspects of his pitching at the gym. This off-season effort paid off. He was in the best shape of his career, throwing the ball hard, and perfecting his curveball. In Florida he left for the park early and stayed late. I whiled away my hours basking in the Florida sunshine, sitting by the pool at the Fort Lauderdale Hilton. We were not lodged in the lush Hilton resort (we were camped inside a cozy efficiency across the street), but the owner of the Hilton was a Yankees fan and offered the use of the pool to the team. I was one of the few wives who took him up on the offer. I spent a lot of "quality alone time" reading about New York and pondering where to find an apartment in New York. Yankee Stadium was undergoing repairs, and so the Bronx Bombers would be playing their home games at the Mets' Shea Stadium in Flushing, NY, for the 1975 season. The options seemed endless.

About a week into the spring training game schedule, I began to get a little concerned about Skip's spot in the starting rotation when he had not been scheduled to start a game. As long as I had accompanied Skip to spring training, he had been assured a spot in the starting rotation and worked on perfecting his timing and endurance during the exhibition games. Last year's banishment to the Angels' bullpen at the end of a successful spring season came as a shock. I recalled other springs, empathizing with some of my friends as they watched their fringe-player husbands try to work their way into a starting position, and I began to feel more than just a little uneasy. Why was Skip not scheduled to start? How many starters did the Yankees intend to keep? How would he adjust to becoming a relief pitcher? Did the Yankees even need another relief pitcher when they had Sparky Lyle? The answers my stressed psyche was spouting were not encouraging. Skip appeared so confident about the season and so excited to pitch to a catcher with the talent of Thurman Munson, I did not want to damper his enthusiasm. Being new to the team, I had no personal support group and did not know whom I could trust to voice my concerns, so I kept my fears to myself and prayed things would improve. A gnawing knot in my gut suggested that this latest career move was heading us in the wrong direction.

Afternoon golf outings were put on hold as Skip stayed longer and longer at the ballpark. Not being scheduled to pitch meant that he had to be ready to pitch in relief every day. He had often warmed up in the bullpen, but had rarely made it into the game. This fact might have gone unnoticed if it were not for the New York press. The press coverage of both the Milwaukee Brewers and the California Angels was minimal at best. A small summary of the game was included with the box scores, and an occasional human interest article might appear, but the sportswriters generally covered the game, not the players. Baseball coverage existed on a different level in New York. The papers competed to see who could fabricate the most interesting scenario. Speculation spurred rumors, which sold papers. Most of these stories reappeared in the Fort Lauderdale sports pages where New York fans came to spend the winter months. I tried not to worry about the daily articles that omitted Skip's name from the list of anticipated starters. Outside of baseball, no news is good news, but no news from the baseball diamond can signal disaster.

Skip finally got a chance to pitch towards the end of spring training. All his conditioning paid off, and he threw the ball well. True, he was still not starting, but he was getting into quite a few games and striking out a number of batters. I finally felt I could let out my breath. During this time we became friendly with a gregarious young New York priest named Father Joe Dispenza. Fr. Joe worked with young, inner-city New York athletes and was a confidant to many New York professional athletes. We shared many meals with Fr. Joe as he introduced us to the mindset of the New York fans and the press. Perhaps our most memorable dining experience took place on Good Friday night. Skip had gotten a chance to "show his stuff" for the past week and had had three good outings in a row. He had just pitched four innings of no-hit ball, and we were all relieved that he would definitely now make the team. Since it was Good Friday, we waited until midnight with Fr. Joe to order, so we could enjoy a steak and a bottle of wine in celebration. The false hopes of last year's California dreaming were slowly fading away. Here was a new team in a new town with a new opportunity to shine. Another great adventure was about to begin, and we were ready, willing, and able to take on Manhattan.

You cannot imagine our shock when Skip received a call the next morning informing him that the Yankees had decided to release him. Not sold, not traded, but released. This was unbelievable. The timing could not be worse. With only a few days left before the season began, it would be almost impossible to sign on with another team. A sympathetic coach confided that the Yankees had not anticipated Skip would pitch so well and had planned to let him pitch himself out of a job at the end of training. Perplexed by his success, there was still no room for him on the roster, and the decision to cut him and his meager salary stood. We spent the morning staring at the phone while disbelief, shock, and anger took hold. How could this be happening? Skip was only 29 and had been playing professional baseball for twelve years. His "great potential" was finally coming to fruition. His career could not possibly be over before it began. What were we going to do and where were we going to live?

A mid-day phone call from Charlie Finley answered all those questions. Charlie O. Finley had signed Skip directly out of high school and had always related to Skip more as a benefactor and friend than as a boss. Mr. Finley asked only one question of Skip: "Be honest with me, son, can you still pitch?" When Skip replied with an unequivocal yes, Charlie assumed full control. The Yankees had neglected to place Skip on waivers, as required, and were in violation of the basic agreement. Mr. Finley was furious with George Steinbrenner for luring Catfish Hunter to the Yankees (after Charlie's own flagrant contract violation) and told Skip that, with his help, Charlie could reap a substantial fine from George for this omission.

In a cloak-and-dagger move, Skip was instructed to fly directly to Phoenix, Arizona, and hide in a designated hotel for a week until the waiver period cleared. He was instructed to "lay low, order all meals in, and not talk to anyone for the week." The wearing of a raincoat, sunglasses and a fake mustache was suggested, but we assumed this was in jest. At the end of the week, Charlie promised to sign Skip to the Oakland organization and pay him his major league salary. He could not assure him a spot on the Oakland roster at that time because they had just finalized their own pitching staff, but Charlie promised that he would not let Skip flounder in the minors and would sell him to a contender if the Athletics did not require his services. Skip's first inclination was to say goodbye to baseball and just go home. After attending college part-time during the off season, he had finally graduated. Maybe it was time to hang up the cleats and join the real world? While I could understand the frustration he was feeling, I also knew my husband was not ready to leave baseball. Too much effort had been spent over the winter to give up now. I insisted he give it one more shot. We were still young and had years ahead of us before we really needed to grow up. I would go visit my parents for a week, and he could play super spy and hibernate in Phoenix during the same period. I would then fly to meet him wherever our next adventure would take us. Enthusiasm can be contagious, and my Pollyanna persona softened the blow. He called Charlie Finley back and accepted his offer. An hour later we headed for the airport, flying off in different directions, yet united with a common bond.

We ran up a rather expensive phone bill that week between Arizona and Massachusetts. I found it hard to comprehend how an organization that appeared so anxious to have us on the team in December could write us off so easily a few months later. Was all that hype about Steinbrenner being a new breed of owner out to bring commitment and loyalty back to baseball only a media ploy? Skip had been plagued by terrible defense in Milwaukee and constant trade rumors in Anaheim. This was supposed to be his year to shine. What had happened? What did the future hold? We agreed to enjoy one last summer in baseball, wherever the season might take us.

I Get Knocked Down, but I Get Up Again

I had not shared in Skip's early minor league experience. During the years we dated, Skip was up and down between the big club and various levels of minor league teams, along with serving occasional stints in the military, but I was at that time comfortably ensconced in my dorm room. Skip held fond memories of his early years in the minor leagues. He had played AA ball in Modesto, CA, with Rollie Fingers, Joe Rudi, and Rene Lachemann when they were all at the beginning of their careers. They were young, enthusiastic, and supportive of each other. Skip was Joe Rudi's best man the summer of '66 as they all attempted to improve their baseball skills while playing for the love of the game. Despite my disappointment at not playing in New York City, I was resigned to relish the camaraderie that was rumored to be part of the minors.

Like Dante's Inferno, the minor leagues are divided into different levels. While fast friendships and great camaraderie might exist in A or AA ball, competition and jealousy appeared to run rampant at the AAA level. The 1975 Tucson Toros AAA team was composed of a few young phenoms on their way up who were on the fast track to success. There were also a handful of career minor leaguers who had played a number of years in Tucson and were content with their lot. These lifetime lost boys were school teachers or carpenters during the off-season and reluctant to give up their dream quite yet; one couple was even being investigated by the IRS to determine how a professional athlete could exist on such a low salary. Surely they must be doing something illegal and hiding income somewhere, or why would they continue to play for such a small pittance? There were players on the team recovering from injuries who needed time recuperating before returning to the big club, and finally there were the seasoned veterans desperately hoping to return to "the show." Skip was in the final group.

We had spent a number of spring trainings in Arizona enjoying the warm winter weather and the amazing desert sunsets. Cool mornings would turn into warm afternoons, and evening breezes encouraged great nights' sleep. The atmospherical ambiance in February and March far surpassed that of the sweltering heat of May and June. Tucson, Arizona, was unbearably hot in the summer. The average daytime temperature was over 110 degrees, but it would "cool down" to 98 degrees for the games. The players all lived in the same complex, but the scorching pavement and the scalding sun made it way too oppressive to congregate by the pool. I never could get over the claustrophobic sensation of our air-conditioned apartment. Sitting inside watching the winter wind blowing snow was fine. Trapped inside while tumbleweeds, fueled by hot Santa Ana winds, tossed by made no sense to a native New Englander.

At 26, I was the matriarch of the team wives. Less than a week after arriving in Tucson, I was thrust into the role of peacemaker and marriage counselor. Toddlers on big wheels terrorized the sidewalks while harried young mothers complained about the lack of spousal support from their husbands. One wife complained to me about being more stressed out when her husband was home because she had to keep her two little children quiet before the game and entertained during the game. The strain of being a single parent while her husband was away for a week at a time was almost easier to take. Not having children myself, I was unaware at the time of the constant demands of motherhood. In the past, all my friends with children had hired a sitter whenever they needed a break. Paying for a baby sitter was considered a needless extravagance for someone subsisting on a minor league salary. I became sensitive to the constraints of raising a family in a crowded apartment on a very limited budget. While we had never made the "big money," by maintaining a relatively modest life style we had always had everything we needed. It never occurred to me that I might have to make a choice between buying groceries or putting gas in the car. I realized that money is only a problem when you don't have any. I almost felt a little guilty that we had not been forced to take a cut in pay like most players when Skip was sent to the minors although I tactfully did not share this with the struggling wives.

I had always dreaded road trips; now I began to despise them. I had yet to find a volunteer program flexible in Tucson enough to fit our baseball schedule and did not have that much in common with many of the wives. The more I tried to blend into my environment, the more I stuck out. I even felt the need to monitor my casual conversations. One day I jokingly complained about having ironed five shirts and Skip wanting to wear the only one that wasn't pressed out. A disgruntled wife quipped to her friend—look at her bragging about owning six shirts when we can barely afford one!"

Personal safety was also an issue. Tucson sits near the Mexican border and drug trafficking in 1975 was rampant. Alone at night, I watched the late night news filled with stories of dismembered bodies being buried in the desert. Not a pleasant image to have on the way to a lonely bed. I did value the company of a few wives with young children, and I would occasionally go to another apartment to listen to the radio broadcast of the game (no game was ever televised). One night, as I walked back across the complex, I heard gunfire ring out behind me. That was the last time I ventured out after dark unaccompanied. Self-pity has never been my style, and so I forced myself to get back into Wendy's mindset and "think happy thoughts." Sure, our present situation was not what dreams were made of, but we had already experienced the majors and were pretty confident of returning. We might be down right now, but I was confident that we would be up again. I replayed some

Skip and Kathy on AAA Hawaiian Road Trip, June 1975.

of the insightful conversations we had recently been involved with at the prayer breakfast in my head, reiterating the fact that staying positive and remaining focused on a goal was crucial to success. Like Aretha Franklin, I knew I would survive.

ALOHA

The Tucson Toros were scheduled for a week's road trip to Hawaii, and the wives were welcome on the trip as long as they paid for their own trans-portation, of course. I was one of the fortunate wives who signed on without questioning the $250 cost. What better use could there be for our emergency American Express card? One young wife at first agonized over using their entire savings account to pay for the trip—then she decided to go. She and her husband reasoned that they would probably never have another chance to see Hawaii together. If they had such a meager nest egg, why not put them all in one basket and enjoy the moment?

Hawaii lived up to its idyllic island reputation. We did have to take time out of our sightseeing to play games most nights, but even the games took on a festive mode in the huge arena. Our decision to rent a car and explore the island paid off in spades. Breathtaking foliage in every imaginable color adorned the roadsides. We strolled down tree-laden, dirt paths and under cas-cading waterfalls more magnificent than Mermaid's Lagoon. At the time I could not understand why anyone would attempt to barrel into the enormous ocean swells, but thanks to the tutelage of my surfer son, I can now appre-ciate the unique skill and fearless energy required to work the waves. I guess there's a little bit of Peter Pan in every young man.

Professional baseball players compose a very small fraternity inside a very big world. It's amazing how often those worlds intersect. As we were walking down a palm tree lined boulevard in Honolulu, we heard a loud, "Hey, big guy" from across the street. The only person who referred to Skip as "big guy" was our second baseman from the Milwaukee Brewers who was memorable for his tendency to stop by the mound on his way to assume his defensive position in the field, before the first pitch was ever delivered, and whisper to the starting pitcher, "Hey, big guy, don't let any balls come my way today. I've got a really bad headache from a really bad night, and my reflexes are not the best." This lackadaisical attitude was not conducive to peak athletic performance, and the party life took its toll on this gifted athlete. I inquired about his (excessively forgiving) wife and he shared that she had left him. It seems that he was playing for a team last year and was called into the office and told that he was being released. "Here's your plane ticket, go home" he was instructed. That's precisely what he did. He went directly to the airport and flew to his childhood hometown, totally forgetting that his wife was waiting for him to return to their "in-season" apartment. Two days later, he recovered from his binge and realized his latest blunder. He called his frantic wife, pleading for forgiveness one last time, but by then it was just too little too late. Even a truly devoted wife with the patience of a saint has a breaking point. He was now a single ballplayer, playing for Hawaii, and relishing the laid-back lifestyle. He's one lonely lost boy I'm sure will never grow up.

The excitement of traveling to Hawaii made the trip over fly by; in contrast there was no joy in Mudville anticipating the trip back. We all had a tough time leaving this tropical paradise to return to the barren desert. It was going to be a challenge staying upbeat once we returned to reality. The serene sienna desert I so admired the first time I set eyes on a cactus flower now appeared eerily drab compared to the lush landscape of the islands. It was going to take some pretty potent fairy dust to keep flying.

On the surface, nothing had changed back in Tucson, but inside my husband's psyche a change was a-comin'. The day after returning to the mainland, Skip was playing catch with Charlie Sands, his catcher, and the ball just started to pop. Without fanfare, without warning, without any apparent divine intervention, there was new life in Skip's old fastball. At first, Skip thought Charlie was pulling his leg when he said the ball was coming in so hard it was hurting his hand, but the look of astonishment in Charlie's eyes registered confirmation that his fastball had resurfaced. Baseball people love clichés and perhaps one the most commonly repeated phrases is "don't think, you'll hurt the team." Skip had spent the last few months analyzing his delivery and pondering his arm positions to no avail. Totally relaxed after a wonderful Hawaiian trip, he forgot about thinking and was merely out playing catch in the yard with his friend enlivened with boyish enthusiasm. Unencumbered by baseball theories, his natural talent was given free reign and his fastball ruled the plate. He was having fun again. That night Skip faced three batters at the end of the game and struck all three out. No one had come close to even fouling a ball off. Driving back to our dreary apartment in our rented, unairconditioned, VW bug, Skip was elated. "We're heading back to the big leagues," he promised. His fastball had become unhittable. Someday soon, he promised, our lives would change for the better.

I had not known Skip in high school when he was one of the top prospects in the country and the center of the media's attention. During our five years in baseball, Skip was a good team player on some very bad teams. All of a sudden Skip's fastball was the topic of the day in Tucson. Forget a shaky economy, forget the mounting tension in Lebanon, forget racial tensions and border disputes, the question of the day on Tucson's talk radio show was how fast was Skip's fastball? Night after night he would strike out batter after batter. While I couldn't help to be caught up in all the enthusiasm, a small part of me was afraid that this newfound success might some night leave as quickly as it had arrived. Ten saves in two weeks was incredible. But the fact that the majority of the outs came on strikeouts was unbelievable. Power pitching was beating power hitting, and the fans loved it. The team was going to Phoenix for the weekend, and I went along to enjoy the ride.

Only a few months ago, Skip was hiding out in a hotel in Phoenix after being released from the Yankees. It seemed like an eternity ago. Returning to Phoenix with a resurrected fastball was exhilarating. After striking out the side and racking up another save the first night back in Phoenix, we ordered a pizza and sat out on the deck of the hotel room with a pitcher of Black Russians. Soon, very soon, we would return to the big leagues. One huge obstacle did exist, however, and that would be the continued success in Oakland of another of Skip's old roommates, Rollie Fingers. Rollie was having another great year in the bullpen, and it would be almost impossible to take his place as the #1 reliever. Would Charlie Finley keep his promise and trade Skip? By his third drink, Skip was potently positive that Charlie was an honorable man and would stick by his pledge.

We were startled by the ringing of the telephone in our Phoenix hotel room at 7:30 A.M. Pacific Coast Time. I answered it in somewhat of a fog and was not prepared to hear Charlie Finley on the other end of the line. Try as I might, I could not wake Skip out of his deep sleep to speak to Charlie, so I mustered up my courage and began to negotiate for our future. Mr. Finley said he had been following Skip's success for the past few weeks and had been hearing rave reviews from his scouting department. He was apologetic at not being able to offer Skip a spot in Oakland's bullpen, but acknowledged the promise he had made in April and told me he was happy to give Skip the opportunity to return to "the show." Protecting his own organization, he would only sell Skip's contract to a National League team. The Chicago Cubs, the New York Mets, and the Philadelphia Phillies all were interested. He was asking my advice on where we might like to go! While I was pretty knowledgeable about the pitching staffs on many American League teams, my insight was negligible on anything to do with the National League. I needed more information before making such an important decision. I asked Charlie for his suggestion as to what team was most in need of a closer. He advised me that Wrigley Field was a tough ballpark to pitch in and that the Phillies had recently acquired Tug McGraw. The New York Mets had great starting pitching, but could really use help in the bullpen. While it seemed like a no-brainer to me, I felt that Skip really should make the final call. I pleaded for a little time to make such an important decision. Charlie said sure, we could get back to him anytime within the next hour. Deals don't stay on the table long in baseball.

I hung up the phone, put on a pot of coffee, grabbed the Excedrin and a large glass of water. Being a sports agent had not been part of my job description. Despite the feeling that the Russian army was marching through his head, Skip woke up. A monumental decision had to be made in a moment's time. Analyzing our options, we concluded that his best shot would be with the New York Metropolitan Baseball Club. The irony was not lost on us that we had started off the spring expecting to play in Shea Stadium for the New York Yankees, and we were now electing to play for the New York Mets in the same Shea Stadium. Well before the allotted time expired, Skip returned Charlie Finley's call. Thanking him for giving us both a chance and a choice, Skip conveyed our decision to join the New York Mets. Looking back, I can safely say that it was one of the best decisions we have ever made in the shortest amount of time.

Of course, nothing in life ever comes without a few complications. The Mets had to option a player to make room for Skip on the roster, so Skip would need to report to the their AAA Tidewater team for a few days. The Tidewater team's schedule had them on the road during most of that period, so Skip flew to Virginia while I opted to visit my parents in Massachusetts. Skip left the next morning from Phoenix, and I returned to Tucson to pack up our apartment and return our un-airconditioned 1967 VW beetle. I admit that as much as I loved my husband, I did not mind bypassing another AAA bonding experience. I was content to return to my family and regroup. Skip was in heaven. He pitched one inning the day he arrived, striking out two and hitting a home run to win the game. Baseball was fun again. The reorganization of the major league roster was completed by the end of the week, and Skip was called up to the Mets.

NEW YORK, NEW YORK

New York, New York. So impressive it had to be named twice. The Statue of Liberty looms proudly at the entrance of the harbor of New York and beckons the world to send its tired, its poor, and its huddled masses yearning to breathe free. The world responded generously by sending strongly energetic, richly talented, and ambitious individuals anxious for the opportunity to thrive in the land of the free. The pulse of New York beats faster than that of any other city in America. A subliminal energy exists that rivals the speed of the subway system at rush hour. Everyone moves in fast forward. People talk faster, people walk faster, and they definitely drive faster. You have to be aggressive to survive in New York. Couple that emotional aggression with physical talent and you have what it takes to succeed in the Big Apple.

After languishing in the minor leagues for the last few months, Skip was ready to conquer New York.

Visitors perceive New York City as one colossal city. The buildings are massive. The sidewalks are congested. New construction and building renovation block the walkways as New Yorkers weave in and out of pedestrian traffic rushing to their jobs. The noise of jackhammers drowns out regular conversation, so New Yorkers have grown accustomed to speaking louder. There are so many streets and avenues that the city planners ran out of names. Many roads are merely numbered in an incredibly organized fashion. More people are squeezed into the skyscrapers and subways of New York City than populate the rural towns of many of the visiting tourists. The body odor of this tightly packed population can certainly challenge your olfactory sense. Looking down from the top of the Empire State Building, the site of my middle daughter's employment for a number of years, the city resembles one huge maze of grey concrete, interspersed with square green patches of landscaped life and deep blue streams of water stretching from Central Park to the Brooklyn Bridge.

Those who live in New York realize that the city is really just one large metropolis composed of many small towns. The fan base of the New York Metropolitan Baseball Club, better known as the Mets, is a microcosm of this metropolitan population. The Mets are regarded by their loyal fans as the local neighborhood team. No one really expects them to succeed, but everyone pulls for them anyway. Rooting for the Mets is a family affair. Men, women, and children from all ethnicities, all ages, and all walks of life embrace the Mets as their hometown heroes. They even have a theme song that plays before every game: "Meet the Mets" by Ruth Roberts and Bill Katz.

Die hard Yankee fans have a long history of elevated expectations from their Bronx Bombers. Since 1903 the Yankees have fielded contending teams, and their fans expect no less than excellence from the celebrated athletes on the roster. Mets' fans base their support not on talent but on faith. "Ya gotta believe" is their mantra. The Mets originated as a 1962 expansion team and lost their first nine games en route to an unbelievable 40–120 record their opening year. Beloved by New York fans despite (or perhaps because of) their losing ways, the early Mets became famous for their ineptitude. In 1969, the Mets again had a miserable start but halfway through the season the fates smiled kindly on the talented young pitching staff and, in an unbelievable push to the finish line, the Mets won their division. The Miracle Mets of 1969 rekindled faith in miracles and instilled hope in underdogs and lost causes. With so much faith and hope inherent in heart of every Mets fan, it naturally follows that you will also find a measure of charity. Mets fans have the rare ability to give the team a break. Win, lose or draw, they come to cheer for and support their hometown team. After all, doesn't everyone tend to forgive and forget family foibles?

After one more mini-separation, Skip and I were reunited in early

August. Skip flew into LaGuardia Airport from Virginia and, having recently retrieved our car from Boston, I drove to New York to meet his plane at the airport. I was familiar enough with the traffic jams of Boston to negotiate my way through the expressways of New York. I did, however, discover that while New York drivers are a bit more courteous than those in Massachusetts, they drive closer to the speed of sound and engage the horn much more often than they do the brake. With a sigh of relief, I finally left the Long Island raceway behind and pulled into a parking space at LaGuardia. A multitude of ethnicities maneuvered fluidly across the parking lot. More than a little overwhelmed at being part of this mass of humanity, I warily entered the terminal and, to my great relief, found that while New York can be overpowering, it is also very organized. Overhead signs and color coded symbols guided travelers directly to their destinations. I located the right gate in the right terminal in record time. In a minor miracle, Skip's plane arrived on time. I was thrilled to hug my husband; I was relieved to hand over the car keys.

We entered Shea Stadium with a new sense of appreciation for being a part of major league baseball. Skip was no longer a promising young starting pitcher secure in his role in the starting rotation. He was now one of the new breed of specialists—a relief pitcher. Every day was going to be a new adventure with a new opportunity to contribute to the team. Gone were the mentally scheduled off-days between starts. It was now imperative to be "on" every day. There would be no more days spent sitting in the dugout carefully charting the game the day before a scheduled start, scrutinizing the line up of the opposing team, and planning a nine-inning strategy of his own; a call to the bullpen could come at any time, and the relief pitcher had to be ready to rapidly respond. We marched into the stadium bolstered by the words of General Douglas McArthur: "There is no security on this earth, there is only opportunity." Skip was being given the opportunity to pitch once again in the major leagues, and he was determined to make the most of it.

It did not take long for that opportunity to arrive. The Mets were currently in a downwardly mobile slide, and the bullpen was overtired and overworked. Skip pitched for the losing side in both games of the doubleheader that first day. In the first game he struck out the side but gave up a "just over the fence" home run. He fared better in the second game, striking out four in an inning-and-a-third. The team lost both games without scoring a run, and the manager, Yogi Berra, was fired at the end of the day. Yogi Berra has been credited with many famous quotes including "It ain't over 'til it's over." Yogi's managing career with the Mets was over the day Skip's playing days with the Mets began. While the fans in New York might be forgiving, the management would demand results.

The New York metropolitan area is home to a myriad of magnificent hotels. The Traveler's Inn in Flushing, NY, is not one of them. It is the job of the traveling secretary to take meticulous care in finding the best hotels in the best locations for the team when it travels on road trips. In an aberration of good judgment, arrangements had been made for us to stay that first night at the Traveler's Inn located in Flushing, New York. While its location was very accessible to the ball park, I do believe additional factors other than mere convenience should have been taken into consideration. Situated in a truly run-down section of Queens, the hotel was erected decades before Mr. William A. Shea envisioned bringing National League baseball back to New York. We cautiously parked our car under one of the few working street lights and crossed the parking lot to ender the lobby of a very unimposing concrete building. While the lobby itself was rather drab, the "ladies" lounging on the circular ottoman in the center of the lobby were anything but. I could not remember ever seeing so much leather and lace together in one place. I got the distinct impression that the rooms were meant to be rented by the hour rather than by the night. The front desk clerk was obviously a Mets fan. Welcome to New York. "I'm giving you the best room in the hotel," he insisted. Who said New Yorkers were born with a bad attitude? The warmth of his greeting comforted us even after we opened the door to a decidedly less than one-star hotel room. Faded curtains covered grimy windows, a tired teal blue flowered bedspread clashed with the vintage green-and-gold striped curtains. At first I thought the patterned carpet had an unusual design, and then I realized that pattern was merely a random hodgepodge of scattered stains. After a discreetly detailed inspection, I determined that the sheets and the towels had, in fact, come straight from the laundry and the tub was meticulously clean. If this was the best room, what did the rest look like? We considered leaving, but we were both exhausted and besides, how could we hurt the feelings of the friendly front desk clerk? We had put up with a lot during the past few months, so one more night couldn't hurt. The Traveler's Inn turned out to be a very "happening" place. Music, laughter, and merriment continued down the hall until the wee hours of the morning. Getting a good night's sleep at this hotel was not in the cards. New York was certainly going to be exciting!

Early the next morning, we both decided that sleep was totally overrated. Anticipation of our new beginning (along with the constant commotion in the room next door) kept us up most of the night. Realizing that getting any more rest was out of the question, we agreed that we needed a good meal. The hotel was serving a "complimentary breakfast" in the lively lobby, but a cup of coffee from a styrofoam cup and a stale donut was not exactly our idea of nutrition. Luckily, the neighborhood was lined with dining options. Since we had never been to a famed New York diner, we opted to give one a try. What a great introduction. At first we felt we had entered a New York Mets gift shop. Mets banners, pictures, and memorabilia hung everywhere. Most of the early morning patrons seemed to know each other, and many were seated at the counter discussing the plight of their beloved team. Our waitress seemed to be scrutinizing us as she took our order. When she returned with our coffee, she continued to stare at Skip and finally inquired as to why we were visiting New York. I guess it was pretty apparent from our dress and speech patterns that we were not native New Yorkers. I jubilantly volunteered that Skip had just been purchased by the Mets, and we were joining the team today. She flashed us a huge grin and yelled over to the regulars at the counter, "See, I told you. He's not a young professor; he's the new pitcher for the Mets." A chorus of "Welcome to New York" followed along with a wonderful breakfast "compliments of the house." This was the first time Skip had been recognized outside of the ballpark in all his years of playing baseball. I realized the rumors of everything existing on a larger scale in New York were true.

Tug McGraw echoed the spirit of the organization when he shouted "You Gotta Be-lieve." The Mets wanted to believe that everyone was just one big happy family and took measures to accomplish that ideal. The family waiting room had been designed with the families of the players in mind. Comfortable furniture was arranged in seating groups to bolster post-game conversations, and there was plenty of room for the children to let out some steam after harnessing their energy for two hours sitting in the stands. There was even a television in the room where the parent of a hyperactive toddler could retreat to and follow the game, unconcerned about disturbing those seated next to her in the stands. The wives' section was thoughtfully placed behind the home plate screen so that they had both a great view of the action and were never in danger of being hit by foul balls in the rare occurrence that they concentrated more on their conversations than on the action on the field. Undoubtedly due to the motherly influence of Mrs. Joan Payson, great care had been taken to protect the wives from the more obnoxious elements at the ballpark.

A unique camaraderie bonded the Mets' wives. Here was a group of women who had grown up together in the organization, surviving the bad times and relishing the good. They shared a family history and a kindred concern with one another. Immature, petty jealousies seemed nonexistent as they all appeared to appreciate the talent and tenacity of their respective spouses. This was the closest thing to being part of one big happy family that I had ever experienced in baseball and a significant step up on the satisfaction ladder from the back-stabbing jealousy I had encountered in the "fun-loving" minor leagues in Tucson over the past few months. These wives were a little bit older (in their late twenties) and a little more sophisticated; after all, they were New Yorkers.

The players arrived at the ballpark from every corner of the Metropolitan area: Manhattan, Long Island, Staten Island, Brooklyn, Queens, and the Bronx, Westchester County, New Jersey, and Connecticut. They lived in communities and had roots. They connected with friends from outside the confines of the baseball world. While these women were certainly committed to their husbands' baseball careers, they were also committed to their children and their local communities. Believing in miracles came easy to the

Mets' wives, and they welcomed the opportunity to make little miracles happen in their respective neighborhoods. Giving back to their fan base was part of their life. Whenever one wife became involved in a cause, she knew that with one phone call, the other wives would volunteer to help. What a privilege to join a team with a community conscience.

IN A NEW YORK MINUTE

Legend has suggested that the Paris Opera House was haunted by Gerard Butler, better known as the Phantom of the Opera. This musical genius lurked in the shadows and encouraged a young and talented songstress to perfect her talent and achieve her dream of mastering her craft. I have no knowledge of any misguided, deformed, wannabe athlete lurking in the back corridors of Shea Stadium, but there was a definite undercurrent of bizarre behavior that radiated throughout the stadium. Mets fans have been conditioned to expect the unexpected. Fickle flukes of fate happened every day between the lines at Shea Stadium. Routine ground balls would take mystifying hops and turn into triples. Fly balls got caught in inexplicable winds and changed directions. Players collided racing after infield pop-ups, and umpires missed obvious calls all the time. While I do not believe in ghosts past, present, or future; there was definitely something larger than life controlling our destiny in 1975.

We had opted to play for the New York Mets because we understood they were in desperate need of a relief pitcher after losing Tug McGraw the previous winter. Of course, the management of the Mets was also cognizant of this fact and had bolstered its relief staff earlier in the season. Our good friend, Ken Sanders, had been acquired by the Mets during spring training and was having an excellent year out of the bullpen. I was delighted for the Sanders. They deserved to catch a break after being on the move so often. As unsettled as my life had been for the past two years, at least I only had my husband and myself to worry about. Maryann had three exceptionally energetic children to both physically and emotionally sustain during this period. The Sanders continued to live in Milwaukee during the off-season, but in the past three years they had been traded from Milwaukee to Philadelphia to Cleveland to Anaheim and now were living in New York. Maryann had become amazingly adept at cramming books, blocks, baby dolls, trucks, trolls, and tiny trinkets into one large traveling activity trunk. While I fought hard to stay positive for Skip, Maryann personified the quintessential baseball spouse. Her Italian roots grounded her to nurture her family. She managed to produce fabulous meals in less than an hour with whatever basic ingredients might be in her pantry. A few more players dropping in for lunch, no problem. And, of course you can bring your children, the more the merrier. She had that rare ability to make everyone feel at home even if that home had rented furniture and unpacked boxes in the hallway. I'm certain that Maryann could have tutored Wendy on how to maintain a comfortable dwelling both in her townhouse in London and her tree house in Neverland.

The Sanders had subleased a small house near the beach in Long Island, and the children thrived as they relished the freedom of spending day after day chasing waves, building sand castles, and finding starfish on the beach. Everything seemed to be finally falling back into place. We were invited to dinner at their house shortly after we arrived in town. Our paths had crossed so many times in the past, we related to each other as if we were part of an extended family. I contacted a real estate agent and tried to find a short-term rental nearby. What could be better than spending the summer at the beach with good friends? Sticker shock soon followed. I spent two days viewing one dilapidated dwelling after another. A "luxury apartment by the beach" was anything but luxurious. Chipped paint and worn furniture was considered shabby chic. Linoleum floors and wood paneled walls appeared to dominate the decorating decor of the town. Mildew seemed to be the one constant feature in every rental. After inquiring as to whether or not one pest-ridden apartment would be professionally fumigated before occupancy, I was informed by the landlord that "everyone has their own standards of cleanliness" and I could hire and pay for a cleaning service if I so desired. For a two-month stay in an efficiency apartment, we would be required to sign a six-month lease and pay upfront the first month, last month, and a security deposit totaling twice our monthly salary. Subsisting in New York on a $20,000 salary was going to be quite a challenge. I was hoping to spend the rest of the summer near the Sanders, but I would have to content myself with catching up on old times during the games.

In a New York minute, the fates of two relief pitchers changed dramatically. Skip had been pitching well, but he was not first in line for the closing role. He was anxious to pitch when the game was on the line, still he had been in baseball long enough to know he would have to work himself into that coveted role. Ken Sanders deservedly held the top spot. Tom Seaver, Jerry Koosman, and Jon Matlack anchored an excellent starting pitching staff that kept the team in contention most games, but according to National League rules, the pitchers took their turn at bat, so the starter was often lifted for a pinch-hitter in the late innings, and that meant more opportunities for the bullpen staff. About a week after our arrival, Ken Sanders came into the game to relieve in the eighth inning. On that day, destiny played a determining role in both our lives. During his warm-up pitches, either the glare of the sun or a flash from a photographer momentarily blinded Ken as the ball got lost in the protective glass screen in front of the cameramen. In a totally fluke accident, Ken was hit in the eye by the return throw from his catcher. Ken never saw the ball coming. A direct shot to the eye socket knocked him out. In a split second, Ken's career was temporarily tossed aside, and Skip's was given the opportunity to catapult. Ken was taken out of the game and rushed to the hospital. It would be almost a month before he would return to the bullpen. Tragically for Ken, while his eyesight returned in time, his opportunity to be the closer with the Mets was lost forever. Skip replaced Ken on the mound that fateful day and pitched two scoreless innings. By the end of the month, Skip had appeared in eleven games and had an ERA of 1.27. While I do not believe a phantom phenom haunts Shea Stadium, some mysterious glaring flash of light gave Skip's star a chance to shine, and he took full advantage of this amazing season in the sun.

The velocity of Skip's fastball continued to mirror the speed of light in our new lives. We were still in transition, moving from one hotel to another and surveying short-term apartment rentals at the suggestion of Skip's teammates. After exploring our housing options during the next home stand and listening to Rusty Staub's enthusiastic endorsement of life in Manhattan, we decided to live in the city while the team was in town. For the same price of subleasing a flea infested efficiency apartment in Long Island, we were housed in a charming boutique hotel in the middle of Manhattan. On road trips I would pack our clothes back into the car and return to my parents' house in Springfield, Massachusetts. This plan not only saved us two weeks of hotel costs, but it enabled me to avail myself of my parents' magical hamper and return to the city with clean clothes at the beginning of each homestand. For the remainder of the season, when the team was in town, we lived at the Tuscany Towers on Seventy-third and Third.

I adjusted easily to living the life of a native New Yorker. We lazily breakfasted during the late morning hours outside at corner cafes as the city rushed by. Relishing the freedom of being able to walk almost anywhere, we wandered down streets, marveling at the architecture of the brick townhouses. Each individual domicile was differentiated by a unique entrance and could be identified by a distinct doorway or window box. The inhabitants of this outwardly impersonal city had made a great effort to claim their own personal space. Carving out an individual niche in the city was worth the effort to industrious New Yorkers, and we had many long conversations concerning the excitement of carving out our own home in the heart of this city. Overnight, Skip had been embraced by the New York Mets. He had made the most of the opening he had been given and was reaping the reward of respect.

Early autumn arrived in Manhattan with welcoming winds and sun-filled skies. We would take walks through Central Park and visit the Metropolitan Museum of Art or stroll along the circular stairway of the Guggenheim. Skip's fastball continued to strike out batters at the end of the game, and his newfound success resulted in a heightened level of pre-game anxiety. He woke up relatively relaxed. By noon he was already starting to pace a little, anticipating the night's action. We had better be handed the lunch check by 2:00 or his patience (or lack there of) would be stretched to its limit. He went along with my current cultural whims, but all he really wanted to do was to go to the park and play ball. He would catch the subway out to Shea Stadium about 2:30 and arrive at the park in plenty of time to get mentally prepared to pitch to one or two batters around 10:00 at night. I spent quiet September afternoons alone after he let for the park, window shopping and planning what I might purchase if another miracle occurred for the Mets and we made it into the playoffs. As luck would have it, I never did get that whimsy wardrobe.

After the worst of the evening commute had raced out of the city, I would retrieve our car from the parking garage and proceed to navigate my way to the stadium. The drive on the first few nights was more than just a little nerve-racking. Taxi cab drivers take ownership of the streets of New York, and their racecar mentality can be very intimidating. As soon as the light changes, yellow vehicles spring forward at an alarming rate, only to slam on the brakes at the next intersection. Swerving in and out of traffic, they seem intent on terrorizing the timid on the tarmac. Realizing I had to adjust my driving demeanor to meet their challenge, I joined in on the aggression on the avenues of New York. However, after crossing the 59th Street Bridge, the motorists change their demeanor. Courtesy takes over, and some drivers even acknowledge the yield sign. The players' families entered the ballpark through a separate gate and were cheerfully welcomed into a secure parking area by a long-time Met attendant. While the trip usually took less than twenty minutes, it certainly seemed a lot longer, and I always felt relieved that I had arrived safely back home when the gate attendant flashed his winning smile while waving me into the safety of the players' parking lot.

A light breakfast and an angst-inspired lunch did not fully satisfy our nutritional needs. Our main meal of the day was always eaten close to midnight. In the past it had been challenging to find a decent restaurant still serving dinner after a night game. In New York there were endless options. We became regulars at two of these. My favorite was a very small corner restaurant with a piano bar. Just like in Billy Joel's famous song, a piano man would pound out notes to requested songs, as the regular patrons mingled with newcomers to the ivory-inspired emporium. As much as I loved to sing, I resisted this impulse and enjoyed the talented musings of the many undiscovered, one-day Broadway singers who frequented the establishment. Skip had become an overnight success in New York, and we were trying to stay as anonymous as possible. Skip's all-time favorite food could be found at Rusty's. Owned by Rusty Staub, a *bona fide* celebrity chef far ahead of his time, it offered the world's best veal saltimbocca. The problem with going to Rusty's was that we were a little too recognizable there, and it was hard to relax when customers constantly stopped by to comment on the night's game or ask for an autograph. Being considered a "star" was a new experience, and we found that a little adulation could go a long way.

After a valiant attempt to make the playoffs failed, the season suddenly came to a disappointing halt at the end of September. We said our farewells to our new teammates and their families and headed back to Boston for the winter. It was time to leave New York's Neverland behind for the winter months. So much had changed since we had left the cold winds of Boston in February. As the crow flies, we had traveled over 10,000 miles and had been taken on a truly wonderful adventure. While we had no idea what the future was going to bring, for the present we were content to enjoy this best of times. After all "it was the epoch of belief … and … we had everything before us."

6

I Love New York

HERE COMES THE SUN

Talk about an exhilarating ride! I felt like I had been tossed onto the boat with Odysseus and journeyed past epic predicaments during the past year. We had reveled with royalty and then were thrust into the depths of despair where we had survived the sirens, overcame our doubts, triumphed over adversity, and finally returned back home with our spirit and our marriage still intact. The grey skies had cleared up, and we were entering into the sunshine of our lives.

A week after throwing his last pitch of the season, Skip was back at Emerson College, pitching his research thesis to his communications professor. The fact that this noted scholar was also an avid baseball fan eased the process of Skip petitioning the college for leniency in missing the first month of the semester. True to his word, my MIT boss had kept my part-time position open, and soon I was back in my supportive role at academia's noted technology institution. As we turned the clocks back in October, it seemed that a time machine must have spirited us off to an unknown world over the summer. What would the future hold? Up early to catch the commuter rail into Boston, we treked into the city together where I would switch to the Red Line and Kendall Square and my MIT office and Skip would transfer to the Green Line towards Boylston Street where his communications classes convened, occasionally meeting up for lunch before Skip left town early to work on an assignment deadline or to join other off-season athletes working out at a local high school. Most nights would find us at home, collapsing hours before our normal "in season" dinnertime. I loved Boston, but I was beginning to miss Manhattan's soulful "New York State of Mind."

Skip's invitation to the 1975 New York Baseball Writers' Dinner brought us back to the Big Apple. Leaving the ten wheelers to cut each other off on I-95, we crossed over to the Hutchinson River Parkway and wound our way back into the heart of Manhattan. For the first time in a long time, it felt like we were heading back home. The city was ablaze with holiday lights. Rockefeller Plaza glittered in brilliant beauty, and the animated window displays at Macy's rekindled childhood memories in every passer-by. Much to my chagrin, I was left to fend for myself in the city. It never occurred to either of us that players' wives would not be included in the dinner invite.

Left to my own devices, I opted to indulge in an up-scale window-shopping adventure. Rather than hit my usual bargain hunting haunts downtown, I headed uptown towards the fabulous fashions of Fifth Avenue for an hour or two of fantasy. Looking back, I'm sure that the prejudicial peering I envisioned was all in my mind, but at the time I felt I was the only female in Bloomingdale's not encircled in fur. Undoubtedly it was more a function of my sifting through the sale racks rather than the lack of animal hide on my prudent, double-breasted, camel's hair coat that had the manicured sales staff rolling their eyes as I browsed through the haute couture designer departments. Since I hit the measuring tape at only five feet tall, the designer apparel was cut too long and lean for me to be concerned with their lofty price tags. I kiddingly reported to Skip later that evening that there was no way I could go prowl the aisles in New York again without being decked out in fur. While I had never given that particular conversation another thought, Skip must have stored the scene in the back of his mind. Two years later, with his first performance bonus check, Skip surprised me with a beautiful, long-hair beaver coat. While it might be a tad politically incorrect, on cold winter mornings with the wind howling through the trees and the temperature below zero, his loving investment in my happiness still warms my heart and my body.

GLORY DAYS

The 1975–76 off-season sped by as Skip pressed hard to complete his undergraduate degree and pushed himself even harder to report to camp in game-winning shape. Dismissing the implausible threat of a possible lockout at the beginning of spring training by the owners, we headed south in February filled with confidence. The final two months of last season where he compiled a 1.50 ERA in 24 games, pitching 48 innings while striking out 61, were still etched in Skip's memory. To reward his efforts, the Mets had skyrocketed Skip's salary from $20,000 to $32,500 (would that he could be pitching in today's lucrative salary structure).

After scraping off the frost from our windshield, we pulled out of our driveway and were on our way towards the bright sunshine of Florida. With Steppenwolf blaring from the radio, we headed down the highway, looking for adventure, from whatever came our way. As soon as we arrived in St. Petersburg, Skip insisted we locate the ball field and check out the dimensions of the park. The New York Mets held their spring training in a lovely stadium overlooking the water in downtown St. Petersburg. The ballpark did not look quite so inviting when we arrived to find barricades blocking the entrance to its doors. The rumored lockout had become a reality.

The players had been advised of this possibility over the winter, but after the financial pain inflicted on all parties concerned four years earlier, no one seriously thought the owners would go through with their lockout threat. Skip's salary had almost doubled over the winter, but two times zero is still zero, and there would be no salary until the baseball season got underway. Stalking around the stadium, Skip found Tom Seaver standing outside the locked clubhouse doors. After exchanging a few barbs, Skip sought advice from Tom regarding housing suggestions. Tom and his family had settled into a rental home for the spring season, and he generously invited us to stay with him for the night, certain the matter would be resolved by the following day. One night turned into a week as the lockout lingered on. I guess there's some truth to the "pay it forward" concept because Skip and I were now at the receiving end of the housing hosting detail during this latest player/management dispute.

Memories of the many meals we had prepared (and cleaned up after) during the 1972 strike surfaced, and while accepting their hospitality, we insisted on being allowed to pull our own weight. Nancy Seaver excelled in the home cooking department, effortlessly whipping up creative concoctions on a daily basis for her family. At this point in my childless culinary competency, I was still reading more menus than cookbooks. On most nights we left the meal preparation to the more culinary-gifted Seavers and happily covered the clean-up detail.

Sharing an occasional dinner, couples get to interact superficially. Sharing a home for an extended period of time provides a greater opportunity for that interaction to transform into friendship. Both pitchers were frustrated by the lockout. Professional lifetime Little Leaguers view life through tunnel vision. As February rolls around, major league athletes start champing at the bit. Competition fuels their well-being. Skip and Tom could not compete on the mound, but they could ponder the finer aspects of pitching. The recurrent theme of the power pitcher's need for "controlling the plate" was debated during long, post-dinner dialogues. I did not fully appreciate the input at the time, but looking back, I'd wager a bet that Tom Seaver's insightful observations of the strengths and weaknesses of many of the premier National League sluggers, thoughts that he shared with Skip over a glass of wine at the beach during our lockout stay, played a large role in the phenomenal success Skip enjoyed during his first full year with the Mets.

I was blown away by the spontaneous hospitality of the Seavers. Spring training is a special time for families to bond before the season interferes with family life. The Seavers had two beautiful daughters and, as much as I enjoyed their company, I did feel just a little guilty intruding on their sacred time. Only another baseball wife can understand the impact the family has on a player's psyche, and I'm certain that Tom owed much of his success to the fact that he was able to leave the pressures of the game at the ballpark and return home to revel with his delightful two daughters at the end of the day. Not having children of our own, I envied the interaction of Tom and Nancy

Kathy, Skip and her parents, Fran and Eileen Murphy, leaving Shea Stadium, 1976.

with Sarah and Ann Elizabeth. The Seavers might have been portrayed as larger than life in the New York press, but at home they were just two young devoted parents managing to maintain a normal life for their children—a modern day Peter Pan and Wendy tending to the upbringing of their young-sters. Joining the Mets last year enriched us with priceless new friendships that proved far more precious than the organization's philanthropic mone-tary compensation.

Once the lockout was over, spring sprang forward. We secured a small cottage on Treasure Island beach for the month. For a devoted ocean lover, it was a dream come true. Other than some strange parrot-like apparitions in the morning mist, I never did encounter the likes of Long John Silver. We hovered in a cute, little, cathedral-ceiling cottage that stood on stilts on top of the beachfront sand, architecturally designed so that the high tide waters could cover the sand dunes and then flow freely back into the ocean—a significant step up from Jim Hawkins's stockade or Ben Gunn's cave. Trea-sure Island totally lived up to its name. Leisurely morning walks and moon-light strolls through the warm sand surrounded days filled with intense physical exertion on Skip's part and total beach-front relaxation on mine. Unlike the mutinous pirates of Robert Louis Stevenson's imagination, we were not left marooned on the Island; on the contrary, impromptu barbeques with old and new teammates cemented us firmly into the center of the Mets family.

Every day on the way to the ballpark, we monitored the pedestrian progress at the Sunshine Retirement Home. A time-weary Colonial Revival mansion had been renovated into an assisted-living facility. One particular elderly patron caught my attention. A very dapper aged gentleman, always adorned in a crisp white shirt with dark suspenders, would slowly shuffle across the left portion of the large veranda as we passed by around 10:30 in the morning. On our way home from the afternoon workouts, at approximately 5:00 pm, this same engaging elder would be working his way back from the right wing of the porch. As we questioned how long it must have taken "Mr. Senior Sunshine" to get from point A to point B and back again, we applauded the caring staff that made sure there were no irksome obstacles impeding his progress.

Over the years of our spring training adventures, my parents altered their travel schedule to coincide with spring training. I'm certain that my father, an excellent golfer, could never have tired of sinking a sixteen-foot putt on the pristine, Bermuda grass greens of the Mid-Ocean course in Tucker Town where they had typically taken a spring break from their New England winters for a number of years, but combining their love of golf with their enjoyment of baseball, not to mention their desire to spend time with their daughter and son-in-law, they expanded their horizons to stay at some wonderful golf resorts throughout the southern half of the United States of America. Without a reason to fly halfway across the country and land in a virtual oasis in the desert, I'm sure my father would have never scored a sub-par round on the forgiving fairways of Scottsdale's Camelback Mountain resort or come to the conclusion that, even though they both might have had the best rounds of their life on the links of Sun City, an active adult senior citizens complex did not fit their image of retirement. This particular year my parents had reserved a fairway villa in nearby Clearwater Beach. My mother, who happened to be approaching her fifty-fifth birthday, was not a very relaxed air traveler and, to calm her fears, she had purchased a copy of *The Fear of Flying* at the airport newsstand, only to be shocked to discover that the story line had nothing to do with relieving her flight anxiety.

DREAM MAKER

The average fan has a much better chance of securing an autograph from a ballplayer during spring training than at any other time during the season. Players are more relaxed, schedules are more flexible, and athletes are more accessible. Quite often the crowds that congregate outside spring training camps are only vaguely familiar with the ballplayers. Still, the desire to get a big league ballplayer to autograph a ball is a paramount pursuit of many spring training tourists. It is the dream of many a youngster to capture an autograph, and who the signer of that autograph is doesn't always matter much to a six-year-old. Stealing a line from *Joseph and the Amazing Technicolor Dream Coat*: "Any dream will do."

When my folks visited, they would schedule their golf rounds in the morning in order to join us at the ballpark in the afternoon. One such afternoon we were all leaving the players' parking lot together when Skip stopped to sign balls for a slew of Little League sluggers; my parents and I were patiently standing near our car waiting for the line to end. One anxious autograph seeker must have gotten tired of waiting in my husband's line, and he came over to my father with stars in his eyes and pleading with a worn-out looking ball cradled in his outstretched hand, "Are you anybody, sir?" My father was a self-made man. He had lost his mother at the age of three, was brought up by a taxing step-mother, picked raspberries for the CCC, freed prisoners from concentration camps in World War II, returned home to marry my mother and work full-time during the day while attending college full-time at night. He took a calculated risk starting his own engineering business, which grew and prospered over the years to eventually become a thriving success. My father was involved in Rotary International, the United Way, and served on the advisory board of a community bank. Yes, he was somebody, but undoubtedly not the kind of somebody this boy had in mind. My dad's first impulse was to shake his head and refuse to sign, but seeing the look of absolute awe in this child's face, he took the baseball, illegibly scribbled his own name, and handed the ball back to the appreciative fan. We laughed imagining that this child's parents would be having a hard time that evening trying to decipher whose name was smudged on the old dirty ball, but the child himself was gloriously pleased with his acquisition.

At the end of a strong spring season, it was time to head back to New York. We had signed a lease on an apartment in White Plains, near enough to the ballpark for an easy commute and far enough outside the city to enjoy some peace and tranquility. Clear skies were ahead of us as we entered another new season. The dark clouds of the past two years had passed us by, and we were looking forward to a fresh season filled with untold possibilities and the promise of glorious days ahead.

Sports Illustrated
May 17, 1976
FIRST EVER SI PLAYER OF THE WEEK

SKIP LOCKWOOD: In 5⅔ innings of clutch relief, the Met pitcher struck out eight batters and chalked up three saves. Twice he came in to fan Cincinnati's Johnny Bench, first with the bases loaded and next with two runners on.

THAT'S LIFE

It's impossible not to let the pressure of pitching in tight situations get you down. Akin to the claims made by a certain high-end manufacturer of hot dogs, professional athletes must answer to a higher authority—the impossible expectations of the home town fans. The cheering crowds, the Mets manager, and the sportswriters for the *New York Times*, the *Daily News*, the *Sporting News*, and *Sports Illustrated* all demand perfection. Let slip any sign that you are a mere mortal with human limitations, and expect to find your failings headlined in the newspaper the next day. Skip's job description, as a late-inning relief pitcher, was to come in to the game in precarious situations (*i.e.*, two men on base and no outs) and put out the fire of the opposing batters. A strikeout was the most exciting option of executing this task and almost mandatory if an opponent happened to be entrenched on third, but alternative out opportunities such as a double play, a groundout, a fly ball, a fielder's choice, or even a successful pickoff attempt would also work to appease the peanut gallery.

On perfect nights, the loudspeaker would broadcast that a pitching change was being made and, buoyed by the bellowing cheers of the boisterous crowd, Skip would emerge from the bullpen, strike out the first batter with a blazing fast ball and retire the side without further ado. Realistically, he was "only" able to accomplish this feat about 95% of the time. In the course of normal human events, this statistic charts exceedingly well, but in the eyes of the fanatic fan, any hint of human frailty is cause for raucous concern.

John Dean, in his book *Blind Ambition*, suggests that it's not power, but the fear of losing power that corrupts. As a relief pitcher, it's that fear of losing your power pitch that can cause intense anxiety at the onslaught of even the slightest slump. To put this pressure in perspective, if a hitter were to maintain a .500 batting average, meaning that he would be successful only one out of every two times he stepped up to the plate, he would be considered an extraordinary talent by his adoring public and be greeted by a standing ovation every time he stepped into the batter's box; but if a relief pitcher on that same team allows even one weak base hit when he enters the game, he can expect to be bombarded with a caustic chorus of boos. Skip technically portrayed the pressure he faced daily coming in from the bullpen in a newspaper article entitled "Lockwood: It's a Science" written by Mike Marley in the late seventies. Skip explained to the sportswriter "the process" that goes into being a successful closer. Skip argued that relieving could be considered a science and proposed that "it helps to be a bit of a mad scientist. You're put out there in emergency situations. These pressure situations can't be looked away from. There's a sense of urgency, of dynamism, to it. You've got to be a little crazy because of the situations you're held accountable for." Skip continued to explain that "relief pitching is the process of reducing the assemblage of impingement, the barriers. You have to go out, day to day, and be very, very aggressive. You have to show consistency in getting people out." After detailing his post-game, lactic acid, milking-down regiment, the icing ritual, the next morning scorching hot showers, and the psychological mind games to both relax and gear up his emotions, Skip concluded by stating that his "job never changes. It's to maintain the status quo.... (He admitted to) having more fun than ever before. I'm throwing the ball well and it looks like I'll end up with good numbers. I've scratched my whole career. I'm short on sense and long on tenacity but it works. A sensible person would have quit this years ago."

Advances unearthed by the scientific community have been discovered by innovative individuals who refused to be held down by the mundane rules. If a mathematician studied the odds of achieving success in major league baseball, he would discourage any reasonable youngster from pursuing his dream. In fact, very few truly sensible people stick around long enough to realize success in the sporting world. Almost every ballplayer who dons a professional uniform and steps onto the "A" ball field for the first time has been accustomed to star-like status. These phenoms have been the best and the brightest from the beginning of their baseball careers. For most rookies, their initial intro in pre-season training unnerves them with the shocking awareness that their athleticism does not outshine everyone else on the field. Accustomed to being a big fish in a small stream, the young player is suddenly a very small goldfish in a stream full of aggressive sharks. Suddenly he finds himself competing against all-star competition not only from the opposing team but also against his own teammates for a spot in the lineup. Hot-shot high school superstars who had rarely missed an inning of play find themselves cooling their heels as permanent bench warmers, pacing inside the dugout, bothered and bewildered by their side-lined situation. For many, a few years in the minor leagues are enough of a reality check to conclude that the life of a baseball player is not for them. Many of these young men pack their bags at the end of a season or two, go home, grow up, and become productive members of society. The athletes who continue to hang on generally are blessed (or cursed?) with the Peter Pan mentality of viewing life as one great adventure and fighting the inevitability of having to grow up. It's that "living on the edge" mentality that fosters greatness, but the traits that promote proficiency on the field are not always conducive to a serene family life.

A baseball wife needs to understand and accept the mood swings of her husband if she is going to maintain her own sanity. It's not only her husband's personal performance that can initiate an irksome attitude for an indeterminate amount of time. An undercurrent of energy permeates a team and ebbs and flows with the tides that connect to the team's winning percentage and its standing in the league. There were many days early on in our marriage that I just couldn't comprehend why the same sequence of events, occurring in the exact same order, could result in such diverse outcomes. A burnt piece of toast could get a laugh one day and be highly criticized the next. Oversleeping and running late was no big deal on Saturday, but might be viewed as a catastrophe on Sunday. One day sitting stalled in traffic was just the price you paid for living in a big city, while the same traffic jam on the same freeway the following day might result in a frustrated tirade on the senseless dependence the American public had with the automobile. Slow, deep breaths calmed me down to put the edgier side of my husband's personality into perspective. It's a known scientific fact that pressure needs to be released somewhere to avoid an explosion. Once I figured out that acting peeved over petty little problems freed his psyche to deal with the pressures on the field, I was able to ignore the occasional annoying outbursts and wait for the sun to rise on a better day.

A good friend of mine confided in me once that it was not easy being married to the "golden boy" of the family. Family life always centered around the sports schedule and whims of the larger-than-life special son. I'm willing to wager a guess that this white-glove treatment is much more the rule rather than the exception for the exceptionally talented athlete. Similar to the early support systems surrounding other professional baseball players, Skip's family had fervently encouraged his career and had taken an active part in his development as a player. Skip's dad, Claude, had been his little league coach during his early years and continued to cheer on and critique his skills from the stands as Skip moved up the ladder of success. As far as Skip's mother, Florence, can remember, his dad never missed a single baseball game Skip played until he graduated from high school. Occasionally his mother would join him on the ride over to the game, but her nerves generally got the best of her and barred her from viewing her son's performance on the field. Instead she would pace behind the bleachers whenever Skip was up at bat or on the mound and wait for the roar of the crowd to indicate the end of the inning before returning to the stands. Meals were always planned around "Skipper's" schedule, a fact that I'm sure must have annoyed the digestive system of his much younger sister, Betty. Betty joined in the family adoration of her big brother while always inserting her own spunky personality into the family dynamics. She certainly made her presence apparent on the day he signed his first professional contract. As Skip met with over a dozen scouts at his house, one at a time, to decipher each organization's offer, Betty was ensconced on their couch with a severe case of the measles. I imagine that more than one scout had misgivings about entering their living room, and I am positive Betty got a great kick out of their discomfort. While Florence kept her contagious daughter content during the long day of negotiations, Claude sat counseling his son throughout the crucial contract consultations.

This fatherly devotion continued after Skip turned pro as his dad would randomly show up unannounced in New York, Baltimore, or Cleveland during Skip's first year with the Kansas City Athletics. The Lockwood family was thrilled when, eleven years after their only son left to play professional baseball, Skip was traded to the New York Mets where, on just a tank of gas, his family could reconnect with their hero/son and participate in the excitement of his new role of a relief pitcher. His dad became a regular weekend resident at Shea Stadium.

It's not only the players who continue to engage in perpetual childhood pranks. The first day that Skip's father knocked on the clubhouse door and introduced himself to the mildly mischievous manager of the clubhouse, Herb Norman, Mr. Norman took it upon himself to initiate Claude into the mayhem of the Mets locker room. When Skip came in from batting practice, he asked the jovial jokester if his dad had had arrived yet. Immediately an impish grin spread over his face as he motioned Skip to follow him into the supply closet. On the spur of the moment, Herbie assessed the congenial constitution of Claude and assumed he could take a joke. On Skip's first day with the NY Mets, his dad had driven down to New York to witness the doubleheader action. Upon his arrival he followed his son's directions and wound his way around to the long brick hallway outside the home team's locker room. Claude had been warmly welcomed by the security guard outside the clubhouse and was directed to "just go on in inside and introduce yourself to Mr. Norman. He'll take good care of you." Following the friendly advice, Claude sought out Herb Norman and proudly introduced himself as Skip's dad. Rather than the hearty hand shake he was expecting, he was greeted by a panicky personality shouting at him "How did you get in here?" Taken back by this outburst, Claude motioned that the guard sitting outside the door had opened it for him. "Oh, no," Herbie retorted, "We're both going to lose our jobs. Give me a minute to figure out what to do with you," he quipped. Then, shifting to a conspiratorial tone, he cautioned Claude that family was not usually allowed in the players' locker room, but he would "do him a big favor" and hide him in the closet until Skip returned to the clubhouse. Skip's dad thanked him profusely and quietly followed the eccentric clubhouse attendant into the storage closet and waited patiently until his loyal son came to rescue him from this ludicrous location. To his credit, Herb immediately sought out Skip and, in a fit of laughter, relayed the encounter and dispatched his son to rescue Claude from the bats and balls. I'm certain that this was not the first or the last childish hoax that was played on Claude as he skipped around the country traipsing after his son, but his affable acceptance of the joke endeared him to the clubhouse clown and allowed him unlimited access to the locker room for the next five years.

Succumbing to the favorite-son role bestowed on Skip by his adoring parents, Skip was always the center of attention and the focus of all conversation when his family joined us for dinner after a weekend day game. He was expected to be their affable star/hero and did his best to live up to those expectations, even if he was not in the mood to be sociable after a less-than-stellar performance. Halfway through the very stressfully successful 1976 season with the Mets, Skip's dad decided to take time off from work and join us for an entire home stand. Unfortunately, his timing coincided with an uncharacteristically shoddy stretch of athletic accomplishment by the New York Mets. Other than a complete game win pitched by Jon Matlock, the Mets came up short at the end of the scoreboard for the entire week. Their crisp fielding wilted, and the power pitchers lost command of their control. For the first two days Skip did not get a chance to pitch to even one batter. Having lived with the intensity of my husband for a number of years, I was in tuned to his innate need to release the aggression he so scientifically managed to gear up for daily by hurling "heat" into Jerry Grote's glove on a nightly basis. Not having the opportunity to let loose his fast ball against the opposition, he had a tendency to unleash his pent-up enmity on the horrendous drivers zooming down the Hutchinson River Parkway. Claude was more than a little stunned by his son's atypical aggressive driving on the way home, while I calmly hung on to the seat of the car and closed my eyes until we arrived safely back home.

On the third night of Claude's vacation, Skip did get a chance to pitch, but did not live up to his own standards and gave up a base hit to the first batter he faced, allowing the runner on third to score. While he managed to finish the game effectively in a losing cause, his ego was still slightly bruised by the bloop single. Unsure how to deal with his son's seemingly aberrant attitude, Claude attempted to applaud Skip for striking out two in the ninth, only to be rewarded by a caustic retort concerning his frustration over the initial errant fastball. This was a side of his son's personality his father had not experienced.

Every morning Claude would rise early, ready to engage in companionable conversation with his son. He fondly recalled their Saturday morning chats during Skip's childhood and how they would sit together around their kitchen table and plan their strategy for the day's game. Skip had been eager to take note of his dad's expertise, and together they would drive over to join their Norwood Little League team on the local sandlot for a generally successful stint on the field. Early on in Skip's professional career, father and son could be found sharing a few beers, instigated by Claude's spontaneous excursions to a number of farm towns in the minor leagues. Together they would stay up late dissecting the finer details of hitting (at the time Skip was still struggling as a third baseman) and brainstorming how Skip could adjust his 20/400 vision to the inadequate lighting of the minor league fields. After Skip was transformed into a starting pitcher in the big leagues, when Claude came to visit for a few days, Skip knew when he was scheduled to pitch and geared his behavior and sleeping schedule to coincide with his turn in the rotation. A genial round of golf the day after Skip's turn on the mound was a given. Such relaxing scheduled off-days were now a thing of the past. It took me a while to adjust to the psychological changes in my husband's personality when he was thrust into the role of a relief pitcher, an adjustment his father was having trouble understanding. Instead of stepping up to the plate three or four times a game or pitching nine innings once every five days, the relief pitcher has to be ready to perform under pressure-cooker conditions where his every pitch is of utmost importance on a nightly basis. This new role intensified the stress of an already stressful occupation. Family routines and dynamics required tweaking to accommodate his changing role. Now my husband would normally sleep until about ten in the morning and, when he did finally stroll into the kitchen, would not feel like talking at all for the first half hour of his waking day. He would sit quietly with a cup of coffee, read between the lines of the sports section to see what batters were on a hot streak, and slowly begin preparing himself mentally to pitch again sometime after nine o'clock that evening.

This professional preoccupation was not very conducive to a friendly, family tête-à-tête. Upon hearing Claude moving around the living room of our high rise early in the morning, I silently slid out of bed and joined him for coffee. I would then try my best to keep him entertained until his son, and the Lockwood he really wanted to converse with, arose. Having been up for two or three hours, Claude was full of enthusiasm and anxious to trek to the nearest local diner for a big breakfast of steak and eggs the minute his son sauntered into the room. Skip, on the other hand, was still half asleep and not really up for any more action than lifting his coffee cup to his mouth. With all the *faux* enthusiasm Skip could muster, the three of us would go out for a cholesterol-clogging breakfast. Our apartment was located in an eclectic neighborhood, and after our late morning meal we would stroll around the city blocks, stopping at the butcher to select a fresh cut of meat for a post-game meal and at the bakery for some mouth-watering chocolate chip cookies. Once back inside our individual unit, Skip would retire to bed for his pre-game nap, and I would again attempt to keep my father-in-law from becoming exceedingly bored. Certainly this somewhat arid agenda was not the fascinating father-son bonding vacation Claude had envisioned.

By mid-afternoon, Skip would be up again and ready for a light meal before heading to the ballpark. Skip, his dad, and Ken Sanders, whom Claude had befriended years ago and who lived in our building, would carpool down to Shea. As noted above, Claude had found a home away from home inside the Mets clubhouse and was undoubtedly happier hanging around the ballpark than hanging out with me at our apartment. Maryann Sanders and I, along with her three children, would head out to the park closer to game time and reconnect with Skip's dad under the protective netting section behind the plate. On the fourth night of this nerve-racking vacation, Claude, who could be the poster child of composure, was starting to resemble his restless wife as he paced back and forth behind the concessions. Yes, he was eager to watch his son pitch, but he was not sure if he could handle the elevated emotions if the results were not to his son's liking. The Mets were struggling again, stranding a number of runners on base, and it appeared as if Skip would be brought in to pitch in the seventh inning. False alarm. The starting pitcher threw a double-play ball, and the inning ended without further damage. We could all breathe a sigh of relief for the moment. Skip was brought in to pitch the eighth. He walked the first batter, but then managed to pick him off at first. Struggling with his control, he had a 3–0 count on the next batter who gratefully swung at ball four and popped it up into the infield. A line drive to right on a 3–1 count brought the boo-ers to their feet. Thankfully, the inning ended with a strikeout as Skip appeared to gain a little more control of his pitches. Fortunately, the Mets started hitting in the bottom of the eighth and had two men on base with only one out. Unfortunately, Skip was the next scheduled batter and, as any odds-playing manager would do, he was lifted for a pinch-hitter. The pinch-hitter was unsuccessful in driving in the runners, and the Mets lost. Skip's dad locked eyes with mine, and I could sense that he was less than excited about the prospects of another uncomfortable long ride home. He offered to let me sit in the front seat for our return trip, but I insisted that the pleasure of putting up with his perfectionist son's melancholy mood on the way home was all his.

Claude's bags were packed and standing in the hall when I joined him in the kitchen the next morning. My husband had never been superstitious, however, his father was certain that he was bringing the team back luck which was, in turn, spilling over to rain on Skip's parade. Never one to criticize his golden prodigy, he did quietly mumble something to me about "not knowing how I could put up with the mood swings" on the way out the door. The answer, of course, was with love and a whole lot of understanding. That was the last time Skip's dad came to visit us for an extended period of time although he did continue to drive down to the Big Apple every weekend. I believe he enjoyed the freedom of cruising home in his Cadillac whenever he sensed the mood was right (or wrong!).

Thankfully, the tides turned for the better when the Mets took off for the West Coast the following week. Success in baseball boils downs to a matter of resiliency. The moment the last strike is thrown, that ball game is history and the pitcher must prove himself all over again on his next outing. During the course of a season, wives of professional ballplayers face many ups and downs. The key to surviving this emotional turmoil is found in their capacity to jump back into the ring after a tough round. After all, that's life, and both my husband and the rest of the Mets team were indeed back on top of their games in June. The long baseball season can be likened to running a marathon. It doesn't really matter how fast you start, it's how you handle the hills and adjust to the down slopes that matters. The lyrics of Frank Sinatra's signature song symbolize the buoyancy an athlete must engage in to overcome the confidence-shattering fear of failure that is inherent in the game; whenever you find yourself flat on your face, it's time to pick yourself up and get back in the race.

ON BROADWAY

You cannot live in New York without falling in love with the theater. The weekend we joined the New York Mets, Skip was offered tickets to the stage production of *The Wiz*. Instantly I became captivated by Broadway and its magical musicals. From my early tap dancing days, I endeavored to keep in sync with the rhythm with varying degrees of success. An active participant in both my high school and college glee clubs, I piercingly belted out a passable rendition of "If I Loved You" in our high school *Carousel* production. Sitting in the fifth row of the audience, amidst the elegant ambience and the marvelous acoustics of the Majestic Theater, the lung power and stamina of the ensemble was awe inspiring; just like a baseball team, a Broadway cast is dependent on every member of the entourage. Identifying with Dorothy and her quest for courageous direction and heart-filled knowledge as she made her way down the yellow brick road, I felt the refrain of a brand new day reverberate within me. Hopefully we had found our way home with the NY Mets. It was time to "believe" once again.

Throughout our amazing New York Mets years, we were fortunate enough to attend a number of outstanding plays and privileged, at times, to meet some of the best and brightest on Broadway. In reliving our time in New York, one particular afternoon sprang to mind. While the New York Mets baseball team was doing battle with the Cubs at Wrigley Field, a very generous corporate executive invited the Mets' wives to a luncheon in their private penthouse dining room followed by an evening performance of the musical *Chicago*. This day stands out so clearly because it was one of the few instances that an event was organized solely with the pleasure of the wives in mind. While I can't recall the entrée presentation, I do recall the entrancing presence of Roxie Clark's stage interpreter, Gwen Verdon, who was a surprise guest of honor at our luncheon. What enormous energy was packed into this petite personality! Ms. Verdon, a rumored introvert, was the one initiating most of the conversation. Years before sports psychologists emerged on the support staff of organizations, those in the entertainment industry appreciated the mind/body connection that exists in performing. Gwen Verdon quizzed us all on the coping skills we employed to help our husbands stay focused and had some suggestions of her own on dealing with the demands of our husbands' career while trying to maintain some sense of our own identity.

Ms. Verdon rushed off to get ready for her evening role, but our group lingered around the table, thinking about her insights. We strolled over to the theater district, passing the hectic combustion of street vendors, honking horns, and haughty hookers that collided in Times Square and reinforced the importance of providing a calming environment for ourselves and our husbands in this fast-paced city. Leaving the turbulent Times Square world behind, we regained our composure the moment we stepped inside the regal theater. As the lights dimmed and the orchestra's melodic strains floated over the room, the audience was transported back to the Chicago in the Jazz Age. Gwen Verdon's performance that night was a masterful model of razzle-dazzle. She compelled the audience to fall in love with her less-than-lovable character as her vociferous vocal chords convinced us all that her illicit lover truly did "have it coming." Her fluid limbs gyrated across the stage, exerting an energy most actresses half her age would envy. I had a hard time relating to the fact that this high-powered diva was the same low-keyed, solicitous redhead we had dined with only a few hours before. Broadway performers excel in a variety of venues. As the lights dimmed on the final act and our evening came to a close, the Mets wives went their separate ways and, like Mr. Cellophane, anonymously blended into the mass of humanity striving to hold onto true love in this fame-obsessed society.

During our B.C. (before children) years, we spent numerous Saturday evenings attending a bevy of Broadway productions. From the silly to the sublime, we viewed the world from the eye of the playwright. We battled imaginary dragons with Don Quixote, questioned the loss of traditions with Tevya, sought to maintain sanity with *Equus*, and recognized that freedom was basically a "state of mind" in *Shenandoah*. Occasionally, a quiet evening at the theater became a little too serene for my husband. While I sat entranced by Emily Dickinson's meanderings during *The Belle of Amherst*, Skip dozed off in the seat next to me and caught up on some much needed sleep after a grueling doubleheader. After that, I made a greater effort to choose a play my husband could relate to a little better, such as *I Love My Wife* or *Guys and Dolls*. We were not alone in our obsession with the theater. I remember Sandy Swan raving over Ann Reinking's performance in *A Chorus Line* months before it showed up on everyone's must-see list.

We enjoyed the same singular sensation the night we took our seats in the audience of *A Chorus Line* for the first time. Still riding high from the afternoon game where the entire fan base of Shea Stadium had given Skip a standing ovation as he entered the game and remained on their feet cheering loudly until the final strikeout, we headed over the 59th Street Bridge and on towards the theater district. As we entered the lobby of the Schubert Theater, it seemed that every eye was turned in our direction. They probably were, but it was not our presence but that of our companions, Tom and Nancy Seaver, that had heads turning. I don't quite recall the how or why, but Nancy had become friendly with Anne Reinking, and the incredibly talented dancer had left her four tickets to the night's performance. We had been invited to join the Seavers at the theater even before Skip had saved Tom's game in the last inning that afternoon. Maybe it was my imagination, but it appeared that the entire cast was spotlighting its performance to the gregarious gentleman whose name was synonymous with the Amazing Mets. The play was every bit as entertaining as we had been told, and Ms. Reinking's dancing far surpassed the superlative praise Sandy had given it. As heart-stopping as the theatrical experience had been, the most exciting portion of our evening was just about to begin. The star of the show, Ann Reinking, joined us for dinner after the play. At the time she was in the midst of breaking up with a famous Broadway producer and anxious to leave the drama of the theater behind and share a meal with a few out-of-industry "normal" individuals. I guess we fell on the fringes of that category.

The most poignant line in *A Chorus Line* is spoken by Diana when she questions what she would do if she is never be able to dance again. Ann, Tom, and Skip all were at the top of their profession at the time and thrived on the adrenaline rush they received from each evening's performance. The concept that this joy could be suddenly taken away was a very sobering. No one at the table was ready for it to end. Whenever I hear the refrain of "Kiss Today Goodbye," I'm transported back to the days when Skip was given the extraordinary gift to do what he did for love for such a long time.

While the lights of Broadway shone softly on summer evenings, they glared gloriously during the winter holiday season. My parents drove to Connecticut to partake in a pre–Christmas New York holiday spree every winter we were with the Mets. My mother and I would hop on the morning commuter train in Cos Cob and depart at Grand Central Station to head over to Fifth Avenue and delight in the intricately creative window displays at Saks, Lord & Taylor, and Bergdorf's. An expensively exhausting day in the city ensued, mingling with other suburban wives who invaded mid-town Manhattan on bustling December Saturdays. Late in the afternoon, when our worn-out pocketbooks and tired puppies had both exceeded their limits, we would renew our spirits inside Saint Patrick's Cathedral and then limp across the street to Rockefeller Plaza. The plan was always to gaily glide over the ice, but somehow our aching feet swelling inside our high-heel leather boots always encouraged us to opt to simply sit and sip a glass of wine at a table overlooking the amateur athletes sashaying in pairs on the skating rink of the Plaza. Skip and my dad would drive into the city later to join us for an evening at the theater. Inevitably the four of us would wind up at Rusty's Restaurant after the show and muse over the night's musical while fondly reliving the previous season and anticipating the upcoming one. Within moments of our being seated, a bottle of wine would magically appear at our table, the generous gift of some anonymous patron. Yes, it was great to be somewhat of a star in a city that thrives on celebrity sightings and where the lights are constantly shining bright on Broadway.

As much as I was enthralled by the bright lights of Broadway, downtown Manhattan could get a little overwhelming. When it came to choosing a community in which to put down roots, we opted for the back country of Greenwich, Connecticut. At the end of the 1976 season, Skip and I bought a "contemporary colonial" cedar home in the middle of the woods in Greenwich, Connecticut, within jogging distance from the Seavers and just across the street from Dave Kingman. Adjacent to our backyard was a 400-acre nature preserve. Trials and tribulations occurred daily at the ballpark, but tranquility prevailed at the end of the day. After years of upheaval and uncertainty, we had found a home. This world was centered on our participation in a very special church community staffed with an odd mix of priests: an elderly, old-fashioned monsignor, an eccentric, Jesuit college math professor, and a young Franciscan communications specialist who televised a daily mass. For years, we had felt like anonymous outsiders at Sunday services, and we had now become welcomed into a close-knit church community. An eclectic gathering of high-powered lawyers, doctors, stock brokers, business moguls, IBM (*i.e.*, I've been moved) employees, Junior League volunteers, third-generation homeowners, and sports personalities worshipped together in a renovated, old carriage house. Preparing dinner for a sick friend's family or watching a neighbor's child for a few hours so the mother could take a nap was the rule rather than the exception. Informal toddler playgroups were formed there along with adult social gatherings in the quaint, stone-walled social center. Leaving the cold war political problems and deadline-oriented personal pressures of the outside world behind, we gathered on Sunday mornings to reflect on our blessings and recognize what truly mattered in life—love, faith and family. I cannot begin to explain how much this fundamental connection meant to the quality of our lives.

Greenwich, Connecticut, was home to countless women whose husbands traveled as much, if not more, than my own. These ladies taught me that baseball wives did not corner the exclusive rights to loneliness. The business world could be just as hard on family life, resulting in the same level of insecurity and anxiety. The rise and fall of the stock exchange could be as distressing to family dynamics as the failure of a fastball to rise over the plate. I actually had an advantage over the business wives. The ups and downs of Skip's career were immediately visible to myself (and of course everyone else). Corporate wives were rarely privy to what went on behind closed boardrooms, but the emotional highs and lows of their husbands' personalities affected the quality of their home life as much as it did ours. Many baseball wives, myself included, had envied women who could prepare dinner at 6:00 P.M. rather than waiting until midnight to cook. Living in Greenwich, I discovered that many a dinner might be ready at 6:00, but if a last-minute problem came up at the office, it could be hours later before it was served. Baseball schedules were set in stone at the beginning of the season, but the traveling schedules of the corporate executive were subject to constant change, and similar to the sports world, birthdays and anniversaries were never taken into consideration. Wives were expected to be flexible and understanding. "What's that? You're not going to make it home tonight for Jack's three-year-old Indian party? No problem, I can corral all those wild braves by myself," or "Of course you have to fly to Florida tomorrow to play golf with clients. Don't worry, I'll deal with Jill's chicken pox and make sure the driveway gets plowed during the impending blizzard." Tiger Lily's stoic demeanor had nothing on the suburban mother of two who might be required to whip up an elegant dinner for a visiting business associate with a few hours' notice. A freezer stocked with Omaha steaks and twice-baked potatoes was essential to any unflappable hostess. Major adjustments were made to my idealized conception of a "normal" life outside of baseball.

We purchased a spec home nearing completion and moved in before the paint was dry on the foyer trim. The quaint country home the Seavers owned was getting just a little too cozy after the arrival of their second daughter, and Nancy Seaver fell in love with a beautiful old carriage house off the beaten path in Greenwich that needed a few minor repairs. As their architect's plans developed, these minor repairs turned into major renovations. A generous fellow Greenwich Country Club member offered the Seavers the use of their home for the summer, as they would be residing on their Argentinian ranch. Instructed to "enjoy it as if it were your own home," the Seavers did as they were told, and Skip and I thoroughly enjoyed their host's extended hospitality. "So this is what Neverland looks like," I thought to myself the first time I drove up the long, tree-lined driveway that framed the entry to this elegant estate. The guest house out back was about the same size as our new home. Sitting around the pool one afternoon, I was startled when what I thought to be a buffalo appeared through the lush gardens. Understanding that the owners were great outdoorsmen, I was still not sure what to make of this up-close-and-personal encounter with wildlife. Trying to get Nancy's attention without either spooking the wild animal or alarming her young daughter, I suddenly saw four-year-old Sarah look up and delightedly run over to give this big beast a huge hug. Apparently the caretakers of the estate owned a big, black Newfoundland dog who aimlessly wandered around the property looking for handouts and hugs wherever he went.

Baseball players are extremely competitive on the field, but once they cross the white line, these grown-up little boys prefer to leave the game behind and socialize with old teammates and friends. One such night before leaving for the ballpark, Nancy mentioned to the affable caretaker of this exquisite estate that she was having a few players back after the game and could he please open up the bottle of wine on the counter to breathe before dinner? When we arrived around 6:00 accompanied by an opposing Philadelphia Phillies couple, we all were flabbergasted to discover that two bottles of Chateaux L'Efitte Rothschild had been brought up from the wine cellar and were already opened for our dining pleasure. Once opened, there was nothing for us to do but enjoy the exquisite fruits of the vine. I'm not certain if it was the tender steak or the glass or two of extraordinary wine that made this one of the more enjoyable dining experiences I can remember. Perhaps the time spent perusing the host's wine cellar gave Tom the idea of growing his own grapes. The Seavers have passionately plunged into a new venture in the cabernet wine industry in Calistoga, California. With knowledge and hard work, I'm certain their efforts will bear fruits leading them to the hall of fame of vintners.

Speaking of dining experiences, George Herbert (Herbie) Walker, Jr. and his wife Mary (original co-owners along with Joan Whitney Payson of the New York Mets) also lived in the Greenwich community. During the 1976 off season, Skip and I were invited over to their home for dinner. Though the Walkers were considerably older than my husband and me, we had met at several events and enjoyed their lively insights on life. As excited as I was to be joining them for dinner, I was having a little difficulty getting dressed as my wardrobe choices were limited by my blossoming, pregnant body. Pulling up to their front door, I was impressed with the elegant simplicity of both the size and design of their lovely home. Just like Mary herself, the home resonated of understated good taste. Over cocktails (mine of course having to be of the non-alcoholic variety) the conversation sprang from baseball to politics to the economy and back to baseball again. A lovely watercolor hung on the wall, and I inquired if it had been done by a local artist. It turned out that the painting had been a thank-you gift from a grateful spouse of a minor league ballplayer. The Walkers owned a lovely summer cottage in Kennebunkport, Maine, and had an interest in a minor league affiliate in the area. At one time they had allowed the players to live on their property for the short season, and an artistically-gifted recipient of this kindness had painted this wonderful replication in appreciation. On the table below was a photo of their nephew, United Nations Ambassador George Bush. The Walkers were proud of their extended family's commitment to service and felt strongly about the need for everyone involved in this great all–American sport of baseball to become equally involved in making America a great nation to live in.

For all the differences in our ages and circumstances, I felt a common bond with the Walkers. As I was recounting to Mary all the different apartments we had lived in, she commiserated about her own first, small, two-bedroom apartment in Manhattan—one bedroom for the newly-married couple and another for their maid. Okay, so while the emotional memories might be somewhat similar, the economic staging of those memories were on a different playing level. My starving stomach became enthralled by the olfactory aromas emanating from the kitchen as we sat down for dinner. A simple salad accompanied a melt-in-your-mouth beef tenderloin with béarnaise sauce surrounded by fresh vegetables from their own garden. I could have easily devoured the entire roast; however, I politely placed two slices on my plate and passed the platter on. Once we all had filled our plates, the platter was removed to the kitchen and emptied into the dog bowls of their two adorable pets. It took all the manners instilled in me at an early age, and all the self restraint I later acquired to keep myself politely smiling at my seat and not screaming to bring the meat back to the table.

Driving home after this enchanting evening, I couldn't help but reflect on how, in our democratic country, there still existed such a definite class system. Anyone could work hard and achieve the American dream of success, but an invisible barrier still limited access to the upper class. More than a decade later, we were vacationing in Kennebunkport, Maine, with our (at the time) three children and overheard a clerk in a Dock Square boutique mentioning that the charming Mary Walker had been in shopping that very morning. Since moving away from Greenwich, we had not been in contact with Mary other than a sympathy note after Herbert's death. On the spur of the moment, we decided to pay Mary a visit. The Walkers "summer cottage" came into view as we rounded the cove past Kennebunkport Beach. The watercolor hanging in their Greenwich living room had captured the architectural ambience of the building, but I'd wager a guess that even Claude Monet would have had trouble doing justice to the many shades of blue emanating from the sky and blending into the ocean. Prompting our girls to be on their best behavior as we wound our way up the long driveway, we were not prepared for the greeting waiting for us at the top of the hill. A less-than-friendly checkpoint guard stared at our Suburban, our sandy, sun-lotioned daughters and scoffed at our supposition that we could just drop in and say hello. He politely, yet firmly, informed us as to where we could turn our car around and vacate the premises when we could not produce any proof of our connection to Mrs. George Herbert (Mary) Walker. An invisible barrier had quickly turned into a permanent barricade once the title of Walker Point had been handed over to the President of the United States of America and the Secret Service was now in charge of security. On Broadway, Orphan Annie was welcomed into Daddy Warbucks's world, but there were considerably more obstacles to encounter when attempting to make a similar transition in the real world.

FOREVER YOUNG

New York throws a party like no other city in the world. Tall ships with their splendid sails billowing off of the yard arms glided down the Hudson River by day while magnificent multi-colored starbursts boomed and lit up the evening sky as the city celebrated the Bicentennial of the birth of our nation. Caught up in the midst of these festivities, we began to question our own place in the universe and our plans for the future. By now the serendipitous existence of the baseball world was very clear. After cementing our personal relationship in Milwaukee, and surviving the uncertainty of 1974 and the upheavals of 1975, by the end of the 1976 season we felt secure enough to consider adding a new wonder to our life. Of course, we had a master plan in place. This child would enter the world during the off-season, preferably late autumn, so as not to interfere with post-season play or spring training conditioning.

In my very first year of marital bliss, I had watched in disbelief as my friend and neighbor, Nancy Hegan, delivered her second child without the support of her husband by her side. This inconsiderate baby arrived two weeks before the due date while her husband, Mike, was away on a road trip. Nancy's mother-in-law, Claire, the wife of a major league baseball catcher-turned coach, understood the uncertainties of baseball life and had come to spend the road trip with Nancy "just to be on the safe side." Nancy's late afternoon contractions combined with Claire's "mother's instinct" led to my spending the night at the Hegans' apartment. Good call. Claire drove Nancy to the hospital in the middle of the night while I stayed at their apartment to watch their young son, Shawn, and contact her husband.

Shawn cooperated by sleeping like the baby he was, but I was not so successful with my second task. Years before cell phones allowed instant communication with our spouses, the hotel operators controlled who could and who could not get connected to hotel rooms. The night operator had been cautioned by his supervisor to protect the privacy of the baseball players staying at his hotel. Impressed with his position of authority, this control freak had no intention of divulging the location of Mike Hegan's room to a young female on the phone. "Sorry, dear, but I do not have a master list of the players' rooms," he pedantically replied. "You'll just have to wait until the morning to leave a message." He erroneously assumed that I was a baseball groupie employing a new ploy to gain access to the players. Putting myself in Nancy's place, fretfully waiting to hear from my husband in between contractions, I was not willing to take no for an answer. A few assertive phone calls later, I got through to the hotel manager who tracked Mike down and informed him of the impending arrival. This ordeal had taken over three hours, and I could only imagine the apprehension Nancy must have been experiencing waiting to hear from her husband. Mike finally did speak with Nancy in the hospital, but it took another two days before the schedule allowed him to fly home to embrace his wife and their second son.

Over the years I have given a wealth of unsolicited advice to my own five children to help them survive the daily traumas of life, especially during those dreadful middle school years. I'm sure they all tired of hearing me say that you can never be in complete control of events, you can only control your response to those events: "It's not the situation, but your reaction to the situation that's important." Try as I might, I could not quite understand Nancy Hegan's easy acceptance of her solitary childbirth situation. Obviously she was disappointed that Mike was not at the delivery, but she was resigned to the idea that it was to be expected. After all, our lives were controlled by baseball schedules. I, on the other hand, was not so understanding. I couldn't believe that the world wouldn't come to a grinding halt as soon as this miraculous beautiful baby was born. Less than two months after joining the baseball world, I vowed, with all the certainty of those who still believe in fairies, that I would never be driven to the hospital by a friend to experience this miraculous life-giving event all alone. Unfortunately, life rarely seems to go along with my meticulous plans.

Flu season does not usually begin in October and so I was more than a little concerned when I started "losing my lunch" before breakfast every day for a week. My annual physical was not scheduled until mid–November but when I explained to the nurse (Carol) on call my worry that I was coming down with the bubonic plague, I was told to come down to the office right away and the doctor would fit me in. Too green to negotiate the winding back roads of Greenwich on my own, Skip drove me to my appointment. My queasy stomach lurched as we rounded each sharp bend in the road. We arrived at the stately, stone, medical building in record time where I was ushered into a private room. After a thorough examination the doctor told me to get dressed and have Skip join me in his office. We nervously entered the confines of the doctor's elegant office. As we lowered ourselves down into the rich, cranberry, leather wing-back chairs to find out what rare disease was at the root of my illness, Dr. Prangley sauntered in with a knowing smile and sat on the edge of his ornate mahogany desk. "Good news," he quipped. "You do not have the plague. We'll have to run a blood test to confirm my suspicions," he advised, "but I think congratulations are in order. You'll be adding another little New York Met to the family day roster next year." Pregnant! So soon? Wonderful! Incredible! Unbelievable! But, impossible! The timing was all wrong.

Doctor Art Prangley was one of the most highly regarded doctors in the area, and he was also a huge New York Mets fan. Appreciating our desire to confirm the results as soon as possible, he directed his nurse to rush the blood test over to the lab. (Being a professional athlete did have a few perks in the New York area.) We were then instructed to "relax and enjoy the rest of the beautiful day outside." I was handed a business card by the doctor with the number of the lab printed on the back to call after 4:00 P.M. to obtain the results. With my digestive system still in a state of flux, we found a quiet corner café that served my current favorite food—tea and saltines—and joked about what we might name the baby who might be growing inside of me.

Checking my watch for the umpteenth time, it finally reached 4:01. Cell phone convenience was still a decade away, so we found a phone booth located on the outside back wall of the corner drug store. I took a deep breath as I dialed the number of the laboratory. A brusque and business like voice answered the phone: Yes, the results were in. My blood had tested positive for pregnancy. These words were followed by an emotionless response: "Are you okay with the results?" "Pardon me," I replied. "Is this situation acceptable to you? Or do you need a number to call for options?" the voice droned on. "Of course it's more than okay," I smiled through the phone. "We're thrilled. Thank you so much," I replied and hung up the phone. Only after I placed the receiver back on the hook did the meaning of the callous receptionist's response sink in. I was appalled that the first person to share the news of this miracle with me was suggesting I end the life I was so excited to begin. What in the world was happening to our civilized world? My glowing expression confirmed my growing condition. Skip ran over to embrace me and our new life. Now that was the reaction I was hoping for. Our life truly was incredible, and we would joyfully bring a perfect little being into this wonderful world.

Our friends laughed at our naïve enthusiasm. Both avid readers, we sped off to the bookstore to research the latest developments in childbirth preparation, convinced that if I followed all the dietary and exercise advice being touted at the time, I would deliver the perfect child. I was clearly insulted when my chart read that I was an "Elderly Prima Gravidas." At twenty-eight, how could I possibly be considered an elderly anything? (I do, however, admit to feeling exceedingly elderly when I delivered my 5th and final child at the age of 41.) I soon discovered that morning sickness does not confine itself to the morning. Many an autumn afternoon was spent sipping club soda and speculating as to what my constitution might keep down for dinner. Luckily for Skip, since we lived in the middle of the woods and a good fifteen minutes from any grocery store, I never developed any unreasonable dietary requests, although I did acquire a new appreciation for the blandness of baked potatoes.

With pillows and exercise mats in hand, Skip and I joined other parents-to-be in neo-natal classes held in the main conference room at the Greenwich Hospital. The focus of the class was geared towards drilling us in the deep breathing techniques of "natural childbirth" on the way to a drug-free delivery. Greenwich was an affluent suburb where women tended to be pampered. "I want you all to pay close attention and learn the concentration techniques I will be teaching" voiced our instructor, "but remember," she said, "the majority of books explaining painless childbirth were written by men who never actually had to endure the experience. Practice these techniques, but remember that no one needs to be a hero. Always be aware that help [in the form of anesthesia] is there if you feel you need it." A very receptive audience nodded with relief at the back-up option. Dr. Prangley had delivered both of Nancy Seaver's daughters, and so I sought out her advice on what to anticipate during labor and delivery. Evidently Nancy did not want to scare me because she always kept her answers on the vague side, telling me that "once you see the smile on your baby's face, you forget all about the pain." I spent half of the winter reading up on what to expect and confirming those fears with my child-bearing friends, and the other half trying to put those expectations out of my head. Tom kept kidding Skip about the sleepless nights ahead, but of course there was no way we could have comprehended the total exhaustion that lay ahead.

By the beginning of June we were prepared for the blessed event. Every book on the subject of pregnancy and childbirth had been read, pre-natal classes were completed, the tour of the hospital had been taken, and the baby's room decorated in a gender-friendly lemon yellow. The exhilaration I felt was tempered only by the dread that Skip would not be around for the delivery. Baseball schedules are, after all, totally inflexible. Even though Skip would be home for the entire week surrounding my due date, my fastidious friends insisted on a back-up plan. Checking out the Mets' road trip schedule and our family's vacation schedule, there was only one night in the six weeks surrounding my delivery that I would be home alone, June 23.

Early on in our scrupulous planning phase, Nancy Seaver volunteered to be my surrogate spouse for night. Of course I welcomed the opportunity to stay in the guest wing of the beautiful barn they had just renovated and spend the night with Nancy and her two adorable girls. However, baseball life had confirmed the truism that the only certainty in life was change. I would have to alter my contingency plan for the evening since the Seavers' stable existence was in chaos. In a shock to the entire New York Mets family, Tom Seaver, the heart of the Mets franchise, had been traded to Cincinnati. Tom, of course, had joined the team immediately, and Nancy was at home in Greenwich packing up to leave early the next morning. Having moved myself countless times, I empathized with the stress Nancy was dealing with and felt I couldn't possibly impose on my friend. But the best baseball wives look out and support each other, and Nancy was one of the best. She convinced me to stay, stating the obvious: If anything was ever going to go wrong, it would go wrong when your husband was away. Acutely aware that life was constantly throwing us change-ups, I gave in to her generous insistence.

There really was no reason to suspect delivery was imminent. My due date was over two weeks away and I was feeling great—or at least as great as one can feel with an extra 25 pounds in her abdomen. Skip dropped me off at the Seavers' on his way to the ballpark and made Nancy promise that she would contact him the minute I went into labor. He phoned an hour later when he reached Shea Stadium. He called again before the National Anthem, "just to be sure." I guess the telephone in the bullpen was only accepting incoming calls from the dugout, because I did not hear from him again until after he had pitched the 9th inning. I assured Skip that the only change in my well-being was the fact that I was being trounced in a marathon Go Fish card game by Sarah Seaver. He checked in before the plane left La Guardia, once again when it landed at O'Hare, and one more time when he arrived at the hotel in Chicago. Since I was taking a nap, Nancy took the final call and gently told him to "relax, nothing's happening." Things were fine. She reminded him that she had promised to call him if anything changed. Nancy's cousin had come to Connecticut to help with the move, and the three of us sat up late that night reminiscing about good times we had shared in the past year and laughing at the obsessive compulsive behavior my husband was exhibiting at this present moment.

At about one in the morning a very strange sensation woke me up. Somewhere between temerity and terror, I realized that my water had broken. My first response was that of mortification. I was going to have to change the sheets and create more laundry at an extremely inopportune time. Excruciating pains started soon after, but since they were all in my back, I was confused but not all that concerned. Trying not to wake up the household, I stood up and paced back and forth for over an hour. Logically, I reasoned there was no way I could be in labor. Number 1, my due date was over two weeks away; 2, I had no pain in my abdomen; and a big 3, my husband was in Chicago. Not able to withstand the stabbing back pain that was getting increasingly stronger and recurring every seven minutes, I woke Nancy up about 3 A.M. seeking her advice. I was not at all comforted by the concern I saw in her eyes. Nancy herself had experienced back labor, and so she calmly insisted we head to the hospital ASAP. Leaving a note for her cousin on the table, we took off to the hospital.

As luck would have it, our other teammate and neighbor, Dave King-man, had also been traded that week and had left his car by the Seavers' front door. Not wanting to waste the time moving Dave's car, Nancy jumped into the driver's seat while I stuffed my bloated body in the passenger side of the little car and headed to Greenwich Hospital, unaware that Dave had left the car with a virtually empty gas tank. Dave was single at the time and did not have a wife to take care of all the little details of his life. Arriving at the hospital in fumes, I was quickly ushered into the waiting wheelchair to begin a scary and solitary labor. Ignoring her own pressing problems, Nancy stayed with me until I was "comfortable" in the delivery area. It was there that she confided in me some of her horror stories of back labor. Since back labor was relatively rare, she saw no reason to scare me ahead of time, but since it appeared that, like it or not, I was in back labor, she decided to impart some of her tried-and-true tips on getting through it. By changing positions frequently to take the weight of the baby off my back, alternating sitting, leaning forward and putting my weight on my elbows, and kneeling on my hands and knees, she suggested, the pain might not seem quite so intense. I looked at her in disbelief. What in the world was I getting myself into? Why was this not covered in childbirth classes? There was no way my enlarged body could maneuver into those positions. How could I possibly do this on my own? I was more open to her suggestion that I put a hot water bottle or an ice pack on my back. As soon as we were certain that yes, I was definitely in labor, Nancy put a call through to Skip in Chicago. By now it was after 5 A.M. and she had no other choice but to leave. It was time for her to go back home to wake up Sarah and Ann Elizabeth to join Tom in Cincinnati.

Scared, lonely, and in excruciating pain, I was not a happy camper. Nurses, hoping to catch a glimpse of my husband, kept peeking in my room but did not stay for long when they realized Skip had not yet arrived. The cold steel gray walls of the room did nothing to brighten my mood. My only company was the constant beating of the baby's heart monitor. Taking slow deep breaths in between breath-stopping contractions proved to be quite a chore. Things were definitely going a little too fast for my liking. Try as I might, I could not recall this solitary scenario playing out anywhere in my master plan.

Doctor Prangley entered my room at about 6 A.M. Finally, a friendly face. It only took him a few minutes to assess the situation and to call down to anesthesiology. I gained an understanding as to why my doctor was so well respected. "I do not like to be in pain, and I don't like my patients to be in pain," he announced, "Please get the anesthesiologist to Room 5 immediately." I must admit I did nothing to argue against the administration of anesthesia, and I never experienced a sensation quite as lovely as the deadening of my back pain, compliments of an epidural. *Good news. Bad news.* Ultimately *great news. Good news:* My back spasms were under control. *Bad news:* The anesthesia caused my labor to slow down. *Great news:* If my labor slowed down enough, my husband might make it home in time for the delivery.

Meanwhile Skip was in a race to get back to New York. He took a cab from downtown Chicago to the airport, got the last seat on the first flight back to New York, and grabbed a cab at La Guardia to pick up his car at Shea Stadium. Incredibly the cab driver had no idea how to get to the stadium (although you can see it across the road), so Skip switched places with the cab driver and drove himself to Shea. A few speed records might have been posted that morning on his trip from New York to Greenwich, but he did make it to the hospital in time and was there to hold my hand in the delivery room as promised.

By the time Skip arrived, the anesthesia had taken hold and I was "relatively" comfortable. My breathing was somewhat under control, and my anxiety level was rescinding with every update of Skip's imminent arrival. I finally relaxed when he entered the room and sat down next to me. Oblivious to my disheveled appearance, I mistook the look of concern on Skip's face to assume that there must be some complication in the delivery. The only actual complication at the moment was keeping the hospital's NY Mets fans out of our room. I have never felt the need to be the center of attention; however, I was getting a little piqued at all the fuss that was being made over Skip's arrival. Hello? Who do you think is in labor? Suddenly our baby decided she had waited long enough, had given her father enough time to arrive, and ready or not she was coming. With approximately another hour of heavy breathing and labored pushing, I delivered a 5 pound, 8 ounce, beautiful baby girl. Skip was handed our daughter right after she had scored a perfect 10 on the Apgar scale. Meghan stopped crying as soon as she grabbed onto her father, and he's been wrapped around her finger ever since.

Family leave is very limited during the season. Skip returned to Chicago the next day while I stayed in the hospital to receive private instructions on the best way to bathe a newborn. In true family form, the Mets wives shared in our celebration. While I was more than happy to have delivered in the sterile hospital environment, I welcomed the insightfully comforting visits of Dee Matlack, who had just received her mid-wife certificate, during Skip's absence. Five days later my husband had us all buckled up in our seats as we slowly maneuvered the winding roads of Greenwich back home, never to get a good night's sleep ever again.

Mets wives group photograph before the players/spouses game at Shea Stadium, 1978. Kathy is in the front row, sixth from left.

GIRLS JUST WANNA TO HAVE FUN

The 1978 New York Mets wives fielded a competitive team on the charity softball circuit. Raising a great deal of awareness along with some monetary support to a wide variety of causes, we caravanned around the greater New York area engaging in some low-level competition and good-natured fun.

In contrast to the spousal squad I participated in with the Angels which, like everything else in California, had more sparkle than substance; there were a number of accomplished athletes on our New York roster. The granddaughters of Joan Payson and Beebe and Whitney De Roulet, had inherited not only their maternal grandmother's love of the game, but also some long lost relative's awesome athletic talent. Mae Mays, Carol Kranepool, and Mary Valentine, the daughter of Ralph Branca, could also hold their own on the playing field. Decades before Reality TV took real life individuals and placed them in situations totally out of their comfort zones, the publicity director of the New York Mets convinced our group of wives that we had the ability to graduate past the yearly husband vs. wife game and the occasional TV sitcom exhibitions to expand the family-friendly image of the New York Mets out into the surrounding islands (Long Island, Staten Island, etc.) and compete against other female fielding forces. The good will and good publicity we generated eventually led to a benefit-laden booking on the beautiful Island of Bermuda.

This trip was the brainchild of Dani Torre, Joe's wife at the time, who was not one to sit around and sulk while the team was away and decided it was time for the wives to enjoy life a little while their husbands were off on the California coast. How she convinced a sponsor to organize the trip and pick up all the hotel and flight costs still remains a mystery to me, but in no time at all her ingenious suggestion turned into a week long, adults only, exhibition itinerary.

I had a slight twinge of guilt leaving my one-year-old daughter behind for the week, but I had no doubt that she would be content with the onslaught of attention she was sure to receive from my parents and her two young crawling cousins. As much as I hated to admit it, I knew that out of sight, out of mind was a psychological reality to a happily tired and fully fed toddler.

And so it was that I joined the other New York Mets wives in mid-June at JFK airport, checked my suitcase and equipment bag through, and boarded a southern-bound flight towards Bermuda. In less than two hours our plane was being beckoned by the beatific beaches and began lowering its landing gear and descending onto the tropical tarmac. Normally it was our husbands who were off on new and exciting adventures. This trip was our chance to fly. More often than not, a baseball spouse is referred to not by her own name but by the rather condescending nomenclature of "the better half." Imagine our astonishment as we walked through the mosaic encrusted corridors of Bermuda's International Airport to find banners welcoming the New York Mets wives as a whole, accompanied by our individual names scattered around the perimeters of the elongated signs.

Walking out into the brilliant sunshine, we were captivated by the soothing simplicity of the island retreat. Immaculate sidewalks sparkled in the summer sun, contrasting with the brilliant blue sky and the lush landscape. Good-will ambassadors of the island welcomed us to their "home" and guided us to our team transportation for the week—a two-tiered spacious vehicle with enormous windows allowing us unlimited views. This motor bus was driven by an engaging Bermudian who would spend the next week relating bits and pieces of fact and fiction about his native island in a spell-binding manner. What a treat it was to not be the one in charge for a change. All of our needs were being looked after. Our luggage was collected and reappeared inside our individual rooms an hour later. Feeling that we had been transported into a pampered wonderland, our group boarded the bus and bounded out over the coastal causeway. The soft blush emanating off the countryside calmed our pounding hearts. Not only were there acres of flowering bushes filled with fuchsia flowers, the homes themselves were painted in a plethora of pink patinas. In contrast to the lovely little mauve cottages lining the pink sand, the turquoise water could have flowed right out of an Impressionist watercolor. The winding roads of the island were punctuated with colorful golf courses and dotted with white-attired tennis partners volleying on terra-cotta clay. As we rounded the round-a-bouts (on the wrong side of the road), we were struck by how few cars and how many motor scooters graced the roads. To ensure both the safety and the serenity of the island, tourists were not allowed to rent cars, leaving the mopeds and bicycles to ramble over the highways in relative peace. There was no doubt we had left the bumper car traffic on FDR Drive back in Manhattan. Slowly, but surely, our scenic ride concluded at the inviting inn, seated upon a spectacular beach on the outskirts of St. George's Parish, Bermuda.

A warm gust of wind greeted us as we stepped off the bus and made our way into the hotel lobby. We picked up our room keys from the smiling concierge and were shown up to our cozy rooms. The concept of customer service must be ingrained at an early age in the local culture for it to be so pervasively consistent. When the bell hop inquired "if there was anything he could do to make our stay more pleasant," he actually waited and listened for an answer and was willing to accommodate them. Roommates had been assigned by the travel agent (undoubtedly with some subtle suggestions from the Mets management), and I was delighted to find myself rooming with Mary Valentine. In this "wow, what a small world we live in" society, I found that I got along with Mary as much, and perhaps even more, than I had Bobby's first wife, Roxanne, in California. I never became privy to the cause of Roxie Valentine's break-up. Suffice it to say some women are just not born to bear the brunt of a baseball wife's emotional burden.

After unpacking our bags, we took a leisurely stroll around the property. Soon it was time to return to our room and dress for the 6:00 "Welcoming Cocktail Reception" on our agenda. Mary and I outfitted ourselves in our best Big Apple attire and walked down the garden-inspired hallway heading towards the elevators. Stepping onto the lift, I pushed the starred button to whisk us up to the top floor. When the steel grey doors opened, we were struck with awe as we entered an enormous, pale pink ballroom. Floor-to-ceiling windows surrounded the room and allowed us to survey miles and miles of sumptuous scenery. This tranquil moment was quickly transformed into one of abject panic when we were introduced to our competitors for the upcoming tournament. Luckily I had a good grip on the stem of the fragile flute of Waterford crystal I was holding when I first came face to face with our powerfully-built opponents.

To say our competition was not exactly what we had expected would be a cosmic understatement. We had assumed that we would be scheduled to play against teams similar in size and talent to those of the charity circuit in New York. We envisioned vying against a team of fair-haired, British-born, Junior League socialites. While this debutante description suited the organizers of the tournament to a tee, the participating athletes appeared to be scarily more skillful. There had been some miscommunication between our New York booking agent and the Bermuda Department of Tourism. In some cruel quirk of fate, we had been scheduled to compete in a round-robin tournament against the Bermuda national team and the All-Star Caribbean national team. From the first "so pleased to meet you" introductions at this opening party until the last "strike three" in the ninth inning of our final game, I was fearfully fascinated by our opponents. I had never brushed shoulders with such an imposing group of women exuding so much confidence and exhibiting so many muscles.

Cleats. The Bermuda National team wanted to wear cleats. Who in the world wanted to cover second base when a runner slid into the base with cleats on? A suggested list of rules and regulations had been handed over to our manager for our approval; first among their requests was to allow the wearing of cleats. While we did not want to appear difficult, we all desired to return to the States in one piece—there was no way we would consent to the wearing of cleats. Did they really think that we were competitive athletes? The only diamonds we felt comfortable in graced our ring fingers; we controlled the comforts of home, not the conflicts at home plate. Perhaps a little more practice should be added to our itinerary. We didn't want to embarrass ourselves or the Mets organization. We'd have to forget about collecting charming little sea shells on the coral sand for the moment. We needed to corral our team to practice improving our softball skills, or we would be shelled ourselves.

The "possible" morning practice became mandatory. Sun bathing could wait until the afternoon; we needed to work out some survival strategies the next morning. Our insistence on banning cleats was okayed, but judging from the physique of the opposing pitchers, we were going to have more than the absence of cleats to combat. On a bumpy, cow pasture of a softball field, our scared and semi-skillful group of spouses headed out onto the field the following morning and assumed our assigned positions. Initially, to make it easy for the fans to identify with the team, it was suggested that the wives would simply mirror their husband's positions. Soon into the first practice, it became obvious that certain vertically challenged wives (me) did not share the physical proficiencies of their husbands. The first time I stood on the mound, mimicked Skip's set position, wound up, and hurled the ball forward, the ball limply bounced about twenty feet in front of home plate. My pitching career was curtailed and quickly fizzled out all together. Since my husband was the number 1 relief pitcher on the Mets team, it was mandatory that I be in the starting lineup, but the question of the day was: What position could I play without causing too much damage to the team's defense? Ever since elementary school days, my softball position of preference was short field. This was the perfect position for someone who had above average speed, but limited catching and throwing ability. Playing behind a competent second baseman, I became adept at running after a ball that occasionally scooted through her legs or dropped behind her head before it rolled all the way out to the outfield. It was also within my limited range to pick up the ball coming in from center field on a weak throw and relay it to the second baseman.

Major league players are scouted on the basis of their speed, their hitting, and their ability to hit with power. In the book *Moneyball*, Billy Beane is touted as one of the few baseball insiders who would have appreciated my unique contribution to the team—the ability to get on base without the benefit of a hit. Topping the height chart at only five feet flat, I was in possession of an exceedingly small strike zone. I had perfected the fine art of shrinking even more at the plate. By bending my knees and hunching my shoulders I was able to significantly down-size my strike zone to a minuscule target. While my more talented teammates would stride up to the plate, take a level stance to connect for a line drive, or set up strongly to swing for the fences, I possessed a higher on-base percentage because I employed my clever mind to compensate for my limited matter. Three times every game I would scrunch down low and gratefully accept a free trip on four balls to first base. The combination of my speed and the extenuated time I was given by my more powerful teammates to sprint to the next base allowed me to score more than my fair share of runs.

This "wait and see strategy" did not work out very well with accurate control pitchers. I had been married to a pitcher for long enough to appreciate the advantage of critiquing the opposition before facing them. On days when plan number 1 could not be effectively employed, I was forced to employ my number 2 strategy—bunting for a base hit. I had discovered that even when I fully intended to swing away, the ball generally died as soon as it left my bat. Deception lies in the heart of baseball. The pitcher tries to deceive the hitter, and it is only the effective batters who are successful in second-guessing the pitcher. As I walked up to address the plate, I would not turn my body around to bunt, thereby tipping both the pitcher and the catcher off to my true intentions; instead I swung away with my less-than-powerful stroke and pounded the ball midway between the pitcher and the catcher. More often than not, this surprise strategy resulted in an infield hit. Regrettably, it occurred to me that neither one of these optimistic options was going to work very well against this talented team of women warriors. By my own amateur calculations, I assumed I would probably have difficulty implementing my number 1 base-on-balls plan and, most likely, would run into problems with my number 2 bunting strategy which left only option number 3 available—pray for rain.

If games could be won simply on the basis of enthusiasm, we would have held our own. Every partner/player was open to any and all suggestions. Batting against our own pitchers, the meat of our offense had some really great rips. Our fielding still had a few major flaws, but at the conclusion of a grueling grounding practice, we were managing to catch more balls than we dropped. Mentally we had gained a modicum of confidence; physically we were still far from competent. By the end of our two-hour workout, the entire team reached the same conclusion—to avoid being humiliated by our Amazon-looking competition, we needed to implore Chalchihuitlicue, the Aztec goddess of rain, to shower us with precipitation to preserve our dignity.

Our softball squad was not alone on the practice field. A scout from the opposing squads had arrived incognito to scope out our practice and report back on our strengths and weaknesses. Rather than accurately report on the relative ineptitude of our infield, the spy sent back his supposition that we had somehow gotten wind of their attempt to scrutinize our skills and sent a bogus, talentless team out on the diamond to throw the opposition off course. He was not sure where the real major league wives were practicing, but he was convinced that the group he had been watching had never participated in serious softball. While we all outwardly laughed when the story was circulated around the hotel, inwardly we cringed at the truthful assessment of our athletic ability.

After being dropped back at the hotel following the morning practice, my first inclination was to go back to the room and collapse, but there was no time for that. After a long, hot shower and some considerable churning over our conservative clothing choices, Mary and I reconvened in the lobby where our devoted driver was waiting. Our team had been invited to afternoon tea at the Governor's Mansion. What a thrill for a history buff! Set high up on a hill overlooking the north shore of the city of Hamilton, the ivory stone towers and arches of Government House took us back to the nineteenth century in which the Scottish-inspired structure was constructed. The British Governor of Bermuda is appointed by the Queen and rules over this quaint, colonial island with support from the local Parliament. The Honorable Sir Peter Ramsbotham and Lady Ramsbotham graciously welcomed our softball team to their home and introduced us to some amazing art work adorning the walls that had been painted by local Bermudians. We then moved out of the drawing room, through the enclosed-glass sun room and out into the lawn. Meticulously kept gardens surrounded the mansion. Large bougainvillea vines, herbaceous borders, and a stately old rose garden framed the panoramic harbor. A traditional English tea had been set up on the terrace. Crustless offerings of cream cheese and cucumber tea sandwiches along with some rather lovely lemon scones (the clotted cream I could do without) enticed our palates as we made a valiant effort not to let any of the Earl Grey tea spill onto the Wedgewood saucers. The Governor and his Lady put forth a concentrated effort to make us feel at home as we discussed the similarities between American baseball and English cricket. All too soon our soiree with English society came to a close. I would have been content to spend the next few days exploring the pathways amid the thirty-three acres of grounds on the premises rather than attempt to field ground balls on the base paths the following day.

Yes, Virginia, there is a Santa Claus. Our prayers were answered. The skies opened up and rained out our first two games. Severe storms were on the horizon for most of the week, and while we were a little disappointed that we were not able to completely unwind at the beach, we were perfectly relieved that we would not be facing the windup of the six-foot Nationals pitcher that night. The itinerary change in our schedule came as a welcome relief. Instead of heading out to the stadium for imminent slaughter, our bus would be dropping off at Front Street in the middle of Hamilton Parish for the remainder of the damp and drizzly day. I have to say that the shopping in downtown Hamilton, Bermuda, was deliriously dashing, an Anglophile's

Left to right: Sharon Zachary, Kathy Lockwood, Carole Kranepool, Nancy Pig-
natano, Lady and Sir Peter Ramsbotham, Mae Mays, Joy Murphy, Debbie Metzger,
Sandy Swan, Dani Torre in Hamilton, Bermuda, 1978.

dream come true. Unusual items of impeccable quality were smartly displayed
in a customer-friendly fashion. Quaint little shops lined the street with one-
of-a-kind hand-made linens. Wonderful, colorful woolens and soft cashmeres
were gracefully displayed on the counters at Trimingham's. Scottish tartan
plaids (I purchased matching kilts for myself and my one-year-old daughter
and a tie for Skip) came in every imaginable color combination. Dashing in
and out of specialty shops between storms, we ran into other waterlogged
wives flooded with purchases. Perfume, china, crystal—so much to look at,
so hard to decide how we could get it all securely stuffed into our suitcases.

Our luck only held out for so long. The skies cleared up enough to get
in two games. Enthusiastic fans filled the stadium and had a lot to cheer
about as their home town heroes successfully trounced the New York Mets
wives. Very few New York fans had come out to support us, but I'm certain
it was more our lack of talent than our lack of support that mattered. To the
best of my memory, I'm almost certain that I was the only batter to reach
first base. While my teammates did their best to swing away and attempt to
hit the fast-moving softball, I strode up to the plate and subsequently
scrunched down low and was awarded a number of walks by the frustrated
larger-than-life pitcher. Our opponents' intensity decreased rapidly when
they came to appreciate the true limits of our athletic ability. Of course they
wanted to win, but they were not so malicious that they wanted to destroy
us. We actually got along great at the post-tournament party back at the
hotel. We all understood the roots of their competitive nature when they
were playing for their national pride, and we were all relieved that, having

only had to suffer total humiliation twice, we still had a little pride left of our own. We couldn't wait until we got back to competing against our semi-competitive, semi-talented contemporaries again.

The game cancellations gave us a chance to enjoy the night life on the island. One night we ferried over to the South Hampton Princess Hotel to listen to The Drifters, a group whose name we could identify with. Their soulful performance brought all in attendance past the neon lights of Broadway and up to the top of the roof to that peaceful existence, away from the bothers of the world" Our final night on the island found us gathered in a nearby cocktail lounge reliving our quasi-athletic feats and follies. The last time I occupied a stool in a drinking soirée with a group of women I was still in college. From the perspective of a happily married thirty-year-old, it was fascinating to observe the interpersonal connections unfold. Subtle communication is translated through body language. It was hard not to laugh at a few of the egocentric executives who sauntered over to our group offering to buy us a drink. I found it not so humorous when one or two in our company took them up on the offer. Mary Valentine and I made eye contact, nodded, got our check, and left before we witnessed any encounters we might not want to remember later. It was apparent that at least one of the girls in our group had a different idea of what kind of fun girls wanted to have.

Our time in this tropical Neverland was nearing its end. It was time to pack up and return home. With all the rain-outs, which precipitated subsequent shopping excursions, our suitcases were considerably harder to close on the way home. Our hosts, the Department of Tourism, had given us precise instructions as to what purchases needed to be declared at the customs office. One unscrupulous spouse had some bizarre suggestions about stuffing sweaters inside the legs of old pants or wearing home the clothing we bought in layers, but the rest of us agreed that avoiding the small excise tax was certainly not worth the huge hassle to trying to deceive the customs' agent. With our customs forms filled out and our suitcases stuffed to the gills, we stepped in line to go through the customs check and then on to the terminals to board the plane. Random suitcase inspections were conducted, and we assumed we had all passed through without incident. As we gathered in the lounge ready to board our plane, we realized that one member of our party was missing. Joy Murphy, the stylish, diminutive wife of the Mets announcer Bob, was being held up in customs. If any member of our party was above suspicion of trying to sneak anything past customs, it would be Joy. Joy was a little bit older than the majority of the wives and treated us more like daughters. She had semi-lectured us on the importance of declaring any and all purchases we had made. She herself had not purchased anything on the island and I guess that is what caused doubt in the inspector's mind. How could a fashionable lady such as Joy not succumb to the shops on Front Street? Every item in Joy's suitcase had been emptied on the counter and shaken. The lining of her suitcase was even checked for contraband. Finally the authorities reluctantly released Joy and her now disheveled suitcase. Joy was not very joyful about her terse treatment. Since that day, I always get a twinge of trepidation whenever I step up to a customs search. I have never tried to cover anything up, but I realized at the conclusion of our idyllic island odyssey that having nothing to hide does not mean you might not get frisked.

Our dreamy Bermuda-bound adventures ended with a sharp wake-up call as our plane skidded to a screeching halt on the runway in New York. Tired and just a wee bit tanned, we retrieved our packages from the overhead compartments, squeezed down the narrow aisle to depart the plane and headed into the terminal. Back home. Back to reality. There were no banners or cheering crowds announcing our arrival. Trudging our way to the baggage claim, we were on our own to capture our suitcases as they slowly spun around the carousel. The "relax, you're in paradise" mentality had merged into "wake up, you're in rush hour traffic" as we said farewell to our teammates and dispersed in different directions to join the bumper-to-bumper traffic on the Long Island Expressway.

Early the next morning I was back behind the wheel of my own car, traveling from Greenwich, CT, to Springfield, MA, to reunite with my daughter. True to my mother's word, Meghan was blissfully content splashing away in a little plastic pool with her cousins. While she did make an effort to toddle over and give me a big wet hug, she immediately ran back to her water play as if I had been away for only a few minutes rather than an entire week. Later that evening Meghan tearfully waved goodbye to my parents as I strapped her into her carseat after dinner and headed for home. Fortunately she fell fast asleep in a matter of minutes while I joined hundreds of other solitary women focusing on driving carefully with a baby on board as I retraced my route back to the Merritt Parkway.

Carrying my sleepy child up the stairs and tucking her in her cozy crib, it struck me how life enfolds; some of my experiences had changed so much during the past week, but the ones that really mattered had remained remarkably the same. Late the following evening, Meghan and I were back on the road again, this time heading to the airport to meet Skip's plane in the wee hours of the morning. External obligations had forced us in opposite directions for the past week, and now we were being given the chance to revive our internal love. Thrilled to be reunited as a family, Meghan serenaded us with nonsensical nursery songs all the way back to our secluded home in the woods. The weight of responsibility was temporarily lifted off my shoulders as Skip hoisted our daughter out of her holster and up to her room before we collapsed in our own.

ON THE ROAD AGAIN

Baseball wives rarely accompanied their husbands on road trips, and unless the team was scheduled against the home town team of the player's extended family, to find a professional baseball player traveling with a toddler tagging along was virtually unheard of. The sheer madness of rushing from the ballpark to the airport, flying halfway across the country, landing in the middle of the night in a strange city, winding through the terminal, catching a shuttle to a hotel to arrive at a downtown location devoid of playgrounds and playmates did not fit into the rational rhythm of most prudent parents. Skip and I had a tendency to march to a slightly different drummer. Our daughter's second birthday fell at the end of a short road trip—three days in Houston followed by three in St. Louis with an off-day in the middle. Skip had recently strained his shoulder, and the extent of the injury was still unknown. What we did know was that he would be sidelined for the week. He was still expected to travel with the team to take advantage of the daily massage, whirlpool, and ice treatments executed with vigorous enthusiasm by the Mets trainer, Joe Deer. Talking into account Meghan's birthday celebration, the day-to-day monotony of a closer who is confined to the dugout, and the fact that my husband knew I was dying to experience the rumored southern hospitality of the Houston area for myself, Skip secured a spot on the chartered flight for his wife and daughter on the upcoming road trip.

We turned quite a few heads as we trudged into the terminal as a family. I'm not sure if it was the patchwork diaper bag slung over Skip's left shoulder or the matching mother and daughter yellow-flowered sun dresses draping his immediate entourage, mine being of the maternity mode, that really had heads spinning. A gracious stewardess shepherded us onto the plane ahead of the rest of the team and settled us into a quiet corner of the aircraft, hoping against hope that we would not cause any undue commotion during the cross-country voyage. The contents of my canvas bag overflowed with crayons, coloring books, paint-with-water posters, and an entire Weeble family that could rock back and forth on the floor without rolling down the aisles and would hopefully occupy our daughter until she fell asleep, satiated by the small bottles of juice and baggies of Cheerios with raisins I had packed in a small cooler. I feel sorry for today's parents who would find it impossible to make it past security with enough snacks to satisfy a spirited toddler. Miracle of miracles, our daughter was so worn out by the excitement of the afternoon game and the attention showered on her by the savvy stewardess that she fell asleep within a half an hour of take-off. Many of the players on the team were not even aware of our presence on the plane until Skip departed from the plane with a small sleeping bundle in his arms.

Once on the ground, the traveling secretary made sure our bags made it onto the team's bus as Skip, my daughter, and I hailed a cab and hurried to the hotel before she woke up and got a second wind. Within an hour of our arrival, Meghan was tenderly tucked into her crib (which fit nicely into the large walk-in closet), and her exhausted parents breathed a sigh of relief that the initial leg had been accomplished with hardly a hassle.

With the first hint of sunlight the next morning, at an hour when many

major league baseball players were just getting to bed, I was up early endeavoring to
keep my exuberant offspring from spring-
ing out of her crib. Unpacking the tub toys
from my suitcase, I ran a bath for Meghan
and grabbed a cup of coffee for myself.
After listening to his daughter splash and
soak her family of yellow rubber duckies
for over half an hour, Skip realized that any
opportunity for peace and quiet had come
and gone. Morning had arrived, and it was
time to break down, wake up, and order
some pancakes. In the past I had never been
a very big fan of overpriced room service,
but the luxury of enjoying a hot breakfast
without wondering if your toddler is toss-

Skip, Meghan and expectant
Kathy in Houston, Texas 1979.

ing her toast across the formal dining room is, as the ad goes, priceless.

Mid-morning found us meandering around the magnificent shopping
mecca known as Houston's Galleria. Validating the saying "everything is bigger in Texas," an enormous, airy, glass atrium encompassed an immense shopping center. Dressed to the nines, the highly polished spouses of the wealthy
oil executives eagerly examined the latest styles at Versace, Gucci, and Chanel,
their shopping spree mirroring a materialistic version of King of the Mountain. I had never been obsessed with soap operas, but still I could envision
the pencil-thin, overly made-up, exquisitely-coiffed customer base conferring
with the equally elite sales staff at Neiman Marcus in choosing the perfect
costume to wear to a dinner party at *Dallas's* South Fork Ranch over the
weekend. I was rounding in to my new shape and beginning to wedge my
increasing weight into my two-year-old maternity wardrobe, so I felt no
desire to delve into the designer showrooms. I was raised to appreciate the
value of a dollar way too much to even consider the exorbitant outfits at the
classy children's boutiques. As we passed one window display, my daughter
Meghan caught sight of a pair of white ruffled bloomers on a mannequin.
She decided that she had to have those ruffled panties. Easy enough, how
much could one pair of tiny underpants cost anyway? As luck would have it,
the bloomers were not for sale on an individual basis. They came along "at
no cost" with the $150.00, size T-2, white eyelet sundress. Despite her tear-
ful tantrum, we left the store empty-handed without succumbing to the
strong-armed sales pitch.

Towing along a tired toddler, we left before we overstayed our welcome
at the upscale mall and headed back to the hotel to collapse for a nap. The
team bus was scheduled to depart from the hotel around 3:30, and Skip went
down to the solitude of the lobby in plenty of time to hop on the bus with
his teammates. Still recovering from the previous night's flight and the day's

shopping expedition, Meghan slept for over three hours. By the time she awakened, we had just enough time to get dressed, repack my ever-changing bag of treats, and head down to the lobby where the bellman hailed us a cab to ferry us over to the ballpark.

Intense heat has never been my friend. I could feel the starch limply leaving my linen dress as my daughter and I emerged from the taxi to witness the New York Mets battle against the Houston Astros. To my great relief, the oppressive weather outside had no impact on the comfortable conditions on the field. Nicknamed the "eighth wonder of the world" by the Judge Roy Hofheinz, the owner of the Houston Astros, the Astrodome was the first baseball stadium to be enclosed with a climate-controlled domed roof. In keeping with the aura of the Lone Star State, it was big, bigger, and biggest: There was a big parking lot surrounding a bigger circular concrete coliseum which beckoned you to enter the biggest sports area you could imagine. I strolled over to the police officer guarding the nearest gate to inquire where I might find the Will Call window. My slight Boston accent seemed to confuse his Texas twang but eventually he was able to communicate where the family passes were held. A less-than-hospitable ticket teller insisted that I dig down inside my diaper bag to produce my I.D. to confirm that I actually was Mrs. Lockwood. Did she seriously think someone would tote along a toddler to score a free ticket?

Having spent four years shivering inside Milwaukee's County Stadium, I had fantasized an enclosed arena; this magnificent monstrosity far exceeded my wildest fabrications. We could have been sitting inside a Disney attraction. The interior was immense and immaculate. The grass (a.k.a. Astroturf) was bright green, the ceiling tiles reflected a constant daylight hue, and the entire area was devoid of columns to obstruct a spectator's sight. Meghan and I were escorted down to a section that contained comfy red-and-orange cushioned seats. Top this off with the fact that the thermostat inside the stadium was kept at a constantly comfortable temperature, and I felt I could sit down and enjoy the action for hours on end. A few hours later I was woefully regretting that thought. The game was already in the tenth inning, and no end was in sight. Aware that I had a tired daughter sitting next to me and an injured husband glued to the dugout, I managed to make eye contact with Skip in between innings and motioned that I was heading back to the hotel.

Maxwell Smart was the only one in possession of a portable phone at this time. Banks of pay phones lined the interior of the Astrodome, but once you stepped outside the door you were out of luck. I had asked directions to the exit from the nearest security guard and was instructed to follow the orange line down the ramp and outside to the waiting queue of taxi cabs. So far, so good. There, however, is where my troubles began. Once outside I noticed that there were no cabs to be found and no way to contact one. As I turned around to re-enter the stadium the gate had automatically locked and the attendant had given up his post to take in the end of the game. Okay, I thought, now what do I do? First I tried banging on the gate to garner some attention, but the length of the ramp I had just walked down, combined with the roar of the crowd careening off the concrete hallway, was not conducive to conveying my call for help. Failing to arouse any attention at Gate #1, I picked up my dragging daughter and carried her around the exterior of the Astrodome, hoping to find an open gate at the next entrance. No such luck— on to Gate #3. Tired and more than a little bit testy, I continued on my quest for assistance. Suddenly I breathed a sigh of relief as I recognized the sounds of footsteps behind me and assumed help was on its way. Alas, the moment I turned around to attract the attention of my ally, I assessed that the seedy looking man lurking in the shadows was not the kind of help I had hoped for in a dark parking lot. Slowed down by carrying my thirty-pound child on top of the extra fifteen pregnancy pounds, adrenaline somehow managed to help me (almost) sprint to the next gate where I found an attendant arming his post.

Arriving at the gate scared and sweaty, I leapt for joy at the sight of the guard keeping watch over the player's entrance. I should not have reveled with relief quite so fast. "Mr. Southern Hospitality," manning the clubhouse entrance, was not very hospitable. In the late sixties, Dr. Laurence J. Peter and Raymond Hull co-authored a book entitled *The Peter Principle*. The book attempted to explain why things always go wrong. The authors argued that people start out working at a job, become proficient in that job, and then are promoted to the next level. Quite often their past abilities are not suited to their new responsibilities and, consequently, they get stuck in a position they are not qualified for and cannot adequately perform. *The Peter Principle* states that "In time, every post tends to be occupied by an employee who is incompetent to carry out his duties." The ability to follow orders without question does not transform well into a position of having to make judgment calls on your own. This sanctimonious gate guard had recently been promoted to his "important" position and took his sentry assignment seriously. He was in charge and no one, under any circumstances, was going to distract him from his post. Explaining my predicament, I was expecting a warm welcome and a comforting smile, instead I was coldly cautioned: "Sorry, lady, I don't care who you say you are. I'm in charge here, and it's my job not to let anyone past this entrance."

Shocked at his rudeness, I frantically explained that I was being followed by a strange man and needed his help. If he would not let us in, then would he please use his two-way radio to call a cab for my daughter and myself? Not a terribly unreasonable request. "You New Yorkers think you can get anyone to do anything you want," he snapped. "I've been instructed that this radio is to be used only for emergencies, and as far as I'm concerned, hailing you and your child a cab does not fall into that category." By now my annoyance had spiraled into anger. This was certainly not what I had expected of Texas hospitality. Unwilling to chance circling the circumference of the stadium one more time, I demanded, in a tantrum reminiscent of my two-year-old, that I be connected to his supervisor. A Houston police officer was making his rounds and came over to see what the ruckus was all about. Thankfully the local gendarme behaved much more like a southern gentleman. He not only called a cab for us, he personally escorted us to the vehicle. Once back at the hotel a chivalrous concierge helped me out of the cab and into the elevator, restoring my faith in the kindness of most strangers.

Despite my ordeal, I was happy I had chosen to leave the game when I did. The contest went on into the wee hours of the morning, lasting a record-shattering seventeen innings. The next evening I opted to pass up the game in favor of relaxing by the pool with my daughter and then tucking her in early to guarantee a good night's sleep before we hit the road again after the next day's game. When not on the pitching mound, my husband generally possessed a pretty even temper and went out of his way to show appreciation to the visiting clubhouse staff when one went out of his way to improve the players' life on the road. Upon entering clubhouse the next afternoon, Skip went up to the guard and inquired as to whether or not he was the gentleman on duty the previous evening. "Yes, sir," the guard replied. Skip grabbed the guard by his shirt and screamed at him, "How dare you treat my family the way you did," and stormed off to confront the head of security. Shortly thereafter, a sudden switch was made at the security desk. No longer would this "gentleman" be able to offer his brand of Southern hospitality to another frightened family member. The ultimate fate of this guard remains unknown. According to the Peter Principle, "the competence of an employee is determined not by outsiders but by his superior in the hierarchy." For all I know, this callous chap might have been promoted for following his orders and enforcing the letter of the law while ignoring its spirit. Rather than simply supervising the VIP entrance, he might have reached his final level of incompetence, surveying the sedans and station wagons in the player's parking lot.

Our final day in Houston came and went devoid of any further drama. The animated scoreboard kept my young daughter intrigued throughout the game. As soon as the last out was recorded in the top of the ninth inning, Skip met us by the player's entrance to hop into a cab. The Mets had chartered a plane for the next leg of their journey, and it was fueled and waiting to take off by the time our taxi pulled in to Houston's airport. A welcoming stewardess immediately invited us on board. By the time the team bus motored up to the macadam and the rest of the team ambled onto the aircraft, Skip and I were relaxing with a glass of wine, content that our daughter had at long last wound down and fallen fast asleep on my lap. It was time to bid the Lone Star State adios and head toward the golden arch of St. Louis. Much to the relief of her drowsy parents, Meghan slept soundly throughout the flight and hardly even stirred as we departed the plane and descended on the hotel, slipping back to sleep as soon as her head touched the pillow in the hotel's porta-crib. With a sigh of relief and an elevated level of exhaustion, we also fell immediately onto the large mahogany four-posted bed.

True to the adage "no good deed goes unpunished," our daughter was sitting up smiling as the first sliver of sunlight slipped through the sheer curtains. By now accustomed to my role as supervisor of the dawn patrol, I darted out of bed and scooped her out of her crib before she could disturb my sleeping husband. While I knew I probably would regret this new, sunrise tub-splashing, toy-drowning routine once we returned home, in the "whatever works" category, by placing my pillow on the floor of the bathroom and lying there singing silly songs and making up imaginary stories of Meghan's adventures in Neverland, I was able to delay the onset of another energy-filled day inside a hotel room.

Off-days are few and far between during the season, and the scheduled day off in St. Louis was the driving force behind what had prompted us to plunge into this family pilgrimage. Friends in baseball had raved about the St. Louis Zoo, and so our day off would be spent strolling around the fascinating complex. Heading down to breakfast at a still relatively early hour, I was surprised to find so many ballplayers lounging around the lobby. Although he had the good sense not to complain, I could see the longing look in my husband's eyes as he watched his golfing buddies gathering together for an outing on the local links. Like it or not, giraffes, gorillas, and zebras were going to be on his agenda today rather than birdies or eagles.

Both the weather and our daughter cooperated as we spent an enthralling day meandering through the timeless twisting trails with a life-saving rented stroller. Thomas Jefferson would have approved of the accomplishments the architects who envisioned this ecological environment achieved. From the first days of the Louisiana Purchase Exposition in 1904, the giant, elliptical bird cage constructed by the Smithsonian Institution for the World's Fair captured the spirit of flight. Rather than part with it at the conclusion of the exposition, the city purchased the flight cage, and thus began St. Louis' fascination with the aviary population. By the end of the first decade of the twentieth century, the citizens of St. Louis were proud to proclaim the opening of their very own full-fledged zoo—the first municipally supported zoo in the world. Time had been very kind to this valiant venture, and the zoo remains a marvelous example of how research and relaxation can combine to create a compelling compound. Over ninety acres of life-like environments housing hundreds of species pack the park with wonder after wonder. After enjoying one final ride on the Zooline Railroad, a welcome relief for our tired feet, we called it a day at the zoo. Heading back to our hotel, I wondered if there might not be some truth to the silly Simon and Garfunkel song, indeed, there definitely was a lot going on at the zoo. Once inside our room, we collapsed on the couch and waited for the tea cart carrying our dinner to be rolled into the room. What better end to a day than playing hide and seek under a beverage cart? I again reveled at the wonder of room service.

Skip left early for the ballpark the next day to partake in extensive therapy for his sore shoulder. I scoured the hotel's gift shop for reinforcements to my dwindling bag of snack and craft surprises. The Cardinals' ballpark stood within walking distance of the hotel. On a sultry evening, with my tiny toddler in tow, I sauntered over to the stadium earlier than usual to escape the confining walls of our hotel room. I had no trouble locating the Will Call window and attaining admission to the park. More graciously than the ticket takers I met in Texas, the staff inside Busch Stadium exuded warmth. Radiant red windbreakers with the Cardinals logo shone brightly throughout the park, as the welcoming wearers of those jackets politely wiped off the highly polished seats and eagerly ushered patrons to their seats. Our box was located just to the right of the visiting dugout, where my husband could peek out and chat with us in between innings.

Sesame Street had been a fixture on PBS for almost ten years, and Kermit the Frog and Miss Piggy coloring books were some of my daughter's favorites, but Meghan preferred the calming quiet of *Mr. Roger's Neighborhood* to the constant animation of Big Bird and Cookie Monster. The colorful, larger-than-life muppets had a tendency to overwhelm my sensitive child. Soon after securing our seats for the evening, our serenity was shattered by Fredbird, the flamboyant mascot of the St. Louis Cardinals. Fredbird was an animated, anthropomorphized, walking Redbird who delighted in entertaining the children during baseball games at Busch Stadium. Behaving somewhat like Charlie Chaplin in a rooster get-up, this fluffy feathered friend would dance on top of the dugouts and prance up and down the aisles to the delight of the majority of the munchkins in attendance. He had a Pied Piper–like following who trailed him around the park, hoping to get a hug from this gentle giant. He also appeared to have an ego as big as his beak. Fredbird did not take rejection well. Rather than the expected smile, this perky personality housed within the enormous red feathered costume was greeted by a frightened scream from my petrified daughter. Much to my chagrin, this oversized adolescent was not willing to accept the fact that his character was not being welcomed with the anticipated animation he was accustomed to. My patient plea, "Please leave us alone. She really is quite afraid of your presence," was not getting through to this bird brain. Like it or not, Fredbird was determined to win over my terrified toddler. Throughout the evening, he would periodically peer over at Meghan and wave his wing at her. At first his attention was acknowledged by my daughter with a death grip hug around my neck as she hid her face inside my shoulder. His sadistic salutations continued throughout the evening, gradually breaking down her fear, while increasing my own anxiety concerning the mental stability of this rambunctious redbird. He finally stopped stalking Meghan when she returned a half-hearted grin to his gyrations during the seventh inning stretch. I guess his mission to maneuver a smile had been accomplished. For the remainder of the evening, he left us alone to watch the Mets lose another close contest. Upon further reflection I could see why the Cardinals' fans related so well with their mascot. He's an outward representation of the inner spirit of those who come to recapture their youth and relive their own glory days, subconsciously identifying with this larger than life embodiment of the class clown who refuses to grow up.

Rain poured down in buckets the following day. After Skip headed off to the ballpark for his therapy, I headed over to the shopping mall to take one more stab at securing the so far unattainable white ruffled undies we had been searching for all week. A brief break in the rain blessed us with a rainbow outlining the sky and surrounding the St. Louis arch in shimmering colors. Connecting with my Irish ancestry, I hoped we would find our pot of gold (in the form of a clean bill of health for my husband) at the end of this rainbow-colored trip. Success, in the form of a two-pack of white cotton, eyelet, embossed ruffled panties for under ten dollars, finished off my shopping for the week. Splashing through the street with my puddle jumper, I was weighing the possibility of watching the game from the warmth of the hotel rather than fight the rain-soaked elements at the park when the hotel concierge informed me that the game had been called off for the evening. "Would you be interested in taking advantage of the licensed baby sitting service we provide at the hotel?" I was asked. Would I? Quickly securing the service for a time when my daughter would be down for the count and making reservations in the hotel dining room for "two adults, away from any children, please," my husband and I reveled in the peace and serenity of a quiet dinner for two.

The following day our daughter celebrated her second birthday at Busch Stadium. Naturally Fredbird came over to serenade the birthday girl when her name was lit up on the scoreboard, but thankfully, the initial fear had left Meghan, and while not fully infatuated with Fred, at least she could shake his wing without shaking in fear. One more trip to the airport, one more plane ride followed by one last car trip to Connecticut, and we were back in our own home. By the end of this whirlwind week we understood completely why children were not usually brought along on the road! Unfortunately Skip's injury turned out to be a lot more serious than initially assessed. He never pitched another inning for the New York Mets, and the pot of gold at the end of the rainbow sprang from an entirely different source.

7

Didn't We Almost Have It All?

NEVER NEVERLAND

Momentum. Hard to define but essential for success. It's that tiny thrust of energy that develops into an uncontrollable force. It's that small stone that rumbles into a landslide. It's that intangible inner force propelling us to reach for the stars. The baseball career of my husband, Skip Lockwood, had been in motion for a long time and finally had gained the momentum to propel him to the top of his chosen profession in the 1975 season.

After being recruited as one of the top hitting and pitching prospects in the country in 1964, signing with Kansas City as a third baseman, and suiting up as the youngest player on the 1965 Athletics major league team, a series of unfortunate events, including an unanticipated induction into the National Guard during the Viet Nam era, had stymied Skip's career. By the time he had completed his basic training duty in 1967, rookie Sal Bando occupied the coveted corner position with the Athletics. The A's charismatic owner, Charlie Finley, unwilling to give up on any investment, ordered his management to "Get Pat Friday's pitching chart of Lockwood and turn Skippy back into a pitcher." In 1968 Skip found himself at Arizona's winter instructional league, re-learning how to pitch. Blessed with raw talent, his pitch placement, control, and finesse needed some refinement. After a few years on the mound, Skip's pitching career, while moving slowly forward, had yet to find the impetus it needed to take off.

Suddenly the pendulum swung and thrust us into the limelight. Skip's fastball started to explode in his catcher's glove amid the heat of the Arizona desert. This explosion of energy rejuvenated his baseball career and recalculated the course of our lives. By mid-summer of 1975 Skip had been sold to the New York Mets and by season's end had become their top relief pitcher. Our lives had been sprinkled with fairy dust, and we were enjoying the ride. Years of frustration and self-doubt had been replaced with standing ovations and high fives. Inside we were the same loving couple ready to conquer the world, but suddenly we were living in a whole new world.

Baseball directed our days, but when the team was on the road, my young daughter and I would venture out on our own adventures. We'd head down to the dock and board the small boat that would take us to the town's private island. Armed with sunscreen, shovels, and pails, we'd jump on the ferry to spend the day at the beach, joining other young mothers and their children jumping over the ripples in the water, building sandcastles to the sky, and enjoying the gift of just being alive. On cloudy days we'd take long walks in the woods, the length of which was measured in time rather than distance, stopping to examine every bright flower and shiny rock, exploring the small wonders of our peaceful existence. I realized a long time ago that taking delight in the little miracles of life helped put seemingly "big" problems into perspective. In the reassuring words of Fred Rogers, every day was a beautiful day in the neighborhood. On serene autumn days, Skip and I would strap our daughter's car seat onto a cart and play a round of golf. Baggies of Cheerios and cut up apples kept Meghan content while we hit the links. Back at the clubhouse, we would indulge in the best warm chocolate chip cookies in the world! Winter evenings would find us huddled around the fireplace recounting our blessings.

In the last year of a three-year contract, Skip would be eligible for free agency at the end of 1975, but we had no intention of leaving the Mets. After fifteen years of service in professional baseball, our financial portfolio was expected to change dramatically for the better. We loved New York and its fans. Baseball life had transported us all across the country. I learned to rely on inner reserves I never knew existed while I carved out a role for myself in this transient life. A serene English major, I stepped out of the shadows and organized fund-raising fashion shows, played charity softball games, and thought nothing of flying off on my own. The fickle finger of fate had certainly challenged Skip's career, but we had survived that challenge. Fortune smiled and assured us there was no need to grow up just yet.

And then...

Strike one. *Snap. Crackle. Pop.* Something inside Skip's shoulder stretched the wrong way; one minute a tear in a muscle under the shoulder would prematurely tear us away from the baseball's Neverland.

Skip was having another great year as the Mets' closer. He had been pitching often and awesome as indicated by his 1.49 ERA. He had picked up his 7th save on Thursday night, had pitched well on Friday, and recorded his first win on Saturday. The team had been home for over a week and, as I had been doing for almost a decade, I had attended every game of the home stand. The birth of our daughter had made my attendance at the ballpark more complicated, but the connection I felt by attending the games far outweighed the inconvenience.

My daily schedule was a bit hectic. I would wake up Meghan's first cries around 7:00 A.M. and tiptoe downstairs so that Skip could sleep in and get his rest. Breakfast number one consisted of fruit and cereal about 8:00. A second hot breakfast was fixed about 10:30 when Skip wandered downstairs. Meghan needed to be fed again about noon before she went down for her afternoon nap. Skip and I ate a late lunch about 2:30 before he left for the ballpark. By the time I cleaned up the kitchen, Meghan would be up from her nap and ready to play. An early dinner for my daughter was prepared about 5:00, and then we would get ready to take the hour-long drive into Shea Stadium. Thankfully, my young daughter generally fell asleep as soon as we pulled out of our driveway. By the time I had negotiated all the turns on the Merritt Parkway and merged with the traffic over the Whitestone Bridge, Meghan would wake up refreshed and ready to color her heart out at the game. At the conclusion of the game, we would unwind in the family waiting room while Skip iced down his arm, then we would reverse our course and arrive home around 11:30 P.M. Gently lifting our daughter out of her car seat to avoid waking her up, Skip would tuck Meghan into bed while I prepared our midnight menu. The next hour would be spent recapping the night's game and sharing a quiet dinner. The dishes were usually left for the morning, when the entire schedule started over again bright and early at 7:00 A.M. The exhilaration of joining in the emotional high of the cheering fans, combined with the physical exhaustion of keeping a toddler entertained during the late innings of the game had taken its toll on my body. My morning sickness had escalated into an all-day assault, and so I uncharacteristically decided to stay home from Monday's Memorial Day afternoon game to rest. Would the fates have been kinder if I had been in attendance?

The best perk of playing for the New York Mets was the fact that our families could share in the excitement. Albeit a long ride from Massachusetts, our parents and siblings frequently came to visit. As was the case on many summer holidays, many of our relatives had driven down to New York for the Memorial Day weekend series and would join us at our home later for a post-game barbeque. The table was set, the corn had been husked, the potatoes were in the oven, and the steaks were marinating, all that was left was to toss the salad at dinnertime. My 22-month-old daughter had finally worn herself out doing somersaults across the lawn. I grabbed a club soda and a handful of saltines and sat down to "relax" and watch the game. My R & R was short-lived. It was another close game and a call had gone out to the bullpen for #38. For the umpteenth time this year, the fans gave Skip a standing ovation as he jogged in from the bullpen. With a modest amount of Peter Pan cockiness, he took the ball from the manager and started his warm-up. Satisfied with his velocity after only a few pitches, Skip signaled to Jerry Grote, his catcher, that he was ready. On the first pitch Skip threw that fateful Monday, he felt something tear. One pitch. One snap. One pop and suddenly a promising career was at the beginning of its end.

Shea Stadium
Monday, May 28, 1979
NY Mets vs. Pittsburgh Pirates

	IP	H	R	ER	BB	SO
Lockwood	0	0	0	0	0	0

With the first pitch to the first batter in the ninth inning, a small tendon in Skip's shoulder snapped. Skip signaled to his catcher to join him at the mound. Moments later Joe Torre joined in the discussion and immediately signaled the bullpen. The team would not take the chance of damaging their valued closer. Skip retreated to the clubhouse to ice his shoulder. The television announcers spent the rest of the game theorizing about what type of injury might have occurred. Could it be a torn muscle? How long would he be out? Might it require Tommy John surgery? There were no answers, only questions. If my stomach was queasy before, it was now in a terrible quandary. I began to pace, waiting for the phone to ring, praying that he would be all right. We had known many friends whose careers had come to an abrupt end. Skip himself had been given the opportunity to pitch in game-winning situations a few days after arriving in New York due to the career-altering eye injury of Ken Sanders. I recalled waiting with Maryann while the team doctors assessed Ken's injury. Together we had agonized over his injury, neither one of us wanting to consider the possible turmoil ahead. While Ken did recover the majority of his sight, his career never did fully recover from that nosedive. I continued my anxious prayers that this would not be our fate. About an hour after the injury, Skip phoned and, while his words said "don't worry," his voice transmitted a different message.

Determined to stay calm and not overreact, I busied myself with dinner preparations. The kitchen clock appeared frozen in time. Checking my watch every five minutes and peering out the windows for some sign of a car, I recognized the hum of our diesel automobile maneuvering around the winding, stone-lined country roads. I rushed out to the driveway to greet our guests and silently appraise Skip's mood. The weather was perfect for a barbeque, but a cloud entered our backyard the minute I looked into his eyes. A cool breeze swept across the deck as our families joined for a post-game cookout, but there was a storm brewing on the horizon. Skip had put on his game face in front of his parents and pretended that he was fine, but after nine years of marriage and a myriad of muscles strains, I knew that he was worried. Fear only breeds more fear, and I was determined not to allow unsubstantiated fear to take over our lives. Thinking happy thoughts had worked in the past, so I refused to let any encounter with Pirates, even if they be of the Pittsburgh variety, infringe on our safety. Drained from the emotional turmoil of the day, we retired to bed early. Tomorrow would be soon enough to assess the extent of Skip's injury.

Life was throwing us another curveball. Hopefully we could foul this one off and remain in the game. This was not the first time Skip's body had taken a serious blow and hopefully would not be the last. I recalled an incident a few years before where Skip had been knocked off the mound by a wicked line drive that landed just inches from his heart. Somehow he managed to field the ball and throw out the runner at first before collapsing on the ground. In the five minutes it took him to regain consciousness, my world came to a screeching halt. At first only worried about the game, I became fearful for his life. After a short period of time which seemed like an eternity, Skip stood up and walked off the field. Two weeks later he was back to his game-winning form. I prayed that we would be as lucky this time. Living by the motto that "laughter is the best medicine," I tried to alleviate the stress we were both feeling by remembering former formidable foibles. To put this yet-unknown muscle tear into perspective, we stayed up half the night reliving past challenges we had overcome and laughing over our overreactions. A distant memory of Skip triumphing over an apparently life-altering injury at the age of six when he fell through his aunt's window, severely severing his right arm and was informed by the surgeon that he would have only "limited use" of that arm, reassured our restless minds that determination can conquer disaster.

We woke up with the dawn's early light. Our prospects looked a little brighter in the wake of day. Skip's shoulder was a little stiff, but he was able to brush his teeth. Perhaps we had been a little too premature with our paranoia. After all, just because we had struggled so much in the past didn't mean we couldn't enjoy a few good years of prosperity. Putting the nagging doubt that something was just not right behind us, we focused on our task at hand—winning ball games. Never having participated in post-season play, we still remained hopeful that maybe "this would be the year." We tried our best to focus on the positive and keep things light as Skip played his usual hide-and-seek game with our daughter (who kept crawling into his suitcase) while he packed for a 10-day road trip.

Unsure as to when he would pitch again, Skip was very certain about the time he would be spending on the trainer's table. A deep physical and psychological connection exists between a major league baseball player and his team's trainer. A player might admit the existence of a pain or muscle weakness to the trainer that he would never divulge to the manager. The slogan of most trainers seems to be "no pain, no gain." Whether placing your pitching arm in a vat of ice, submitting the ache in your back to the extreme heat of the whirlpool, or having adhesions rubbed out by the masochistic fingers of steel of the physical therapist, the trainer's room is the first and last stop of the day for many athletes. The major role of the trainer is to get the players ready to perform day in and day out, and to this end, he employs every trick in the trade to return an ailing athlete to the lineup. The trainer is paid by the management to field a "healthy" team. At first it appeared that Skip's shoulder problems would be fixed by spending a little extra time on the trainer's table. "Don't worry about a thing, just come in early tomorrow and we'll have you back on the mound by the end of the game," he was told. Amazingly, Joe Deer, the Mets' skillful trainer, fulfilled his promise.

Skip left with the team while I was left home to cope with my own misgivings. By then the majority of the Mets' road games were televised back to New York, and so rather than trying to visualize what was happening through the subtle observations of our colorful radio announcers, I had the advantage of viewing Skip's mechanics close up, thanks to the telescopic lens of the skilled cameraman. I kept my young daughter active all day so she would fall asleep before the televised games came on at night. Alone in my chair, I focused on Skip's pitching form to determine for myself whether or not there was anything serious to worry about, free from the distraction of needing to identify every baby bear in Meghan's picture book. The wife of a professional athlete is more in tune with the subtle actions transpiring on the field than the average television viewer. Every grimace, every hesitation, even the height of every leg kick, is scrutinized by the pitcher's wife as she concentrates on his form. Halfway through the road trip, I let myself relax. Watching the games all week, I thought Skip's delivery appeared normal. His arm showed no signs of distress as he picked up save #8 in St. Louis on Tuesday night and performed well for an inning on Wednesday. A combination of deep massage, ice, and heat, along with an extra dose of pain medication, kept him in the lineup despite the little pinch in his shoulder. Moving to Atlanta, he picked up win #2 with two innings of relief on Friday night and save #9 with a three-inning appearance on Sunday. Okay, so maybe my reaction to Monday's injury was way off-course. I certainly hoped I was wrong. "Sure, there's still a stiffness there, but don't worry, it's going to be fine," Skip acknowledged after Sunday's game. I continued to worry. It's a lot harder to judge the level of pain and discomfort inside another's body, especially when that body is over 400 miles away.

The wear and tear on Skip's shoulder was beginning to manifest itself in subtle ways. Small spasms while performing personal grooming tasks such as shaving and hair combing triggered concern. Retrieving items from the top shelf of the locker resulted in a slight shiver of pain. Skip was relieved to find that he had been give the night off when he entered the Cincinnati clubhouse. Rather than partake in his usual pre-game stretching routine, he took out the crossword puzzle. Instead of running out to the bullpen, he meandered into the dugout. Between handfuls of sunflower seeds, he sipped Gatorade and swapped stories with his bench-sitting teammates. There was no need for him to transform into his maniacal mindset. Suddenly the game started to get out of control. The rested bullpen was having trouble holding off the surging sluggers of the Cincinnati Reds. Skip tried to avoided making eye contract with his manager sitting at the other end of the bench, but eventually he could not ignore the pleading stare and nodded that yes, he could give him one inning—if absolutely necessary. Minutes later, Skip was on his way out to the bullpen to warm up. With minimal preparation and maximum adrenaline, Skip entered the game.

New York Mets vs. Cincinnati Reds. Riverfront Stadium, Cincinnati, Ohio. Bases loaded, no outs. Lockwood comes into the game. Lockwood retired the first batter. One down, two to go. Strike one, strike two....

And then that slight tear that had been an unwanted annoyance for the past week triggered into a full-out assault. The next pitch never made it to the catcher's glove and sailed past the mound and through the infield. As the cameraman's telescopic lens focused in on Skip's painful expression, I knew that something was seriously wrong. He picked up the rosin bag and threw it down with disgust. Something much more distressing than giving up a base hit was unsettling him. Terry Grote threw the ball back to the mound with his usual form. Skip grabbed for it with his left hand and despondently signaled for his catcher to meet him at the mound. This was a very bad omen.

As much as I felt like screaming at the top of my lungs, the last thing I needed was to wake up a tired toddler and deal with a two-year-old temper tantrum. Being an avid reader of pre-natal and early childhood magazine articles, I was aware of the need to remain calm for the health of the baby I was carrying. However, deep breathing relaxation techniques are not that effective when you are watching your husband being led off the mound writhing in pain. Anticipating the emotional trauma I was experiencing, Skip called from the clubhouse and tried to allay my fears. Yes, something in his arm was not quite right, but whatever the problem was, it could be fixed. After all, New York had great medical resources. I heard the words, "Don't worry, everything is going to be fine," come through the telephone lines, but I was not certain if those words were meant to convince me or himself.

Just before we hung up, I remembered to thank him for the lovely foliage that had arrived that morning. Rather than deliver a fleeting bouquet of roses that would wither before the end of the week, Skip had sent a beautiful rose bush that would flourish in our front yard and grow along with our family for years to come—Happy Wedding Anniversary!

Skip returned home and entered the inexact process of medical discovery. The waiting rooms of doctors' offices became our home away from home during the month of June. At first, well-meaning friends jammed the phone lines showing support, but with each passing week of inconclusive test results the calls became fewer and fewer. I continued to attend all the games. Of course I rooted for the Mets to win, but it hurt to see someone else running in from the bullpen with the game on the line. I found that I missed that knot in my stomach that began to emerge around the eighth inning. Sitting in the wives section, I found myself feeling somewhat ostracized. Empathetic with Skip's precarious physical status and aware of its implications to his contract status at the end of the season, most of my friends on the team did not know what to say, so many of them said nothing. I was beginning to feel a little lost in the enchanted forest.

Where Do We Go from Here?

Uneasy summer emotions blossomed into raging hormone eruptions. As my maternity mid-section expanded, so did my anxiety. At the end of the

1979 baseball season, Skip would be eligible for free agency and the possibility of a mega-contract to reward all the sacrifices of the past was almost a given—as long as he was healthy. Skip had started off the season with such promise. A one-man bullpen, he had appeared in 13 of 14 games, and his shoulder was beginning to show the effects of stress. On the fifteenth day, he was given the day off and told there was "no way" he would be allowed to pitch that night.

"A day off" means different things to different people. To a relief pitcher, a day off from pitching means a day on to run extra laps in the outfield and to work out with a few extra weights before the game in preparation for the following evening. During the seventh inning, Skip was approached to see if he might be able to go in for "just an out or two" at the end of the game. The thought never entered my husband's mind to respond, "Sorry, like you insisted earlier, I really need the night off." Instead, Skip grabbed his glove and jogged down to the bullpen to warm up. Instead of warming up in his scientifically ritualistic manner, gradually getting loose over a period of innings, Skip swiftly stretched his sore shoulder muscles and started slamming the ball into the catcher's glove. In a matter of minutes, he was in the game and tossing his final warm-up throws. Sadly, in a matter of just a few more minutes, he had stopped throwing and was calling for his catcher to meet him at the mound. The fickle finger of fate had selected this fifteenth fire-trouncing trip to the pitching platform to fiddle with our future. On June 6, 1979, Skip despondently departed from the diamond in Cincinnati never to return as the commanding closer with the Mets.

Trying to be optimistic, we hoped for the best and assumed that if a shoulder muscle could be stretched so easily from overuse, it must be as easily fixed by rest. After two weeks of rest, which included our "relaxing" family birthday road trip, there was no significant improvement. The only sparkling fireworks on the Fourth of July came from the tin-canned, pyrotechnics variety. We were both a bundle of nerves, likely to explode at any minute, waiting for the results of X-rays and CAT scans. Cautious concern was turning into edgy exasperation. When were the doctors going to diagnose the problem? When could he return to the mound? Didn't the medical profession realize how important it was to our future for him to get back into the bullpen ASAP?

Our families continued to visit on weekends. Post-game barbeques boiled over into unsolicited question-and-answer sessions. We really didn't need to be reminded by Skip's well-meaning dad how much these "incompetent doctors" would be costing us come the end of the season. We were acutely aware of the potential fiscal fiasco. Skip was the ace of the New York Mets bullpen. He was the number 1 reliever in the number 1 media market. He loved New York, and the New York fans loved him back. We had a wonderful home, a beautiful daughter, and another child due in October. We almost had it all. We needed a successful season to be re-signed with the Mets to be financially secure for life.

Skip watching two-year-old Meghan take off to right field, 1979.

While my patience was slowly shrinking, my waistline was rapidly increasing. By Skip's 33rd birthday in August, he had missed over two months on the mound, and we were both troubled at how the season was unraveling. The frequent (and excruciating) cortisone shots never seemed to hit their intended location. There was no let-up in the pain level. The organization deemed it unnecessary for Skip to join the team on road trips. All this free time did was furnish him more time to dwell on him how much his free market value was dwindling. Still, we were confident that the Mets appreciated Skip's value to the team and would reward his past several superlative years with a viable future contract. How little we knew!

The summer sped by with a blur of medical ministrations. Skip's daily torture on the training table, follow-up stress tests, and intense physical therapy combined with my monthly maternity check-ups kept us in and out of doctor's offices. I was rounding into my third trimester and was still losing the battle against the day-long morning sickness that had started in at the beginning of April. It was a relief to have Skip around the house so often playing "Mr. Mom" with my two-year-old daughter and fixing afternoon tea (and saltines) parties for the three of us.

Skip had not pitched an inning in three months. Still, after ten years as a baseball wife, my body was programmed to tense up watching a baseball game. Some habits are hard to break. From the middle of September on, my abdomen would start agitating around the seventh inning of every game the Mets played. A few piercing pains would start in a random pattern, and after about an inning I would start to time the contractions. Just when the pains were consistently about ten minutes apart and I would be getting ready to call the doctor, the game would end—and with it my contractions. I started to believe that, even though my due date was Halloween, my child-to-be was already playing trick-or-treat games with my body. This cat-and-mouse game went on for over two weeks before the Mets season ended on September 30 and my nightly contractions took a short hiatus. The team's successful surge the final week of the season was not enough to propel the Mets into the playoffs.

Back in our earlier spring training days in Arizona, we used to pass an adorable maternity store in Scottsdale by the name of "The Pumpkin Seed." By the second week of October, I made a conscious attempt to avoid wearing anything in an orange hue since my physique now resembled an enormously large pumpkin. During the early fall, the baby merely kicked and hiccupped during the late innings of the playoffs, but when the World Series began again on October 10, so did my stomach spasms. True to form, the Braxton Hicks contractions stopped at the conclusion of every game. Fast forward to October 17, 1979. I waddled into the doctor's office that morning and was told the baby could come at any time during the next two weeks. It was also strongly suggested that, considering this was going to be my second baby and I had been having pre-labor pains for over a month, we not wait too long to get to the hospital. That night, right on schedule, my pains began around the fifth inning. By the seventh-inning stretch, they were eight minutes apart. As instructed, I called my doctor to update him on my progress. Lamenting that he could catch the last inning of the game in my hospital room as well as in his den, he insisted we head to the hospital ASAP. As we traveled over the twisting turns, I was relieved that on this labor-bound trip my husband would be standing by my side, not rushing home from Chicago. With any luck I would be bringing another would-be miracle Met into this world within the hour.

A welcoming staff of baseball devotees showered us with attention at the hospital while at the same time keeping tabs on the seventh game of the series. Some of our friends played on that close-knit Pittsburgh Pirate team, but we were not half as involved in the "We Are Family" mystique of their winning team as we were with delivering another team member into our little family. By the time we were "comfortably" settled into a pre-delivery room, the game had ended and so had my contractions. My doctor was familiar with the peculiar pattern of pain I had experienced over the past month and joked that I had to come to terms with the fact that the baseball season was over. He could not allow me to wait until next spring to deliver this baby. I was instructed to walk up and down the halls for the next hour to trigger some action. If that didn't work, he suggested we secure a copy of a past game and fast forward it to the seventh inning to start up my labor. This on again, off again, pattern continued for the next day-and-a-half while I waddled around the hospital not allowed to eat anything, watching one mouth-watering food advertisement after another. Thankfully, my husband had the courtesy to take all his meals outside of my sense of smell. At long last, after 38 hours of labor (coinciding with the number 38 on the back of Skip's uniform), our second daughter, Maura, wailed her way into our lives. Elated and exhausted, I enjoyed five days of pampering in Greenwich Hospital with my newborn. A steady stream of company, first and foremost being her older sister Meghan, came to share in our joy, bounce on my bed, and have a story or two read, then return home with her grandmother as I collapsed between feedings.

Now a family of four, the time had come to decide where that family would be living the following year. The 1979 season had faded away in shades of concern and confusion. Skip's agent, who had been so exuberantly confident mid-way through the season, was now cautioning us to "be patient"; he would do the best he could to stir up interest throughout the league. Many teams were reluctant to take a chance on a pitcher who missed over half the season and whose future was still unknown. Much to our shock and chagrin, the New York Mets did not make a viable offer. The Mets themselves were in a period of transition. Implausible rumors became reality as the Mets president, Lorinda de Roulet, announced that the team was for sale at the beginning of November. The Mets "one big family" days under the Payson lineage had come to an end as the business bias of baseball took over over the reins.

The last two weeks of October were filled with sleepless nights, partially induced by our newborn who was waking up every three hours for a feeding, but more inspired by the angst of the upcoming draft. Skip was declared a free agent at the beginning of November and was drafted by ten teams, including the Boston Red Sox. Taking the advice of Tom Seaver, Skip had hired Dick Moss as his agent three years earlier and was confident in Dick's ability to broker the best deal available. If we had to leave New York, our first choice would be to move back to the Boston area where both our families still lived. After what seemed to be a lifetime of late night conversations, Dick Moss came to a tentative agreement with the Boston Red Sox. Skip would receive a lucrative contract "if" he could pass a required physical. The upcoming holiday season brought with it more apprehension than usual. Trying to spend enough time with both our families always injected a little stress to holiday gatherings; add a 2½-year-old, a new baby, and a physical exam that will determine whether or not you will continue to have a future in a game that you love, and the seasonal stress level skyrockets expeditiously.

On Thanksgiving Day 1979, we had a great deal to be thankful for and even more for which to be hopeful. Too exhausted from both the physical and emotional drain to entertain both our families in my usual polished-silver-and-crystal fashion, we opted to bring the family to the Greenwich Country Club for their annual Thanksgiving feast. A wonderful dining experience was had by all as the charming staff served up a traditional feast in the understated elegance that could only be found in this stately old building located on top of the hill overlooking the beautiful gardens of Greenwich. Our month-old Maura even cooperated by sleeping through the entire meal. The problem with having dinner out is that, while there are no pots and pans to scrub, there are also no leftovers to snack on for the rest of the evening. Alas, amid every treat hides an underlying trick.

Our newborn daughter subliminally sensed the stress that her parents were under. Despite the supposed immunity of an infant, she contracted a terrible cold the day after Thanksgiving. In an effort to accommodate our incredibly complicated life, Father McLaughlin, St. Agnes' gentle old monsignor, who had devoted his life to ministering to his parishioners and who also happened to be a huge Mets fan, offered to baptize her the Saturday after Thanksgiving to make it easier for our traveling relatives. The way Maura was wheezing during the ceremony made everyone in attendance feel blessed that she was being so blessed! After leaving the quiet sanctuary of the church, many of our friends and past teammates came back to our chaotic home to celebrate this significant event in the life of our daughter and wish Skip good luck in making the grade during his upcoming physical.

The following day we drove to Massachusetts for a final exam that would pass or fail the next chapter of our lives. We left our daughters with my parents and, equipped with face masks and vaporizers, my mother monitored Maura's cold for the next two days while my father became schooled in just how many times Meghan could want to have the same book read over and over again. Skip and I headed down the highway towards Boston and checked into the same hotel my parents had stayed at the night before my college graduation ten years earlier. I hoped that the successful passage of that phase of my life would signify an equally successful passage for us now. Looking forward to a night of uninterrupted sleep away from our newborn, Skip and I unsuccessfully attempted to put our fears to rest.

Early the next morning Skip checked into the rehabilitation center for an anticipated day full of intense scrutiny. An hour later he had passed all the required tests with flying colors. He had no trouble lifting the required weights. After all, that is *all* he had been doing for months. The range of motion exam on the Cybex machine flowed freely as his shoulder moved through a series of complex motions. He had passed! We were elated! He would sign with the Boston Red Sox! The following day Skip signed a four-year, "guaranteed" contract with the Red Sox. We were on top of the world. We had been offered more money than he had made in his entire career. We couldn't wait for our next season in the sun to begin. Yes, we had it all. We believed in the Red Sox, and they believed in us. This was definitely the way it was intended to be. Incredibly, no one asked Skip to throw a baseball.

8

Please Come to Boston

Turn! Turn! Turn

Spring is my favorite time of the year. It's a season of anticipation, a season of optimism, a season of rebirth. Embracing the promise of *printemps*, we arrived early at the 1980 Red Sox spring training facility of Winter Haven, Florida. For a Massachusetts-bred athlete, the chance to play for the Boston Red Sox was a dream come true. Skip had high hopes of recreating that 1967 "impossible dream" pennant-winning season.

Every city had its own unique manner of supporting its team, and Boston's propensity for its excessive love/hate relationship with its players was legendary. True to form, there had been a number of naysayers who questioned the wisdom of signing a free agent who had ended the season on the disabled list. We expected such scrutiny and were certain that once the season got underway, Skip's arm would soon strike back to its intimidating form. The New York Mets' fans had truly been amazing; Skip was greeted with standing ovations for the past five years whenever he entered the game. I had confidence in my husband's physical prowess and in the integrity of the Boston fan base and was certain that, in time, he would forge the same bond with these loquacious lunatics. Granted, I had been shocked on my first visit to Fenway Park as a visiting team wife to hear Carl Yastrzemski getting booed quite so boldly in his home town one afternoon for striking out with men on base, even though he had hit a home run earlier in the game, but Boston athletes accepted the ardor of their fans. Physically, Skip had been pounding the pavement all winter, and his doctorate studies at Columbia relating to the psychology of sports could only enhance his mental preparations.

For the past decade, spring had arrived months ahead of its calendar schedule for us with the beginning of pre-season training in mid–February. Four years of catching the cactus bloom in the Arizona desert followed by six more of shell seeking on the pristine beaches on both Florida coasts solidified my spring fever. With the Brewers, we were able to convince contractors to allow us to occupy a few units in complexes "under construction" in Arizona every spring, as the housing boom mirrored the rising of the Phoenix area in the early seventies. A deserted field one year would be transformed into a landscaped adobe-style complex the next. With all the upfront construction costs, an unanticipated influx of cash was a godsend to a struggling builder. Nearly-finished units opened up to house married spring training ballplayers and their families, who were more than willing to put up with the constant noise of housing construction in exchange for the luxury of spending the spring spread out in two rooms and dining at home instead of climbing the walls inside a hotel room. (I have often wondered whether my breast cancer that occurred twenty years later was somehow related to all the pesticides being sprayed around those instantly landscaped apartment units.)

Pre–season training with the Yankees and the Mets found us moving on to Florida, the snowbird capital of the world. A plethora of efficiency apartments were prevalent in Fort Lauderdale, and endless options of short-term oceanfront rentals had been ours for the asking with the Mets as we reveled in the sun and surf around St. Petersburg. Last year at this time, I was lounging carefree on the beach outside of my stilted beachfront cottage on Treasure Island reading a book while a baby monitor in Meghan's room kept me informed of her sleep activity.

Located in the middle of the state, Winter Haven, Florida, was not a tourist destination. Winter Haven was primarily a haven for retirees in 1980. No emerging businesses spurred new construction, and the town seemed satisfied with its stagnant development. The few apartment complexes in town considered a short-term lease to be six months, not six weeks. After a number of noisy nights in the crowded team hotel, we found a small, two-bedroom apartment in a tired-looking complex that rented to the minor league players during their season. So this was what the reward of a lucrative, long-term contract was all about? I soon discovered that my prior privileged existence of past springs belonged to a former life. Reality, in the form of a sparsely furnished, two-bedroom apartment inhabited by a rambunctious two-year-old and a four-month-old baby who had yet to sleep through the night had arrived. My athletic "older" daughter discovered the art of climbing out of her porta-crib. Equipped with the desperate determination of a harried mother who had not had a good night's sleep in ages, I coerced the manager of the local furniture rental dealer to lease me two cribs for a period of two months, despite their definitive six-month minimum requirement. I was willing to pay anything for the outside possibility of a little peace and quiet.

Cramming one crib in the closet and the other at the far opposite end by the windows, I rearranged the room so that Marua's two o'clock early morning pleas for her bottle would not wake Meghan, who always insisted on a lengthy lullaby to lull her back to sleep. There was no hope at all of getting either child to agree that the day didn't initiate with the rising of the sun around six A.M. It took a week of pre-dawn waking to accept the fact that sleep was just something I was going to have to learn to do without during this spring. Aware of the pressures my husband felt, it never entered my mind that he should share in my somnambulant state. I took refuge in the fact that Skip was home and was able to take the girls for a walk around the complex before dinner every evening. I guess I never fully appreciated the divine luxury of serene loneliness before I had children.

Hope continued to spring eternal, but that hope was being shaded with doubts concerning the possibility of yet another union-mandated work stoppage. We had housed a number of players in our Milwaukee condo during the 1972 strike and had been housed by the Seavers four years later during the '76 spring training lockout. The current basic agreement had expired at midnight on December 31, and the owners were committed to regaining control. The players were seeking a small rise in the minimum salary to reflect the cost of living (the minimum salary being $21,000 in 1979), an increase in pension contributions from the television revenue, and an updated version of salary arbitration and free agency status. Unsuccessful in pushing through a salary cap, the owners were insisting on equitable monetary compensation to reimburse the team that had spent time and money nurturing a young player before losing that perfected talent in the free agent market. Marvin Miller recommended the owners put together a cash fund to compensate the team losing the free agent, but the owners were reluctant to listen to any advice from their powerful adversary. Dissent between the wealthy team owners and those with financial constraints complicated the process—negotiations had stalled and no easy solution was in sight. An undercurrent of unrest permeated the clubhouse and seeped into conversations in the family section. The Boston press had a field day speculating on the ramifications of the seemingly doomed discussions. Skip had been privy to the inner workings of the players association for almost a decade and was distressed that negotiations appeared to be going from bad to worse.

This possible postponement of the season was not a welcome thought coming at a time when he needed to focus on his rehabilitation. After receiving a clean bill of health from his physical therapist, Skip started to rebuild his strength pitching inside the Fairfield University field house (Maura's godfather was both the baseball coach and athletic director of Fairfield). We arrived in Florida even earlier than normal to accelerate his rehab and regain his arm strength. We also looked forward to building relationships with our new teammates. I'm sure Skip missed the camaraderie of the Mets clubhouse as much as I longed for the rapport I had had with the wives. It had been rumored last year that twenty cabs pulled up outside of the visiting clubhouse after a game on the road, but that was last year and who could predict what this year would bring? After all, the one constant in baseball is the certainty of continual change. Life was propelling us in so many directions. We had joined a new team in a new town and were in the process of purchasing a new home for our newly expanded family.

Skip missed the open communication he had with his Mets manager, Joe Torre, but he had been in baseball long enough to understand that each skipper managed in his own eccentric style. Dave Bristol had an in-your-face

confrontational manner, but you always knew where you stood. Del Crandall was a superstitious gentleman who relied heavily on his hunches and concluded that Skip's bad luck had turned into a self-fulfilling prophecy. Dick
Williams was blatantly belligerent and not quite on the same page as my husband, screaming at him once that "he did not need any Bible-reading do-
gooders on his team" during a cross country flight. This was obviously not a
player/manager match made in heaven. Hank Aguirre had given Skip free
rein to regain his confidence and along with it his fastball in Tucson. Since
Yogi Berra was relieved of his duties the same day Skip arrived with the Mets,
he never benefited from Yogi's legendary wisdom. Joe Frazier had a suppor-
tively laid-back managerial mode and carefully critiqued a pitcher's performance after the game so that the pitcher could make the needed adjustments
before the next outing. In the end it was up to the player to figure out how
to conform to the quirks of the manager while improving his own performance. Skip had not yet warmed up to Don Zimmer's prickly personality but
was hopeful he could manage to find a way to deal with his caustic manner-
isms as the season progressed.

Skip never did get the opportunity to slowly work out a relationship
with his new manager. Tensions around the clubhouse got a little testy as
Marvin Miller and Jim Fehr periodically stopped by to keep the players
informed and educated as to the status of the basic agreement negotiations.
There was nothing positive to report on the proceedings. Ingrained into the
veteran ballplayers' conscience was the legacy and the responsibility that each
player had to secure the rights of the future while maintaining the rights of
former, less fortunate, players. There was great resolve and solidarity; there
was also a great deal of apprehension. The coaching staff was being paid by
the owners to field a competitive team and the management team was itself
in transition. How do you choose a 25-man roster from a 40-man squad if
the players go out on strike or if the owners choose to close the club house
doors again? Concentrating on last year's staff made a lot of sense in such an
environment, and Zimmer indicated on more than one occasion his annoyance about not being in on the free agent negotiations, and not being particularly pleased about working a previously injured pitcher into shape.
Through it all, Skip was trying to negotiate some normalcy in his pitching
workouts. As the training season progressed, Don Zimmer's reticence turned
into open hostility about having Skip, who was accompanied with a sizable
salary, on the team. He was not at all interested in discussing Skip's personal
perspectives as to how best he should be utilized. A rational discussion with
an irrational manager was proving to be quite a challenge for my husband.

Spring training games commenced and continued as scheduled through
March, despite the fact that negotiations had stalled. Unwilling to start the
season without a new basic agreement, the Major League Baseball Players
Association unanimously went out on strike during the final week of spring
training, 1980. Just at the time when a pitcher should be fine tuning his skills,

the games ceased. We were in a state of personal panic. How could this night-mare be happening at a time when our dreams were just coming true? Where were we to live? We still owned a home in Greenwich and were scheduled to purchase a new home outside of Boston the next week. Should we go or should we stay? We decided, along with the majority of our teammates, to stay put in Florida until the end of the week, hoping an agreement would be reached. In the meantime, the players worked out on their own without the benefit of training table massages, ice packs for shoulder wraps, or whirlpools for loosening up achy muscles; all in all, not such an optimal arrangement for a recovering athlete.

Neither the players nor the owners wanted to delay the start of the sea-son. A last-minute agreement allowed the season to open as scheduled. How-ever, while the players agreed to take the field as the talks resumed, a deadline of May 23 was set for a new contract to be signed, and the union threatened to strike again if no such agreement was reached. We were finally on route to Boston. Hopefully the future would look a little less murky once we made it back home to the "dirty water" the Standels had made famous on the banks of the Charles River.

So caught up with just surviving the day, I was almost oblivious to the fact that life was not going as smoothly as planned. I was still learning how to juggle quality one-on-one time with my two-year-old while the baby was sleeping with the need to put them down for a nap at the same time so I could get a brief nap myself. It's hard to focus when your mind is so foggy. I longed for the companionship of the Mets' wives, but at the end of the day I did not have the energy left to seek out that much needed spousal support. Even in my semi-conscious state, I was conscious of the pivotal role this sea-son would play in our lives. It was a time we had so much to gain. It was a time to build up our family ties, to laugh with our children and to fully embrace Boston. I fervently prayed that it was not too late for a peaceful set-tlement of the 1980 basic agreement.

Location, Location, Location

1970
1. Brown Deer, Wisconsin
2. Mayaguez, Puerto Rico

1971
3. Tempe, Arizona
4. Greenfield, Wisconsin—Piccadilly Place Apartments

1972
5. Greenfield, Wisconsin—Twelve Bridges West Condominiums
6. Tempe, Arizona
7. Greenfield, Wisconsin

1973
8. Sun City, Arizona
9. Greenfield, Wisconsin

1974
10. El Centro, California
11. Palm Springs, California
13. Costa Mesa, California
14. Norwood, Massachusetts
15. Lynn, Massachusetts

1975
16. Fort Lauderdale, Florida
17. Tucson, Arizona

18. New York, New York (via Tidewater, Virginia)
Various hotels in Long Island
Tuscany Towers in NYC
Springfield, Massachusetts on road trips
19. Lynn, Massachusetts

1976
20. Treasure Island, Florida
21. White Plains, New York
22. Greenwich, Connecticut

1977
23. Madeira Beach, Florida
24. Greenwich, Connecticut

1978
25. St. Petersburg, Florida
26. Greenwich, Connecticut

1979
27. Winter Haven, Florida
28. Weston, Massachusetts

1980
29. Winter Haven, Florida (two rooms in a Holiday Inn with two children)
30. Denver, Colorado
31. Weston, Massachusetts

WHERE YOU LEAD

On April 10, 1980, while my husband was shivering in the freezing bullpen of County Stadium in Milwaukee, Wisconsin, I was trying to keep my cool in a large conference room surrounded by a cadre of lawyers and real estate agents, signing over a dozen documents that would bind us to a twenty-five-year mortgage on our new home in a western suburb of Boston, Massachusetts.

Moving should have been old hat to me by now, having had over 25 addresses in the past ten years, but this move was different. This move would bring us back home to Massachusetts. Skip left his childhood home in Norwood, MA, at the age of 17, less than a week after he graduated from high school, to follow a star and now, sixteen years and twelve teams later, his dream of playing baseball for his home town team had become a reality. A Western Mass native myself, I joined Skip on his cross country journey four days after I graduated from Regis College in Weston, MA. For the past ten years, our lives and our belongings had been in some state of transition.

We purchased our first home, a two-bedroom condominium in Greenfield, Wisconsin, with the eternal optimism of a two-year "veteran" starting pitcher with the Milwaukee Brewers in the fall of 1971. We had agonized for weeks about the wisdom of spending a major portion of Skip's $11,000 salary on the mortgage payments of a $24,000 condo, but in the end we concluded that the investment in our community far outweighed the real estate risk. We felt a deep connection to the Milwaukee area and naively planned to spend Skip's entire career with the Brewers.

I devoted countless hours of creativity decorating our first domicile. Looking back I was imbued with a lot more tenacity than talent, but at 23, I was also unencumbered by the perception of prudence. Not only did I create drapes out of a stylish geometric designer fabric (purchased at a discount outlet), I hung the wallpaper and made lamps for the living room at a ceramic class. A felt wall hanging was assembled with spray glue to match the striped bedspread I had semi-skillfully sewn. The guest room was transformed into a work of art by tacking red and white gingham check fabric up on all the walls, severely bruising my thumb in the process. We planned to be there for a long, long time, and I sought to create a happily-ever-after safe haven.

I grew up indoctrinated by the idea that no home is complete without distinctive wallpaper. The stark white walls of the four apartments I had rented in the past two years solidified that conviction. I searched far and wide for the perfect paper to transform our new condo into a hospitable home; pre-pasted wallpaper had recently been introduced onto the market, but the paper/paste *modus operandi* had not quite been perfected. The tutelage I was tendered in the fine art of wallpaper hanging was derived from the school of trial and error. A safari-inspired covering for the downstairs half-bath was selected solely on the basis of color and design. I had no idea that this delicate paper would disintegrate when dipped into the vat of water provided by the manufacturer. With only the slightest adjustment to straighten out the tusk of an elephant or elongate the neck of a giraffe, the tissue-like paper would tear, causing me to ruin more than one roll of paper and weaken my resolve to hang the rest of the rooms by myself.

Food has always been a great motivator for the boys of summer. Offer home-made spaghetti and meatballs to an off-season athlete and your fondest wishes may come true. An outfielder by the name of Al Yates was spending the winter of '71 in Milwaukee and offered his "expertise" in paper hanging in exchange for a good meal and some Old Milwaukee beer. After struggling with the soggy safari paper the week before, I decided to add form and function to the covering that spruced up the back hallway. I migrated to an extra thick, very '70s, metallic zigzag design—determined that this paper would not fall apart so easily. Al took one look at the paper and cringed. I didn't know that in the world of wallpaper hanging, too thick paper could be as taxing as too thin. I was sent back out for special sizing to slap on the walls before we attempted to attach the heavy foil. I was also informed that this job was going to require another six-pack of beer. I was gaining an appreciation of the do's and dont's of selecting wall coverings. The heavy foil was reluctant to stick to the wall, and the zigzag pattern was all but impossible to match. The two-hour project that had started at noon on Sunday was less than halfway finished by 4:30. My husband and I headed out to the 5:00 evening mass and told Al to take a break while we were gone. Dinner was simmering on the stove and would be ready when we returned. Returning from church, we sensed a few suspicions relating to the well being of our wall the minute we opened the hallway door. Loud music and loud laughter was emanating from our apartment. In the hour-and-a-half since we had left, Al had finished the wallpapering and had also finished the beer. He was relaxing in our living room in the company of our next-door neighbors, waiting to be congratulated on the completed project. Even if Judy Frank had not been an art major with a fine eye for detail, she could have swiftly surmised that I had not intended the zigzag pattern to change direction in the middle of the wall. However, Judy's gracious demeanor did not want to hurt Al's pride by pointing out the obvious flaw when he knocked on their door to show off his work. Cornering me in the kitchen, Judy assured me that there was no reason for dismay—she would help me straighten out the wall the next day. A full plate of pasta and few glasses of Chianti later, I could almost acclimate to the unusual pattern.

I was not alone in learning the logistics of home-owning one mistake at a time. There was a small wall between the two large sliding glass windows in our living room, the perfect spot to install a heavy wooden shelving system to house our stereo, speakers, and a few of our favorite books. With painstaking precision, Skip tapped the drywall an inch at a time to exact the location of the wall studs. He measured and marked and measured again, finally bolting the black cast iron brackets to the wall, reinforced with toggle bolts. Next it was time to secure the thick wooden shelves on the brackets. Success was met with success. Confident that the shelves were centered correctly, he stood back to admire his handiwork. After a little discussion as to which shelf should house the stereo and which one the speakers, Skip placed a copy of Tolstoy's *War and Peace* on the top shelf. In an instant, the solidly secured shelf collapsed and fell down upon the second shelf, which in turn plummeted on to the bottom shelf, sending all the wood and rod iron crashing to the ground and leaving huge holes in the wall where the toggle bolts had been. Should I laugh or should I cry? Our new home now had a gigantic gouge in the center of the room. Fortunately, workmen were still finishing up construction on the far side of the complex. Bribed by box seats to a Brewers game and even more by a bottle of brandy, our wall was repaired within the hour. True to his word, our miracle angel of wall repair returned the following day to professionally install the brackets. We both had a lot to learn about home maintenance.

Much to our dismay, we discovered that job security and baseball were conflicting concepts. A few changes in managers, a constant change in personnel, and a concurrent change (demotion) in my husband's role on the team forced us to face the fact that it was time to move on. Two years after we had so enthusiastically purchased our first "permanent" residence, it was placed on the real estate market for resale.

We left Milwaukee for California at the beginning of the 1974 baseball season with the intention of returning for the winter, but economic reality, in the form of monthly mortgage payments on top of monthly rental fees forced us to reconsider. Since the association rules and regulations prohibited us from sub-letting our apartment, we had no choice but to place it on the market. The Franks, more best friends than next-door neighbors, helped us locate a realtor, and the Cotes, our other munificent neighbors, packed up our belongings, rented a U-Haul, and drove it all the way out to Boston in early autumn. While we still keep in touch through Christmas cards, I regret that time and distance has kept us from retaining the close friendships we shared with these two wonderful couples those first few years in Milwaukee. Financially forced to sell our condo and not at all in tune with the Southern California way of life, we decided to head back to Boston for the off-season and re-group. I have already related my 1974 house hunting adventures, but let me now take you inside of that second home.

The three most important things to consider when purchasing a home are location, location, and location. While a .667 batting average would be incredible, we learned the hard way that two out of three stars in real estate did not constitute a sage purchase. The three-bedroom, ranch-style home that we viewed was located two blocks away from the Atlantic Ocean in Lynn, Massachusetts. We were assured by the real estate agent that the house would easily rent out for the summer. It was also within a ten-minute walk to the center of town where we could catch the Metro North rail line into Boston for Skip's school and my job at MIT. The owner was willing to finance the house herself at a significantly lower percentage than the going rate, and we could move in by the end of the month—what was not to love? In time, we came to understand that there were two things not to love: the taxes and the local juvenile delinquents. At about seven o'clock in the evening, the night before our closing, we received a call from the devious real estate agent to inform us that the $1900 tax bill he had shown us was only a six-month bill. The actual taxes on the property were $3800 for the year. Of course, we should have backed out, but we were so anxious to be back living on our own after having gained over five pounds in less than a month of politely devouring all the calorie-laden baked goodies Skip's mother was baking up that we allowed our hearts to overrule our heads and signed the papers.

Kermit the Frog might have been content being green, but an entire house decorated in dark moss green was a little too much for my taste. Learning from past mistakes, I made more prudent wallpaper choices, and Skip even convinced me to paint the living room and the adjoining dining room an elegant ivory. The off-season sped by as we spent our days ensconced in the Boston collegiate environment and our evenings and weekends creating our own version of *Extreme Makeover Home Edition*. We were relieved when we learned (by the morning paper) that Skip was traded away from the California Angels and looked forward to playing for the Yankees the following year. New York would be an exciting city to play in, but we wouldn't want to live there. My husband and I had mentally adjusted to the lifestyle of the majority of ballplayers. We would maintain a permanent winter residence and rent an apartment during the season. This was not the arrangement we had originally planned for, but then the world of baseball had hardly ever catered to our personal preferences.

The 1975 baseball season challenged us professionally, physically, logistically and emotionally. We left Boston with high expectations of Skip being a starting pitcher for the New York Yankees and returned eight months later with my husband the top reliever for the New York Mets. The months in between were a blur of upheaval and uncertainty. Amidst all our professional anguish, our new home continued to sit empty despite its spectacular ocean access location. I guess we should not have been all that surprised that the assurances of our unscrupulous agent for immediate summer rental occupancy never did come to fruition. Rather than have our house sit vacant for the entire summer, I suggested to my sister that she and her family take advantage of the ocean walk and spend a few weeks enjoying the beach. Anne and Steve welcomed the idea and headed north to vacation. At the time our lives were in a constant state of flux and immediate communication between myself and my family was limited at best. I had alerted Anne that we had contracted to have the exterior of the house painted, but had no idea when the painter would arrive. I was sure that if the house painter happened to show up while Anne and Steve were there, they could all survive.

Players' paths often intersect in the constantly changing world of professional baseball. A few weeks before the trading deadline, our teammate from the previous year, Denny Doyle, a devoted family man with a terrific wife and three adorable little girls, was traded from the Angels to the Boston Red Sox. Through an exchange of Christmas cards, the Doyles knew that we had purchased a home in the Boston area and Denny contacted Skip to see if we might be interested in renting it out to them for the remainder of the season. Of course, we were open to the idea and assumed the Doyles would move in at the beginning of the next home stand. Travel and time zones being a little confusing, we never did get a chance to mention the Doyles' future arrival to my sister. Undoubtedly both parties were totally befuddled by their initial encounter. Denny Doyle was quite surprised to find the house occupied when he arrived earlier than we had expected. My brother-in-law Steve, a huge Red Sox fan, assumed that Denny was the house painter they had been expecting and graciously pointed out to him where the ladder was located. Luckily Denny did not embody the enormous ego ingrained in many ballplayers' brains, and lightheartedly replied that this was not quite the greeting he had expected on his arrival to Red Sox territory. Steve was mortified by his mistaken impression and promptly proffered his hand in a welcoming gesture. I'm assuming a few laughs, along with a few beers, followed this initial introduction. While I did feel badly about the interruption in my families' vacation, I was comforted by the fact that Steve had relished the opportunity to be the first fan to welcome the Doyles to the Red Sox family, albeit a rather inauspicious reception.

Sometime between the Doyles' departure and our own arrival, our home in Lynn was broken into for the first time. Not the homecoming welcome we were expecting, but with the year we had just survived, nothing could dampen our spirits. The policeman who answered our call was non-plussed and sur-

mised that the burglars were most likely just some of the young juvenile delinquents from the projects who liked to prey on the oceanside properties. Why
was this not a comforting thought? Whoever it was that broke into our home,
did not find much to take, but recognized, from photos in the den, that the
home belonged to a professional baseball player. Two weeks after Skip and I
settled back into our home it was ransacked for the second time. Undoubtedly the thugs who broke in the first time assumed that once the ballplayer
was back home, the house would be overflowing with money. This was so not
the case. In fact, I was certain that no money had been taken because I had
spent the morning searching through coat pockets myself for change to bring
to work. The police did locate our television and stereo, carelessly dumped
in the neighbor's yard, and found the perpetrators, who did happen to be the
same thieves as before. Another stint in a JV detention center was all they
gathered for their efforts. Any affection I had previously felt for this dwelling
had come and gone. As we packed up to leave for spring training at the end
of the winter of 1976 we had no regrets in placing this would-be safe haven
on the market. This house would never again feel like home. It was time to
move on.

There was no doubt in my mind that the house we purchased in the fall
of 1976 we would live in forever. After a second successful season with the
New York Mets, we believed we had found a team and a town to embrace.
Midway during the summer, I played in a member-guest golf tournament with
Nancy Seaver at Greenwich Country Club and fell in love with this celestial
Connecticut commuter town. As the summer progressed, Skip also became
enchanted with the area, and we proceeded to procure a property in that
charming town. Nancy put us in touch with her honorable realtor, Candy
Blynn, who, after showing us over twenty of her own listings, encouraged us
to put an offer in on a new home under construction, even though it meant
she would not receive a commission for her time, cementing my faith again
in the basic goodness of human nature.

And so it was that in the fall of 1976 we moved into the home of our
dreams; a cedar, contemporary, colonial, open-concept home situated at the
end of a long, tree-lined driveway adjacent to a 400-acre nature preserve. We
had found our niche in Neverland. Dave Kingman lived on the same street
and had encouraged us to join him in this naturalistic neighborhood. At one
with nature, I felt completely at home. My amateur decorating skills had dramatically improved with prudence and practice. A small kitchen opened up
into a cedar-lined, vaulted-ceiling family room. A dramatic brown-and-grey,
pussy willow paper lined the dining room walls, and a serene silk covered the
living room. We had purchased the house halfway through its construction,
and so we opted to turn one small bedroom adjoining the master into a dress-
ing room with copious built-in drawers and mirrors. The master bedroom
itself, while not overly large, housed a cozy fireplace and magnificent views
of the forest primeval. Our home was simple, but elegant, and I would be

content to spend the rest of my life in this peaceful paradise. We were loving the luxury of living year round in the same community, although this time it was with a new appreciation for that gift of stability. We had good friends and a connected community. We had each other, and we had just discovered we would be having a child within the year—life was almost too good to be true.

Like the saying goes, "nothing lasts forever," and four years later we moved on again. The excitement of returning to our Massachusetts roots was tempered by having to leave our life in Greenwich behind. I adored our home, but it was still only a house made of wood. It was the myriad of little meaningful gestures and the ungluing of bonds that hurt the most to leave behind, the friendships we had forged, the close connection with our church community, and even the friendly baggers at the local grocery store. The week after we placed our house on the market, real estate interest rates jumped dramatically overnight, rising to a high of almost sixteen per cent. How in the world were we going to sell our home in this crazy market and what could we possibly afford to buy in the Boston area without equity for a down payment?

I signed my life away on that April 1980 morning at the beginning of a new decade, deluged with doubts and wishing my husband was there for moral support. What were we doing buying an expensive house when we still had not sold our house in Greenwich? How could we commit to two mortgage payments and a bridge loan when only last week the players had been out on strike and the possibility of a strike occurring midway through the season still hung over our heads? We had been so confident when we had decided together to set up a home in Weston, Massachusetts. Alone I was riddled with uncertainty and shocked by the staggering amount of interest we would incur over the next twenty-five years. Taking a deep breath and saying a fervent prayer that I was making the right decision, I signed my name on the contract, binding us to this last location of our baseball career—a career which ended way too prematurely the following year.

THE GREEN, GREEN GRASS OF HOME

Dorothy only had to click her ruby shoes three times and believe to get home. We believed that once Skips clicked with the Red Sox, we would be easing down that yellow brick road to happiness. Regrettably, neither the opportunity nor the anticipated outcome was found at the end of our Bostonian rainbow.

Instead of slowly sharpening skills at the end of the spring, the players were gearing up on their own for the grinding season ahead. Skip's shoulder had not received the intensive care and conditioning it required in the final days of the spring. The normal anxiety associated with the start of any season had risen to a stress level of unheard-of heights. The 1980 season opened as scheduled, but the tendons underneath my husband's shoulder blades had not responded quite as readily. Trying to ignore the unwelcome pain in his shoulder, he welcomed the opportunity to begin the season in his old haunt of Milwaukee. Playing for the Brewers, we had prayed for the weather not to interfere with Skip's scheduled opening start. As a veteran relief visitor, we now pleaded for inclement weather to wash out the opening series. Opening day was brisk but bearable as the Red Sox won the first game of the season, 3–1. Skip was relieved he was not asked to relieve in the chilly confines of County Stadium. Severe weather cancelled the second game of the season. Nibbling on a piece of pizza while moving into our new home on my own, I felt more than a little twinge of annoyance as Skip called in the midst of an impromptu dinner party at the Franks home to see how the closing had gone.

On Saturday, April 12, the Milwaukee Brewers walloped the Red Sox by a score of 18–1 on a day when the wind chill on the frozen field made the conditions hazardous to healing muscles. Down 15–1, Zimmer called down to the bullpen to have Skip warm up. At first Skip assumed that the bullpen coach was playing a practical joke. There was no way any sensible manager would ask a relief pitcher recovering from a serious injury to warm up in such frigid conditions in such a losing cause. Assured that this was not a joke, he picked up the phone and tried to explain to Mr. Zimmer the folly of jeopardizing his tender shoulder in such an icy environment. If the connection between my husband and his new manager was shaky before, it became downright explosive. Rather than respect the intelligence of a veteran athlete to know his own limitations, Don Zimmer viewed the encounter as a threat to his authority. Skip was cornered after the game and screamed at that "if he was the type of prima-donna pitcher who didn't want to pitch, he could just sit out in the bullpen and rot, for all he cared." He let it be known, in no uncertain terms, that he was the manager and he was in charge of the decision making: "Don't expect to see any action in close games." This offensive altercation, on the opening road trip of the year, cemented the timbre of their caustic relationship.

A week went by before Skip was asked to warm up again. In another losing cause he was sent in to put out the fire at the end of the sixth inning. Successfully striking out the last batter, he faced only one batter in the 7th before being lifted. He was put in for one-third of an inning the next day and then almost got to get into a rhythm by pitching 2⅓ innings in another blowout on the third day. Finally starting to get into a groove, he pitched an unusually long stint of 4 innings two days later and was credited with a win when the team came from behind to score in the last inning. Inconceivably, it was another week before he pitched again in yet another losing effort, and still one more week passed by before he saw action, picking up a second unexpected win in Kansas City. For a top closer to be used in such a haphazard manner was mind-boggling. Zimmer was intentionally setting Skip up to fail. His wish was granted a few days later in Texas when Skip gave up three runs in one-third of an inning. The press had a field day with this lackluster performance. Speculation was all about the status of Skip's shoulder. No one bothered to question his questionable usage from the bullpen.

An entire home stand, followed by a week's road trip, went by without the phone ringing once in the bullpen for my husband to warm up. My home phone, however, was constantly ringing as old friends and well-meaning family members wondered what was wrong. Constant conjecture continued in the press as to the effrontery of Skip being paid all this money and not pitching, but what the press did not report was how he was being manipulated and mismanaged with a series of mind games by his manager. Don Zimmer held true to his word that Skip would pitch only in meaningless games.

Feeling the frustration of this infuriating situation, I was helpless to do anything about it. Sure, I would have loved to give the manager a well-meaning phone call and explain how valuable my husband could be to the team, if given the chance, but the slim chance of my ever getting up the nerve to place the call and the real possibility that Mr. Zimmer would react with even more antagonism to my audacity, stopped me from picking up my phone. Instead I sympathized with my husband and hid the morning paper on days that particularly nasty articles appeared. I continued to attend the home games although I discovered that "enjoying" an evening at the ballpark was quite a challenge with two dynamic daughters. After a few weeks of struggling to entertain my tired toddlers with coloring books and crayons, I secured the baby-sitting services of a Connie, a creatively caring college student matriculating at Regis (my old alma mater) to corral my children at home during many evening contests. The price I paid for their normal bedtime routine was a very early wake-up call for me the next morning.

In the midst of Skip's banishment to the back benches in the bullpen, the Major League Baseball Players contract negotiations came to another impasse. As if I didn't have enough on my mind with a disgruntled husband and two off-the-wall offspring, when I went to bed on the night of May 22, 1980, the players were scheduled to make good on the threatened strike the next day. Talk about overwhelming anxiety! We were responsible for two children, two mortgages and a bridge loan, and in two weeks we would be receiving no salary. My morning prayers turned into nightly pleas to St. Jude. How could coming back home be fraught with so many problems? The power of prayer finally prevailed. At 5 o'clock in the morning on May 23, an agreement was reached between the players and the owners. The tricky issue of player compensation was put aside for further discussion but, at least for this year, the season would continue, along with our paycheck. While I do not normally believe in bribes, the Campaign for Human Development received a sizable anonymous donation a few weeks later.

Breathing a sigh of relief that a strike had been averted, I opted to concentrate on the gifts we had been given, not on the problems we were encountering. We owned a lovely home in a wonderful community, and both our extended families visited on a regular basis. I was starting to make a few friends on the team, and our neighborhood was filled with children the same age as our own. True, the tension at the ballpark was taxing, but life at home was spinning out to be splendidly serene. My seven-month-old daughter had even finally started to sleep through the night!

PLAYMATES

Meghan's third birthday fell in the middle of a road trip, and I invited all my new teammates with children to celebrate. Apparently this was a rather novel idea in this particular club. The children thrived in getting to know each other without restraints as they were allowed to run around the backyard and be as loud as their laughter dictated without being cautioned not to disturb anyone in the stands or wake up a sleeping father. The luxury of laughing with other young mothers sharing survival strategies while participating in a lifestyle that was not very family-friendly was well worth the effort it took to roll up all those peanut butter-and-jelly treats. The camaraderie the children gained swinging wildly in their attempt at breaking the piñata at Meghan's birthday party made day games a lot more tolerable as shy little toddlers stopped clinging to their mothers and took delight in spreading out on a small blanket and stuffing little dolls into the small dump trucks of their new playmates underneath the folding chairs of Fenway Park.

It took having a second child to truly appreciate the challenge involved in being both a baseball wife and a mother. Like Wendy, it was easy to cater to Peter's whims when his happiness was the only focus of her existence, but problems arose when she became responsible for the welfare of the other lost boys. I felt pulled in so many different directions. I was trying hard to encourage my discouraged husband as we dined around midnight and dissected the dynamics of his tedious tenure with the Red Sox. I was trying even harder to jump out of bed with enthusiasm around 6:30 the next morning to create make-believe fairy tales with Fisher-Price's little people in the company of my own little girls. I was also struggling with my own discouragement. I relished reconnecting with my college friends in the area, but I missed the close play group I had been a part of in Greenwich. With all the stress Skip was under, I felt guilty complaining about my own struggles to forge another circle of friends for comfort and support. I placed my negative thoughts in a "do not enter" folder and focused on the future. Like Maria in *The Sound of Music*, I remembered my favorite things, and things seemed better. I realized it was time I reached out into the community at large. One of my new neighbors invited me to join an auxiliary group that supported the New England Home for Little Wanderers, and suddenly my self-pity dissipated as I began to appreciate my blessings. My husband's involvement in baseball came to a close the following year, but my association with this dedicated organization of volunteers continued on.

Having learned my lesson from my exhausting, toddler-toting road trip excursion, I accepted my mother's invitation to take my children for a few days while I accompanied Skip on a road trip to Chicago. Skip and I could both benefit from a few days off from parenting, and we had a number of friends from Milwaukee who were now living in the greater Chicago area. To add to the allure of this escapade, Chicago's Palmer House Hotel served the best oysters Rockefeller, and no one could compete with the Executive House's orange-infused french toast. Similar to other MLB organizations, Red Sox wives rarely accompanied their husbands on the road, and so I was pleasantly surprised to meet Linda Fisk as I was checking into the hotel. Voyaging through the Michigan Avenue shops was infinitely more enjoyable with a female companion.

The Windy City certainly lived up to its well-deserved name. On night two, the wind was blowing straight out of Comiskey Park, and the White Sox were taking advantage of their torrential wind tunnel to torment the pitching staff of the Red Sox. To add insult to injury, every time a player on the home town team hit a home run, fireworks would erupt from the center field scoreboard. As luck would have it, my husband was the fifth, and final, pitcher to be pummeled that evening. He knew when he was sent into the game he was there for the duration. Unfortunately he fared no better on the mound than his predecessors as one more home run flew out of the ballpark accompanied by another round of fireworks exploding from center field. Both Linda Fisk and I were surprised to see Carlton call time and stroll out to the mound to speak with my husband, as it was obvious no one was warming up in the bullpen. More often than not, the conversations that occur on the mound between the pitcher and his catcher have an aura of the theater of the absurd. With his ever-engaging smile, Carlton confided in my husband that he really did not have any pitching advice to give him, but he knew that the scoreboard was running out of fireworks and felt he needed to give the staff a chance to reload. That being said, Carlton strode back to his position and signaled for the action to begin again. As much as I would like to report that Carlton's trip was an exercise in frivolity, the sky did light up one final time in a fantastic display of red, white, and blue skyrocketing blasts.

Both the Red Sox hopes of making the playoffs in 1980 and my husband's hopes of working his way back into the closing position never came to fruition. In the "too little, too late" category, Don Zimmer was fired near the end of the season, but by that time Skip's reputation, his confidence, and his relationship with the fans was damaged beyond repair. Skip was taunted nightly in the bullpen by one season ticket holder who would routinely drag his young son over, point out to my husband and, swearing profusely, accuse Skip of being responsible for the demise of the team and the increase in ticket prices. I never could understand the rationale behind this man's tirade, but I had to give my husband credit for holding his temper and not responding to this fanatical fool.

Skip's initiation into the Boston bullpen fell way short of our expectations, but still it was just one year, and things were bound to improve with a new manager in charge the following year. We sold our Greenwich home mid-way during the season and were relieved to be back to one mortgage payment. My daughter was enrolled in the local nursery school where many of her new classmates' parents also sprang from various corners of the wide world of sports. At the first "three-year-old curriculum night," we were introduced to Peggy and Bobby Orr and Olympic hockey gold medalist Bob Cleary and his wife, Ann. For the next five years I spent many hours squeezed into dwarf-sized chairs with a number of celebrity mothers, gluing yarn hair on paper plate puppets and publishing pre-school artistic picture books.

I did feel some responsibility for the at-home birth of the second child of Robert Parrish and his wife. In response to her inquiry as to how much faster my second delivery had been than my first, I shared the story of my 38-hour labor marathon in Greenwich Hospital one morning outside of the pre-school playground. That very afternoon she went into labor, but she delayed her departure to the hospital, hopefully not due to our morning chat. Unfortunately (or fortunately depending on your perspective), her labor sprang into fast forward and her initial reluctance to rush to the hospital resulted in her delivering in her own bedroom as the paramedics rushed to the scene. From the rumors flying around the playground the next day, I understand that mother, baby, and father were all fine, but her mother-in-law had to be revived from fainting by the ambulance crew when they arrived, post-partum, to offer support. Perhaps the 00 on the back of this Celtic great's uniform should have been a tip to how long her second delivery was going to take. In retrospect, I guess my well-meaning advice was not quite so helpful after all.

The 1980 Red Sox season ended at the beginning of October. Once again we were destined to watch the playoffs and World Series on television rather than being active participants on the field. Two weeks before the season ended, Skip was picking out his doctoral psychology classes at Boston College, but similar to his sports career, he was finding it hard to duplicate his previous courses at Columbia and had to settle for a less applicable academic agenda. I began to acclimate to a normal existence. My children still rose at the crack of dawn, but during the off-season I was able to retire at a reasonable hour and catch up on the sleep my body had been longing for all summer. We lived in a quiet neighborhood where I could take long walks with my daughters and join with other mothers socializing our children and maintaining some sense of adult sanity in our own lives. Our play group resembled a mini–United Nations. The children's ancestry in our neighborhood sprang from China, England, Egypt, Greece, Italy, and my own Irish-American upbringing. Best of all, both of our families lived nearby, and our children could get to know their grandparents as people rather than as occasional holiday guests. From a personal level the move was working out as planned, but on a professional level we were still trying to find our way back to the Emerald City.

THE TIME OF YOUR LIFE

Rest and relaxation did not fit into our off-season schedule during the winter of 1980–81. Skip spent countless hours at the Boston College library delving into published theories concerning the psychology of sports. I implemented my own trial-and error child psychology methodology nurturing our nature-loving daughters. Soon it was time to pack up and head south. Much to our dismay, we were informed that, due to a number of problems with several irresponsible minor leaguers the previous summer, the complex we had stayed in last spring had decided "never to rent to ballplayers ever again." Thus we joined the majority of Red Sox families who called two rooms in the Holiday Inn home for the next two months. This was not a luxury, all-suite hotel. This motel was constructed in the post–World War II building boom from a bare bones blueprint that allowed for two double beds against one wall, a narrow built-in dresser on the opposite wall and a free-standing television set at the end of the open clothes cabinet. No stove. No refrigerator. No privacy.

In their defense, the staff at the Holiday Inn did their best to accommodate the needs of all the cramped couples with children. At my request, they removed one of the double beds and replaced it with a crib, which allowed me just enough space to set up a really tacky set of child-sized, magenta-pink, blow-up furniture that the girls took delight in jumping upon. Next I purchased a (very) small refrigerator that fit under the bathroom sink to house milk and juice boxes. I then procured a Mr. Coffee machine that served up instant oatmeal, flavored cream of wheat, and chicken noodle cup of soup at the drop of a hat. Had only portable microwave ovens been available!

From the perspective of rearing five children, I propose that the toughest stage in a young child's development is the time span between 15 and 18 months. During this tricky period the child is physically running full speed ahead but mentally has not enough common sense to appreciate the consequences of these actions. We moved from our four-bedroom, totally child-proof home in Weston into two adjoining rooms in the Winter Haven Holiday Inn when my oldest daughter was three and my youngest had just stumbled into her sixteenth month of life. This arrangement might have been bearable if the weather had cooperated, but the spring of 1981 would go down in the record books as one of the rainiest in history. In the eight weeks that we spent in claustrophobic conditions, we were graced with a total of seven beautiful days and only a handful more of partly sunny skies. Every morning I would peak out the drab, multi-colored, faded flowered drapes for a sign of blue sky, only to be rewarded with the heavy morning mist that signified another dreary day was coming to light.

My husband, of course, was up and out early every morning in an effort to jump start a more productive season. He was always the first one at the ballpark and the last to leave. While I admired his dedication, I did occasionally wonder if his commitment would have been quite as intense if our housing conditions were a little more opulent. The complex did boast of a beautiful, big, concrete swimming pool, but this proved to be more of a problem than a perk. The shallow end was way over both my children's heads, and the weather conditions being what they were, I was loathe to jump into the cold water myself and monitor their aquatic activity. We could have passed a few carefree hours warmly dressed in sweaters and rain gear at the playground, if only one had existed. As it was, there was a square box of dirt that surrounded a large tree just down the stairs from our room that the children spent many an hour filling up their little trucks with said "sand" and dumping it out again. More than once, my sensitive three-year-old broke down in tears when a dump truck was inadvertently emptied out on top of her head by one of more rambunctious Remy boys. As chaotic as my life was with two little girls, I can only imagine how hectic it must have been for Phoebe Remy trying to contain two similar aged boys in the same space.

If maintaining sanity during the day was a challenge, you can only imagine how "relaxing" it was to take two youngsters out to dinner every evening. There is a pace of life that speeds through a New Englander's being that significantly differs from the Southern-style tempo. With nothing to do and nowhere to go, the majority of retired Floridians seemed satisfied to spend an hour or two leisurely lounging around the atriums of the local restaurants. "Don't worry, be happy" seemed to be the mantra of the mature population. On the rare nights that I was able to secure the services of the only hotel babysitter I trusted, I had no trouble leaving my cares behind and adopting the laid-back attitude. However, most nights we had at most forty-five minutes before one, or both, of our daughters would tire of the toys I had selected for the night's dining experience and feel the need to escape the restrictions of the high chair. For the first few weeks Skip and I took turns doing laps around the parking lot with the girls until the food came. In time we developed a better plan; one of us would enter the restaurant, stand in line for the required thirty minute, wait, and order. Approximately an hour later the other would show up with our daughters as their food was being placed in front of them, and we would all be able to share a hot meal without the threat of an imminent meltdown. My husband and I still share a knowing smile whenever we happen to be dining out near a table with two toddlers. We are never bothered by the utensil banging. When you don't have to deal with the commotion yourself, you view the disturbance in a completely different light.

Children are considerably more adaptable than their parental counter-parts, and the young offspring of the Red Sox players soon grew to look forward to meeting each other around their adopted sand box. One morning towards the end of that interminably long spring, I awoke to a screeching machine sound accompanied by even louder, and more ear-piercing childish screams. The old Holiday Inn was in the process of slowly being remodeled, and the makeshift children's sand box surrounding the tree was being dismantled. As much as all the mothers had complained about the size and the quality of the little, tree-covered sand box, the fact that it was being destroyed in front of their distraught sons and daughters gave us all a new appreciation for its existence. Try as we might, we could not convince the construction foreman to hold off a few weeks until spring training concluded. He had an unexpected opening in the excavator's schedule and decided to make use of it. In the final analysis I imagine the hotel manager was more perturbed with the premature dirt demolition. Rather than quietly digging in the sand, the boisterous boys in the complex took to racing their Hot Wheels up and down the concrete walkways to the peril of both the front desk personnel and the other patrons of the hotel.

With the long hours Skip was putting in at the ballpark, he had expected a little more time on the mound. So far the change in management had not signified a significant change in Skip's status on the team. Physically he was in great shape, and despite (or maybe because of) the less than ideal living conditions, he was anxious to let out some of his pent up aggression on the competition. It appeared that Ralph Houk, the new manager, was focusing his time critiquing the new talent on the team and ignoring my husband's progress. The knowledge that his salary was guaranteed for the year helped us both to sleep a little better at night, and so it was with disbelief that Skip came home towards the end of March after a round of golf with Ken Harrelson. Ken, an old friend and teammate and at the time an announcer for the Red Sox, confided in Skip that, rumor had it, Skip was being released at the end of the spring. This was inconceivable. Skip had signed a four-year contract with the Red Sox and had not yet been given the opportunity to prove his worth. We had moved home in anticipation of ending Skip's baseball career in the area where he had begun as a Little Leaguer, but not quite so soon. There had to be some mistake. This could not possibly be happening. He was too talented. He was too committed. His best years were still ahead of him. After considerable consternation, we both concluded that there could not be any substance to this ridiculous rumor. The story clearly had to be a sensational concoction of some speculative sports reporter.

Nevertheless, the following day Skip went to the ballpark even earlier than usual, hoping to get a chance to spend some quality time with the manager and personally discuss his status. Whether by happenstance or design, the opportunity never arose, and Skip also never got a chance to pitch. As was the case with most afternoon home games, I had driven Skip to the park in the morning, gone out to breakfast and on to the park with my daughters to tire them out, given them a late morning nap, and then showed up to the game in about the fourth inning with my two adorable little girls identically attired. Today's clothing choice of matching white sailor outfits was one of my favorites, mainly because I could throw the dresses into the wash with bleach and get almost anything out. I could sense the built-up frustration in my husband's stride as he came over to give the girls a hug at the end of the game and inform me that he would be a little longer. He had not gotten into the game again and felt the need to run extra wind sprints.

I already had about as much fun as you could have with two toddlers playing underneath the stadium chairs, and so I decided to treat Meghan and Maura to an ice cream cone down the road. Their favorite flavor would have to be mint chocolate chip. About half an hour later I returned with both girls looking a little less pristine after dripping the bright green ice cream all over their dresses. Spotting Skip still running full steam ahead out in the outfield, I suggested my girls engage in a game of king of the mountain on the giant mound of dirt piled high outside the clubhouse. It was at about this time a television reporter walked by and introduced himself as being from my home town of Springfield, Massachusetts. How could I graciously refuse an interview? Trying to comb through my own hair with my fingers to look at least somewhat presentable, I attempted to answer the probing questions of the reporter with as much enthusiasm as I could muster. Yes, I was aware that the team appeared to be going for a youth movement, but, no, I did not feel my husband's job was in jeopardy. Of course he was healthy and ready to contribute and finally, yes, we were happy we had made the move to Boston. Only then did I realize the cameraman had turned the camera on my two, incredibly grimy, red, white, blue, and green-streaked daughters. With an attempt at levity, I smiled and stated that a baseball wife and mother did have to be a little flexible when it came to how many hours her husband spent at the park and how to keep the children entertained while waiting for their father to emerge. The next day I was inundated with phone calls from friends and family who had seen our disheveled daughters on the news the previous evening. Only my mother answered honestly when I inquired as to whether or not their apparel looked as appalling as I had imagined, but she assured me the impromptu exposure could only help Skip's connection with the still somewhat hostile fan base.

In early April, 1981, Skip was called into Ralph Houk's office and greeted with the world-ending words: "Sorry, but you don't fit in with our future plans." One simple sentence that rocked our world. Perhaps Hawk Harrelson's keen insight should have softened the shocking news, but from our perspective, there appeared to be no rationale for this turn of events. How could this be the end when he hadn't yet begun to fight? Skip's fastball had finally started to fly out of his hand, and there is no way that anyone could question his work ethic. We had signed what we had thought to have been a guaranteed contract (although we came to realize that the fine print at the bottom of the document greatly limited the length and depth of that guarantee). Six years earlier, when Skip had been released by the Yankees at the end of spring training in 1975, we had been shocked, but there are no words to describe how flabbergasted we were by this unexpected and unwelcomed legal liberation. Again, the timing was terrible. His release came at the very end of spring training when the rosters of all the other major league clubs were being finalized. Teams were making their final cuts, not looking to add to their confusion. And there was still that groundswell of deep concern throughout the league over the impending strike concerning the unresolved compensation issue. The scale was definitely tipped towards the weight of problems more than solutions. A call to Skip's agent did nothing to soothe our souls. "Go home, relax for a week, I'll see what I can do," did not really bode well to bolster our confidence. Skip did not want to sit around and relax; he wanted to be standing on the mound, in control of the game, pitching in relief in pressure-filled situations.

In hindsight it was easy to wonder why we had jumped on the Red Sox's offer and not held out for other options. Our minds had been sprinkled with the pixie dust of childhood dreams and we longed to leave our wandering world behind and return home. Our emotions had grabbed us by the wrist and directed our decision. It was too late now to question the road not taken. Our present path would lead us towards another unpredictable turning point.

9

Welcome to the Real World

AGAINST THE WIND

After two months dwelling in cramped living accommodations, followed by three claustrophobic days in the car with two toddlers strapped in their car seats, we pulled into the driveway of Buckskin Drive in Weston, Massachusetts, relieved to be home albeit apprehensive about our future. Each of our daughters was tucked into her own bed in her own bedroom with room darkening curtains. While there seemed to be a cloud hanging over Skip's career, I knew that the morning sun would still rise at dawn. After the last few wakeful nights, I would use every trick in my book to squeeze a little more sleep. Miracle of miracles, the children slept in until eight the next morning. If my prayers had been answered in such a small matter, perhaps there was still some hope for our long-range goals.

Thoughtfully, Skip's parents had stopped by the day before and stocked our refrigerator with ingredients to scramble up some diced ham and eggs, my children's favorite. I felt lighthearted and liberated standing at my island stove cooking up a hot healthy breakfast for my daughters who were busy fashioning pillow forts in the family room. The simple pleasures in life are appreciated so much more when you have lived without them for a while. After breakfast I slipped out by myself and drove over to Mr. Big's Toyland in Waltham and procured an extra-large, vintage kite for my husband and two small kites for each of my girls. Hoping to diffuse any oncoming depression, I decided to make lemonade out of lemons; I figured if Skip was told to "go fly a kite," we might as well take the advice literally and delight in the juvenile joy of controlling a small flock of multi-colored nylon birds soaring through the wind at the end of a long string while lying around in our front lawn. It had worked splendidly for George Banks; why couldn't it work for us?

Dick Moss tried hard to broker a deal for my husband's services, but the final results of his effort fell into that "not quite what we had hoped for" category. The majority of general managers saw no rationale for Skip's untimely dismissal from the Red Sox, thus it was assumed that his arm had not responded well to therapy and he was considered damaged goods. His less than stellar stint in the American League the previous year did not help his cause; all the same, a few scouts connected with several National League clubs remembered his five solid years with the Mets and were willing to give him a chance. Unfortunately all of the offers on the table required that Skip return to the minor leagues to confirm his agent's contention that he was indeed healthy.

After a few long agonizing days and even longer sleep-deprived nights assessing our options, Skip signed with the Montreal Expos and was scheduled to join the Denver Bears in Denver, Colorado, the following day. That was the first of several daunting decisions that had to be made in a very short time and with very limited information. Skip was assured this was going to be a brief banishment to AAA, and he should move up to the big club by the end of the month. Seeing how content our children were to be home in their own rooms, playing with their own friends in their own backyard, and dreading the thought of uprooting them again so soon for another tenuous temporary housing situation, we opted for Skip (Peter) to fly off solo to Denver and for me (Wendy) to stay behind and hold down the fort.

I hated to be separated from my husband, but at least I had the support and companionship of both of our extended families. I did feel a little betrayed by my former Red Sox acquaintances. Perhaps they did not know what to say or how to say it, but it still was hard to accept the fact that none of my so-called friends from the year before contacted me once the season began. Fortunately, I had a circle of friends in my neighborhood and in the local volunteer community to offset this feeling of abandonment, but it still seemed so strange that not one single spouse made the effort to reach out and touch my unhinged life. The close female camaraderie among the baseball wives I had experienced in the past appeared to be declining in direct proportion to the increase in their financial fortunes. My past experience had proved that the most giving wives were those of the most successful husbands. It was as if they realized what a wonderful gift that had been bestowed upon them and reached out to pass that blessing on to others. I sincerely hoped the silent treatment I was encountering was an atypical aberration of compassion rather than a general trend in the league. A wife of a professional baseball player can get overwhelmed on her own and it's the support of other "single" spouses that fosters survival during the long lonesome "home alone" times.

April showers nourish May flowers. In the midst of a horrendous downpour in the middle of April, my daughters and I sloshed over the Massachusetts Turnpike asphalt and through the concrete caverns of the Callahan tunnel to drop Skip off at Boston's Logan Airport as he set off to rejuvenate his career in the fresh mountain air in Denver, Colorado. The plan was for us all to rendezvous a few weeks later in Montreal, when the blooming bouquet of May flowers would greet our arrival back to the big leagues. It's good that we had a back-up plan. The cool crisp air of the Colorado Rockies might be wonderful for outdoor hiking adventures, but it was not very conducive to keeping high fastballs inside of Mile High Stadium. It became clear as the mountain sky, to both Skip and the Montreal organization, that after spending a year warming the benches of the bullpen, he was going to need a little more time down in the minor leagues to get his arm back into its proper rhythm. Mother's Day weekend found me presenting my mother with the "gift" of babysitting as I dropped my daughters at my parents' house in Springfield and boarded a flight to Denver for the week's home stand.

My desire for a few restful hours was dashed by the constant commotion of the unruly two-year-old sitting across the aisle. The worn-out single mother seemed to assume that one of the stewardess's jobs was to keep her child entertained and became unglued when she was asked to quiet her child down and keep him buckled into his seat. I usually could overlook the antics of an out-of-control toddler, but in such a confined space, I found the behavior hard to ignore. Fortunately I had forgotten to purge my pocketbook of the plethora of crayons that generally ruled the lining of my purse and, to the relief of my fellow passengers, I kept this little terror contented coloring all over the pages of the airplane magazine until he finally gave up and fell asleep. Many years spent sitting in the family section surveying the quieting techniques of some very creative mothers had taught me more than my fair share of inventive artistic distractions. This quiet kindness did not go unnoticed by my surrounding passengers as I received a generous amount of "thank you's" from heretofore total strangers as I gathered my bags from the carousel. My husband wondered what new cause I had taken upon myself this time as our warm embraces were interrupted by a huge hug from the rambunctious rug rat and his beleaguered mother. Often we don't realize the ripple impact that the simple gift of attention can incur.

ROCKY MOUNTAIN HIGH

Set high on top of the city, the lightness of the atmosphere enveloped Mile High Stadium that housed the Denver Bears baseball club. If I had felt a little more mature than the majority of wives six years earlier in Tucson, I now appeared be ready to apply for my AARP card. Skip had tried to prepare me for this age discrepancy. Upon his arrival inside the clubhouse, the first person he ran in to was Terry Francona, the grown-up son of Skip's Milwaukee Brewers teammate, Tito. The affable Terry extended his hand to Skip: "Good to see you again, Mr. Lockwood. Welcome to the Bears." Skip looked behind him to see if his dad had just unexpectedly walked into the room, and then it dawned on him that Terry was referring to him as "Mr. Lockwood." "Please," Skip pleaded, "lose the 'Mr.'; I'm your teammate." It seemed impossible that at the age of 34 he was more a contemporary of a player's father than he was of the player himself. Remembering how often the ten-year-old Terry had offered to go up and get hot chocolate for myself and the other Brewers wives my first year as a bride brought back longing memories of a time when life was simply an exciting adventure, before I understood all the complicated effort that went into in that escapade.

My husband did have a tendency to embellish certain encounters, and before I entered the Denver stadium, I was certain he had exaggerated his senior citizen status on the team. After picking up my ticket from the will-call window, I had no trouble locating the family section. An animated group of younger-than-springtime girls convened behind the home plate section amicably chatting before the game began. Holding my ticket in my hand, I inquired of the ravishing redhead at the end of the aisle as to whether or not this was Row 5 in Section 8 and was greeted by the strange response of "Yes, Ma'am." For the entire week, try as I might to dispel the notion that I was not a mother hen but merely another teammate's wife, the answers to the majority of my questions ended in a "Yes, Ma'am" or "No, Ma'am." Granted, this friendly female flock seemed to hail primarily from the southern section of our country where such a greeting is common courtesy, but to a northern Yankee with two children under the age of four, it sounded rather perplexing. My week in the Rockies sped by, and in the end Skip traveled even further out west with the Bears rather than east to the Montreal Expos. I returned to Massachusetts satisfied that Skip's arm was finally regaining its former strength and confident that we would be reunited as a family before Meghan's fourth birthday in June.

Back in Boston, the newspapers were filled with doom and gloom about the stalled status of baseball's basic agreement. A strike had been averted the year before by shelving the most contentious issue for further discussion, but time was running out, and no new agreement had been reached. Reading between the lines of the local press, I could not decipher what impact an impending strike would have on our own future in the sport. It would be a cruel twist of fate if Skip were to finally get called back up to the big leagues just as the team went out on strike. Speculation ran rampant and rumors surfaced and were squashed hourly. And then, on May 29, 1981, the Executive Board of the Players' Association voted unanimously to strike over the unresolved issue of free-agent compensation. The deadline was extended, briefly, as the Players' Association's unfair labor complaint was heard by the National Labor Relations Board. And then, at 12:30 A.M. on June 12, union chief Marvin Miller announced that the Major League baseball players had gone out on strike. This began the longest labor action to date in American sports history. By the time the season finally resumed on August 10, seven-hundred-and-six games had been canceled.

Once again our world was rocked with uncertainty. What now? No one actually thought it would come to this, and now no one had any idea when it would end. Negotiations had totally broken off, and neither side appeared willing to give an inch. I was "almost" thankful that Skip was still with the Denver Bears. At least whenever the season resumed, he would be in shape to pitch. On the day Skip left for Colorado, we had no intention of taking the children out to Denver. Now, almost two months later, I found myself packing up two suitcases, one for clothes and the other for toys, and gearing myself up for a long flight with two flighty children. The Denver Bears were scheduled to be home for ten days, including an opportune off-day on my daughter's birthday, and so it was off to Denver for us. My excitement at this prospect was tempered by the realization that I would be traveling by myself with a serenely sensitive almost-four-year-old and an extremely energetic twenty-month-old toddler.

It seemed like ages ago that I had boarded the plane in Boston to meet my husband in Denver. Being both mother and father for a few months had added a few more grey hairs to my already harried hairdo. As I embarked on this new quest with Meghan and Maura in tow, I was cognizant of the comfort of the other passengers and, keenly remembering the ruckus on my last trip, packed a small carry-on travel bag loaded with child friendly activities. Michelle Pfeiffer's purse in *One Fine Day* had nothing on this floating nursery school suitcase. I had the expected crayons, markers, and coloring books, but I also had packed paint-by-number painting books, small scissors, glue sticks, a cardboard pop-up doll house with little people, along with match box cars, baggies of Cheerios, raisins, and juice boxes. But what really kept both girls totally entranced for over an hour was the Play Doh barber set that let them each stuff a plastic patron with colorful dough, turn a lever and watch the canary yellow, magenta pink and day-glow green hair "grow" through the tiny holes in the top. Taking their tiny plastic shears they were able to style the stringy hair into some very creative hair styles. Happy they were, neat they were not. As I packed up and left my cluttered row of seats, I handed the stewardess a tip to hand to whoever would be unlucky enough to clean up after us on the airplane. She assured me that it really wasn't necessary; the mess could be vacuumed up in a minute. The fact that my girls had spent the last four hours quietly content and not bothering the other passengers was worth the clean-up effort. I prayed the rest of my trip would be as peaceful as the flight.

Successfully surviving the plane ride, we paraded into the Denver airport with my twin-attired daughters, looking a little more disheveled than when our journey had begun. As soon as the girls spotted their father, they let go of my hands and sprinted down the terminal hallway to jump up into his arms. Young children develop daily, and Skip was taken aback by the change that had occurred in his daughters over the past two months, not to mention the noise level that had shattered his solitary existence. With a daughter clinging tightly to each of my husband's hips, we maneuvered our way through the airport, procured our luggage, and piled into the rental car Skip had leased for the week. Had he known in April he would still be playing for Denver in June, he would have rented an apartment but, hopeful that his next phone call would be a call-up to Montreal, he continued to live out of a suitcase and had only moved on to an efficiency hotel near the stadium after the call to strike.

Soon as we had settled into the hotel, it was time for Skip to leave for the ballpark. Thankfully the girls were as wiped out as I was after the exhausting trip, and we all crashed for a few hours before we left for the ballpark. The major league strike had also changed the complexity of the minor league system in 1981. There was normally a lot of movement at the triple–A level of baseball, with players being called up to the majors and sent back down on a weekly basis. With the threat, and the ensuing reality, of the work stoppage, there had been little change in the roster in the past month. Most of the wives I had met in May were still residing in Denver in June, and I think the young age of my children confused some of the women who might have thought I was past the childrearing stage of my life. After an unusually long nap, my own two girls were on their best behavior, playing with their Skipper dolls, Barbie's less developed younger sister, and constantly waving to their father as he popped his head out of the dugout in between innings. A little disappointed that Skip hadn't gotten into the game to pitch that night, I was not at all certain my nerves could have handled any more excitement in one day anyway.

The time zone change was not in our favor, but exhaustion was, and we all slept in to the luxuriously late hour of nine o'clock the next morning. Was time finally beginning to be on our side? Knowing from experience that the best way to keep children quiet in a hotel is to get them out and moving before they have a chance to really wake up, I pried my husband out of bed and off we went to the Denver zoo. After acting like a single parent for way too long, I wasn't the least bit perturbed that both girls insisted on holding my husband's hand rather than my own for the entire afternoon. We all felt reluctant to have this enjoyable outing come to an end, and so we stayed on until the last possible moment enjoying a spectacular day in the sun.

Quite out of character, Skip was the last, rather than the first, player to enter the clubhouse on that ominous afternoon. As soon as Skip crossed the clubhouse door, he sensed that change was in the air. His manager, Felipe Alou, called Skip into his office and closed the door. With sincere regret Felipe told Skip he had been informed by the Montreal Expos that he had to let Skip go. "I'm so sorry," his manager sighed. "I told them you were throwing the ball with fire and that your control was improving with every outing. They told me they were aware of that and that there was no use giving a veteran player a spot on the roster this summer who would only improve his value to the open market the following year." There was no major league team to return to at the present time, and the outlook was not hopeful for baseball to resume at all this season. The Montreal Expos organization did not have the backing of wealthy owners, and a decision had been made at the top level to cut their losses for the present season and concentrate of giving young indentured players playing time. Had the strike been settled in a timely manner, Skip would have most likely resurrected his role as a relief pitcher in the cosmopolitan city of Montreal, Canada. The strike situation being as it was, he was unceremoniously released into the wilds of the Colorado Rockies.

Both girls had passed out on their beds, succumbing to the exhilarating exhaustion that came from spending the day at the zoo with their father. Feeling a little hazy myself, I had just decided to let them sleep through the night and forgo the game. I was trying to figure out how to relay that message when the phone in the room startled me into attention. My shell-shocked husband was on the other end of the phone, instructing me not to go to the ballpark and telling me that he was on his way back to the hotel. The word "released" was never spoken. I spent the next hour trying to decipher his unspoken message. Why had we spent so long at the zoo? Had he twisted his ankle there and decided not to mention it? Had he pulled another muscle in his arm warming up? Had someone in one of our families been in some type of accident? Why would he be leaving the ballpark before the game even began?

The moment he opened the door I knew that something terrible had transpired. "Kate, I've been released" were the words resonating from his mouth. Words that just would not register. How could this be happening? His fastball had just started to return to its pre-injury velocity, and he had experience and attitude on his side. I wanted to scream out loud at the absurdity of this action, but instead I merely rushed across the room with a warm embrace. Neither of us spoke for the longest time. We both were trying to render some sense of this senseless situation. After an eternity of silence, Skip finally repeated the conversation he had had with his manger. As much as his manager wanted to keep him on the team, he had no control over the upper level decisions, his own salary was being paid by the organization, and the final roster decisions were not his to make. With the present stalemate in baseball, the past few solid weeks of Skip's recovery became irrelevant, and the decision had been made to focus on the future. If Skip continued his impressive performance throughout the summer, he could name his own price at the end of the season, and the Montreal Expos knew they would most likely not be in the running. Better to cut their losses now and give a younger player who was tied into the organization for a few more years some experience. What kind of reward was this for our standing up for the rights of future players? Somewhere down in AA there was a young pitcher excitedly packing up his bags after being told he was being brought up to AAA. For us it was time to sadly stuff our dreams of a comeback back into our suitcases and head home.

What now my love? After an exhausting day we decided to hold off making any further decisions tonight. We had learned during our chaotic baseball years that life choices always appeared a little clearer come the morning.

TO THE MORNING

The next morning we awoke at the break of day with the shock of yesterday's news starting to sink in. The fiery sun rose over the mountains of Colorado, and we welcomed the new day with a new outlook on life. As devastated as we were by Skip's release, the earth continued to spin on its sphere, and the morning sky blazed resplendent with the colors of the new day. It was easy to succumb to a tunnel vision view of life and blow our own problems out of proper perspective. Yes, Skip had been released—again. The New York Yankees had delivered a devastating strike one to us in 1975. A surprising strike two had been thrown at us at the end of this past spring by the Red Sox, and now we were being rung up by the Expos organization. Skip's career was mirroring his favorite count on the mound: Strike three, you're out.

We were not the only ones flirting with disaster in 1981, and our present predicament paled in the light of what was happening in the world. For 444 days the frantic families of the American hostages held captive in Iran had prayed for their safe return. Their prayers were finally answered through the efforts of the peace-loving Jimmy Carter; however, the timing of their release was diabolically delayed by a political power play of the Iranian government to rob President Carter of the opportunity to welcome the Americans home on his watch. Minutes after Ronald Reagan was sworn into the presidential office, the hostages were released. In war-torn Ireland, Bobby Sands, an IRA activist, had begun a hunger strike that would result in his death two months later, and all throughout the world there were rumors of an epidemic, which would later become known as AIDS.

Pope John Paul II had been shot in an assassination attempt by a Turkish-born zealot. This holy man demonstrated to the world that he practiced what he preached about compassion by visiting the Italian jail to forgive his assailant. President Ronald Reagan had also been shot and gravely wounded by John Hinckley, who insanely thought his action would impress the actress Jodi Foster. While the president recovered fully in time, his press secretary, Jim Brady, was wounded in the head and remained partially paralyzed. The music industry was also changing as fast as the tempo of the times. MTV exploded onto the small screen debuting with the prophetic offering "Video Killed the Radio Stars." Kool and the Gang were urging us to "Celebrate" good times, but the events of the time definitely did not seem to merit much of a celebration.

Back to our present personal dilemma. As the saying goes, this was the first day of the rest of our life; it was up to us to decide what direction that life would take. Other than the two days off over the All-Star break, we had never had the time for a summer vacation. The ballclub would pay for Skip (only) to leave the state whenever he so desired, but the girls and I were scheduled on a return flight a week from now and there would be a significant cost to change those reservations. For the first time in a long time, we had been handed the luxury of freedom. We had just been set free from our place in the competitive world of baseball and had yet to find our focus for the future. Suddenly we had nothing to lose and were being offered the freedom to slow down and smell the roses. We elected to enjoy the clear mountain air for the next week and immerse ourselves into the ethereal beauty of the Rocky Mountains as we pondered our prospects. Perhaps by then we would be able to decipher God's casual reply.

Departing Denver and driving our station wagon up over the winding roads, we cruised towards the mountain crests. Checking into a rustic camp, our children delighted in cantering along side their father as they clung to their slow-moving ponies trekking down dirt pathways and dismounting before jumping off a boulder into a mountain stream outside of Boulder, Colorado. Not once was it necessary to check our watch to see if it was time to leave for the ballpark or keep quiet so that Skip could take his pre-game nap. On the day Megahn turned four, we found a charming country inn that offered her unusual birthday dinner request: stuffed mushrooms and steamed artichokes (what can I say; I started early refining their dining tastes). We basked in a beautiful suite in a Breckenridge resort as Skip and I raced each other, with a child on each of our laps, bicycling the paddle boats across the lagoon in the complex. Maybe retirement wouldn't be that bad after all.

With Skip's career still hanging by a thread, but with renewed spirits, we turned in the rental car at the Denver airport and returned to Massachusetts. We had not looked at a sports page all week, but we were not surprised to discover that nothing had changed in the continuing contract impasse. The owners were publically complaining about how much money they were losing. Privately they were collecting enormous sums from their emergency fund. Before the 1981 season began, the owners of Major League Baseball secretly agreed to spend $2 million on a strike-insurance policy. The policy contained a 153-game deductible, after which the owners would receive $100,000 for each of the next 500 games lost to a labor dispute. After taking a hard line for months, the owners yielded on the central issue just as the strike insurance was about to run out. Coincidence? I think not. The reasonable compensation system that the Player's Association had suggested in 1980 was shelved in favor of a much more complex agreement written by the owner's attorney that proved to be too complicated to work effectively. After forcing a 50-day strike to win the battle over the compensation draft, the owners quietly abolished it in the next labor agreement. So much was lost and so little gained over so much pride.

Closing Time

Some life-changing decisions are made on the spur of the moment and others slowly evolve. Without a team to play for or a league to pitch in, it was impossible to maintain a professional level of intensity. Skip's agent had nothing encouraging to report, and the doors were closing in on our options. After a month spent attacking the fairways and greens of Weston Golf Club, Skip considered an attempt at qualifying for the pro golf tour but, much to my immense relief, he concluded that the constant travel and continual uncertainty of that vagrant lifestyle might be more than we could handle with two small children. Hard as it might be to accept, it was time to leave the carefree games of childhood behind and grow up. The shining glory associated with our National Pastime was severely tarnished by the 1981 strike. Major League Baseball resumed in August, but the country's fascination with the summer game had fizzled. It took many years for the fans to regain their affection for this wonderful sport. This strike also ended our active affiliation with major league baseball. For us, the opening week of the 1981 strike signaled the closing time of Skip's career.

A year later, after an attempt at counseling at the Chestnut Hill Psychotherapy Clinic proved unfulfilling, Skip enrolled in the Sloan Fellow's MBA Program at MIT. In early March of 1982, I spent the better part of ten hours delivering my third daughter, Kara, into the world. No longer considered the wife of a local celebrity, five hours after my delivery, I was still lying in the crowded corridors of Newton-Wellesley Hospital waiting for a bed to open up before being rolled into a semi-private room. The VIP treatment no longer magically appeared for my recuperation.

Much had changed, yet even more stayed the same. No longer was our day centered on Skip's baseball schedule. Now it was scheduled around his course work. He was not traveling around the country; he was moving in the educational world of motivated business men and women from around the globe. Couples from all around the U.S., China, Japan, Brazil, Mexico, France, and Spain moved their families for a two-year tenure at MIT. I was blown away by the support the spouses of the Sloan Fellows received from the Massachusetts Institute of Technology. The families were handed a booklet containing a list of possible apartments, suggested schools, preferred parks and museums, recommended doctors, and even a map to the local grocery stores. What I wouldn't have given for a similar list of the basic necessities of life to help me to adapt to the constantly changing communities we inhabited during our baseball years. The Sloan Fellows program taught me that the need to adapt to change was as essential to a spouse of the business world as much as it was to one in the world of sports. The clubhouse door might have closed on one phase of our life, but we were just beginning to enter another world filled with an entirely new set of possibilities.

Epilogue

Seasons in the Sun

YOU CAN'T ALWAYS GET WHAT YOU WANT

Recently, my extremely competent, twenty-five-year-old, married daughter had a total meltdown resulting in an uncharacteristic eruption of frustrated tears. Earlier on that Saturday spring morning, she woke up by herself, took an honest assessment of the unruly grass growing out of control around the house she and her husband had purchased over the winter, glanced over at her trusty little Italian greyhound companion, and remarked, "Well, Brutus, I guess it's up to me to do something about the yard today." Equipped with the ingrained awareness of a young woman surviving on her own that "if you need something done, you just have to go do it yourself," she headed off to the PX to purchase a lawn mower.

With all the optimism of a first-time homeowner, Kara maneuvered her way to the home and garden section of the PX to locate a lawn mower that would fit her landscaping and budgetary needs. She assumed this device would come fully assembled. Unfortunately that assumption fell into the wishful thinking category. "There's nothing to it," she was told by the encouraging garden center employee. "All you have to do is follow the simple directions and secure the wheels." A muscular helpful hand loaded the large carton into her car, and she headed for home, anxious to pop the wheels onto the mower and get moving on manicuring the meandering foliage overtaking her property. She carefully backed the car into her driveway and set about opening the back hatch of the car to unload. It did not take long for Kara to realize that her finely tuned schedule for the day was going to require some significant amending. The box was much heavier than Kara anticipated, and her size six was having trouble unloading the super-sized carton. Sweating profusely, she finally managed to push and pull her purchase onto the ground. Now came the fun part of prying the staples out of the cardboard container. Fortunately, this was accomplished without breaking any of her finely polished fingernails. The simple directions turned out to be anything but simple. There was no way that the A bolt was going to fit into the red opening or that the round peg was screwing into the square hole. Kara's husband, Louis, was the mechanic in the family, and his tour of duty in Iraq had just been extended; however, Kara was certain that, even with his technical expertise, he would have found it impossible to follow these confusing directions. The labeled parts simply did not match up to the intricate diagram. With considerable effort, she managed to attach the wheels to the machine, but no matter how hard she tried, the wheels refused to spin. She managed to connect all the wires, but even a novice mechanic realizes that smoke streaming out of the motor is not a good sign. More than four hours later, at precisely the time she had expected to finish her lawn maintenance, Kara's optimistic resolve was rapidly dissipating, and she decided to give up on the project for the day. Of course, this left the brand new lawn mower fair game for drive-by thieves and so, summoning up her last ounce of energy, she pushed the heavy mower over to the attached storage shed (which had not seen sunlight in over six months) and unlatched the door. A cadre of cockroaches scurrying out into the sunlight warmly welcomed her. Did I happen to mention Kara is paranoid about bugs? She must have mutilated the mother bugs first, because all the little baby bugs kept circling her feet looking for direction. I'm certain that she must have made quite a sight, jumping up and down in hysterics, crushing lively little black bugs while attempting to roll an uncooperative machine into its new home. It was at about this moment I decided to give my daughter in Kansas a call to see how her day was going. "This is *soooo* not what I signed up for," she screamed into the phone!

Kara's husband, Louis, was not home to assist in the assembly process because he is a United States army sergeant serving in Iraq. While I cannot possibly relate to the year's absence that military families must endure, I can totally relate to the challenge of being on your own for weeks at a time and trying to maintain some semblance of normalcy. At approximately the same age, I admit to frequently feeling those same "not what I signed up for" thoughts. After five challenging years in the major leagues, I found myself the scared and lonely wife of a professional baseball player, down in the minor leagues for the first time, uprooted from my friends and family, and feeling imprisoned in my claustrophobic apartment in Tucson, Arizona, while my husband was on the road again. The intense hot desert sun scorched the sidewalks and made it impossible to walk outside during the day. Earlier that evening I had ventured outside for a leisurely stroll around the complex when my peaceful sojourn was shattered by a scary soaring sound which caused me to quickly scurry back to the relative safety of my rental residence. I hovered in the corner of the living room, listening to gunshots burst across our apartment complex and trying to hold it all together, while inwardly lamenting my present situation. Our "better" baseball days in Milwaukee appeared only a distant memory and I recall wondering how much "worse" the "for better and for worse" part of our marriage vows could get.

Back up in the majors a few years later, I reiterated these "not what I signed up for thoughts" again during a monumental hurricane. The New York Mets airplane, with my husband on board, was grounded in Cooperstown due to a violent weather warning. Alone in a high-rise apartment in White

Plains, New York, the rain-soaked, wind-driven giant trees from the parking lot across the street were banging on the wall of glass on our tenth floor unit, while I cowered in the corner of the bedroom praying that the hurricane would pass quickly and that I would survive this latest storm. Yes, like the song goes, I was afraid and petrified, but I did survive. However, not without a night spent hovering under the covers as the sky filled with frightening lightning.

Somehow Skip rarely seemed to be around for many of the environmental challenges I faced. My skin still crawls when I recall the morning I was woken up by the uncontrollable screams of my children in Weston, Massachusetts, when the Red Sox were on a lengthy west coast trip. During the night the exterior of our lovely gray colonial had been covered with ugly black gypsy moth caterpillars, giving it a sinister bumpy black appearance. After a few screams of my own, I realized that I was not soothing my children's anxiety and replaced my initial emotional reaction with a more rational one, to call my father-in-law and seek his advice. Calmly pleading into the phone, "Can you please come over and see what's attacked our home; dealing with this insect infestation, by myself, is definitely not what I had signed up for." Thankfully, Claude Senior arrived a few hours later with the phone number of a lawn service to attack the creepy caterpillar-clad condition.

True, I had pledged to love, honor, and respect my husband on the day we were wed. What I didn't understand at the time was that I was also pledging to somehow merge my softhearted demeanor with a hard-as-steel backbone. Many of my fellow baseball wives have also survived challenges that far exceeded the realm of experiences they thought they were signing up for. Young brides anticipating a life filled with unconditional love were instead immersed into a world of unimaginable self-sufficiency. Wives who left training camp early to be in town for opening day and while driving, by themselves, on an interstate highway to a major league destination, have been flagged down and pulled over by the state police and been instructed to "turn around"; their husband had been sent down or traded on the last day of spring training. Wives who have hoisted themselves up into a Suburban and driven themselves to the emergency room of an unfamiliar hospital, in an unfamiliar city, to deliver a new baby alone; or worse yet, to suffer a devastating miscarriage without the benefit of their spouse or even a strong family support group nearby. Sophisticated spouses, unaccustomed to small town petty politics, have successfully survived their stint in small town environments and countless number of family-focused country wives, with a basic mistrust of any city, have mustered up the courage to adapt to their current circumstances and provide a little pocket of security for their families in a scary, fast-paced urban environment.

My daughter Kara was not really upset about the uncooperative wheels on the lawn mower. She was upset that her husband's tour of duty in Bagdad was being extended by an additional three months. A certain baseball wife from my generation might have lost her cool over a broken jar of pickles spilling out of her grocery bag and onto the ugly, gold, shag carpeting, but the true cause of her meltdown was her *de facto* exclusion from an invisibly segregated apartment complex. Today's baseball wives are not burdened by the financial constraints we had to juggle in the early years, but they still spend over half of the season alone. These wives still suffer the same shock when their husband, who was one of the most beloved and valuable players on the team the year before, is cold-heartedly traded to the highest bidder the following season. In this era of instant celebrity status, the constant spotlight on their every move and the intrusive scrutiny of the media monitoring their daily lives undoubtedly causes more than one modern day major league wife to utter the words: "This is not what I had signed up for!"

THROUGH THE YEARS

It's true that my life in baseball turned out not to be what I had signed up for; however, it also blessed me with so many unexpected adventures. Embraced by the baseball fans of the world, it was winding up in each other's arms that really mattered in the end. After baseball, Skip left the transitory world of sports behind and joined the supposedly stable world of financial services. Thanks to this security we have "only" moved five additional times. During his investment career we continued to invest in our own family, resulting in four daughters and one son. Educational costs of both high school and college, which have skyrocketed over the years, have dramatically decreased our personal portfolio. Had Skip been pitching in today's lucrative compensation market the year he pitched two one-hitters as a starting pitcher in Milwaukee, or when was awarded numerous New York Mets "Fireman of the Year" awards as the top closer in New York, I would not have had to spend hours filling out financial aid forms on college applications. Skip's first major league salary was a mere $7,500. He played five years in the major leagues, twice starting the home opener, before making $17,500. I do not begrudge the salaries the current players receive; after all, the salaries merely reflect the television advertising assessments, but I do feel badly that a working class family can no longer sit in box seats behind the dugout for $10.00.

As part of the Baby Boomer generation who grew up believing in fairy tales, I still try to keep the faith, even though the realities of life after 9/11 sometimes stretch that faith to the limit. I still harbor fond memories of hopping on the train in Greenwich, Connecticut, to spend the day in downtown Manhattan taking in all the excitement of the big city. It broke my heart to view the rush hour commuter trains return to the Cos Cob station and see the doors open to only a handful of angst-ridden analysts amble off onto the platform. The parking lot was crowded with late model vehicles whose owners would never again return to unlock the driver's side, clearly illustrating

From left: Casey, Kara, Meghan, Erin, Skip, Kathy and Maura Lockwood at the New Hampshire seacoast.

the loss this caring community suffered on that terrible day. Real life is accompanied by real problems, and I believe that it is only a belief in a higher power that helps us to wake up every morning and welcome in a new day.

For almost twenty years, I have resided in a small New Hampshire seacoast town where good people still go out of their way to help their neighbors. The Wendys of the world still keep the fires burning at home. And similar to Mary Martin's flying fey portrayal, both the boys and the girls in town get a chance to strut their Peter Pan–like performances out on to the Little League field with childlike abandon. When I successfully battled breast cancer some years ago, a volunteer army of warm-hearted women brought dinner over to my family for the months that I went through chemotherapy. Catering to the basic necessities of a family continues to enhance the quality of life in a close community.

I have sailed through the changing ocean tides during the many seasons of my life. I have been awed by the inspiring stars and delighted in magical starfish on the beach. As I move into the autumn of my life, I am thankful that my future is no longer manipulated by managerial decisions beyond my control, but I am thrilled that unconditional love and the childlike wonder of our days in baseball remains alive.

Index